THE KRIPALU COOKBOOK

THE KRIPALU COOKBOOK

GOURMET VEGETARIAN RECIPES

ATMA JO ANN LEVITT

THE COUNTRYMAN PRESS
WOODSTOCK, VERMONT

The Kripalu Cookbook: Gourmet Vegetarian Recipes
ISBN 978-1-58157-613-9

Edited by Constance L. Oxley
Cover and book design by Catharyn Tivy
Illustrations by Janice Lindstrom

Published by The Countryman Press, P.O. Box 748, Woodstock, Vermont 05091

Distributed by W. W. Norton & Company, Inc., 500 Fifth Avenue, New York, NY
10110

Manufactured in China

10 9 8 7 6 5 4 3 2 1

TO MOM AND DAD

Acknowledgments

I am extremely grateful for the assistance of community, family, and friends, and it's important to me to acknowledge those who've been part of this book. I want to praise my literary guardian angel, Lucy Kroll, who has persisted in championing my cause through the years and has insisted that I write no matter what the roadblock. Lucy's faith in me is the highest imaginable accolade.

I am grateful to the Kripalu community, and in particular, to the Kripalu Center administration, including Shankar Michael Risen and Narendra Kent Lew, for sharing in the vision for this book and helping it come to fruition. I thank Chandra Dennis Slattery, my very precise, punctual, and fun-poking editor, who has tried very hard to school me in the proper use of the English language, despite my writing idiosyncrasies.

My heartfelt gratitude goes to Kuntal Deborah Howard, the chief recipe tester for this book, who in her own kitchen has generated hundreds of recipes from her many years of experience operating her own cafe and cooking for Kripalu. She is not only a first-rate cook, but also an excellent detective, able to decipher strange notations on computer-generated recipes. I also wish to thank the dozens of Kripalu kitchen staff members who collectively have cooked, served, and nourished thousands over the years. To each of you, I offer my thanks and appreciation.

Several others have contributed to my education or to the enrichment of these recipes. I wish to thank Janet Ballantyne, the author of several cookbooks, for painstaking collaboration on and improvement of many recipes. I also commend Hansaraj Mark Kelso, chef, musical impresario, and cooking teacher, for his gift of cooking and his insights into the creative process. I acknowledge Chandrakant Ernie Heister for his incredibly skilled touch, especially with Indian dishes, and his equally fine-tuned wit; Sona Sheila Fay and Seamus McAtee for wonderful desserts and breads, respectively; and visiting talents Cheri Yuzik, Gloria Drayer, Tami Ronen, and the late Frank Arcuri, who all brought excellent seasoning to this collection of recipes. Also, I toast Richard Bourdon, who helped train us in the fine art of sourdough bread baking.

It has been a joy to work with Berkshire House Publishers and to collaborate in the easy climate of creativity developed by Jean Rousseau, Philip Rich, Madeleine Gruen, and Constance Oxley.

Finally, I offer thanks to Yogindra Richard Cleaver, who has endured countless recipe tests with patience and good humor, continually providing perspective and practical pointers for developing our creative product.

CONTENTS

INTRODUCTION

Here's to Hearty, Healthy Meals!

We Americans have been learning new information about food and diet for many years now. Everything we learn seems to bring us back to the point from which good cooking starts, back to appreciating naturally healthy and delicious food and restoring wholesome and unprocessed ingredients to all phases of cooking.

Even though you may have a very hectic lifestyle with many responsibilities to your family and your job, taking the time to prepare nutritious meals adds not only to the joy of eating, but also to your long-term health and energy. In fact, a modest investment of time and a willingness to learn a few basic dietary principles can yield a significant improvement in the quality of life for you and your loved ones.

To assist you on that path, this cookbook offers many delicious and tempting vegetarian meals that you can prepare quickly, and many others that can be prepared and frozen in advance for heating and serving on short notice. In addition, this collection presents a full array of wholesome natural foods recipes, suitable for daily meals, entertaining guests, and creating special events.

Whole-Foods Diet

This is a book about whole foods, because at the Kripalu Center for Yoga and Health, a community dedicated to yoga, good health, and hearty living, we're about wholeness. Yoga literally means union or wholeness. Everything at Kripalu, including our choice of foods, is dedicated to helping us live up to our human potential as fully as possible.

These are the primary ingredients in a whole-foods diet: whole grains and whole-grain breads, fresh vegetables and fruits, beans and bean by-products, nuts and seeds, natural sweeteners and flavorings. Whole foods make us feel whole, because they contain all of the nutrients our bodies need to thrive and flourish.

We've created countless recipes over many years of serving gourmet vegetarian cuisine to the guests and residents of Kripalu. For us, good health starts with a healthy body, so we care a lot about what we eat. Consequently, we attempt to conserve and take in the optimal nutrition that food has to offer, while avoiding unnecessary or unhealthful elements. By using whole grains, for instance, we benefit from all of the vitamins, minerals, and other nutrients that otherwise get lost in the commercial hulling process. And by avoiding animal products, except for small amounts of milk and butter and an occasional egg, we steer clear of many of the well-publicized health problems associated with unnecessary extra cholesterol and saturated fats, as well as those associated with the pesticides, growth hormones, and other chemicals used in the animal products industry.

Many of us in this country are already well versed in the advisability of reducing calories from fat and avoiding too much sodium or sugar. Even more benefits are available to us, however, when we center our diets around whole foods. First, the foods themselves taste great. (If you've ever eaten a slice of freshly baked, whole-grain bread, it's very difficult to go back to the bleached white, supermarket variety.) Furthermore, when we eat foods that retain their full set of nutrients, we have the personal satisfaction that comes from taking good care of ourselves and our bodies. The better we feel, the more likely we are to make other healthy choices in our lifestyle, which in turn increases our sense of well-being.

The important thing to remember is that you can be healthy and have fun at the same time. There's no need to envision yourself serving bland, unappetizing foods in the effort to keep healthy. This cookbook offers bright casseroles, soups, and stews, elegant party dishes (there's an extensive chapter devoted to cooking for large groups), and desserts that deceive your taste buds with high-quality, yet low-fat flavor.

You'll find recipes you can rely on to spruce up a Sunday barbecue, a picnic at the lake, or an evening dinner party. Though you may not use them everyday, you'll know exactly where to turn for recipes to create an exotic *Vegetable Paella* or *Tofu-Basil Lasagna* or to whip up a superb *Amasake Cheesecake with Fruit Glaze* that dispenses with the heavy calories of traditional cheesecake. Included are chapters on low-calorie cooking and on meals designed specifically for kids, as well as sections on menu planning, kitchen setup, and cooking tips for the chef. So, welcome to the Kripalu kitchen and welcome to what we call "the Kripalu experience."

THE KRIPALU

EXPERIENCE

Chapter 1

 EXACTLY WHAT IS KRIPALU? We've been referred to as an educational institution, a health spa, a yoga training center, and a New Age spiritual community. We combine many elements of the above, without being any one of them exclusively. Founded in 1974, the Kripalu Yoga Fellowship is a nonprofit, educational organization dedicated to promoting personal growth and performing humanitarian service. (The name Kripalu is a tribute to Swami Kripalvanandji, a master of yoga.)

Kripalu is also a community, one that embraces the Kripalu Center for Yoga and Health in Lenox, Massachusetts, host to 15,000 guests per year and home to 300 resident staff members; the original Kripalu residential community in Sumneytown, Pennsylvania; an extensive network of yoga teachers and health practitioners; and over 100 Kripalu support groups and centers across the United States and around the world.

Located in the Berkshire Mountains of western Massachusetts, the Kripalu Center for Yoga and Health is the focal point of this vast community. It comprises a live-in spiritual community as well as a world-renowned educational facility for yoga and holistic health. The center offers programs and individual health services that promote health and well-being. It is here also that we test our culinary talents, serving wholesome vegetarian meals to thousands of people each year. The recipes presented in these pages are a distillation of decades of cooking at the center.

A KRIPALU DINER'S HISTORY

For me, one of the most endearing (and sometimes exasperating) aspects of Kripalu is its continual unfolding into new forms of expression and its openness to diverse avenues for personal growth and transformation. This is as true for us working in the kitchen as it is for us stretching on the yoga mats. From one perspective, you could say that we've been on a roller-coaster ride of dietary choices and experimentation since our community began.

I can recall in the early 1970s waking to a breakfast of granola, bran muffins, dates, toast, and jam. Vegetarian diet in those days was synonymous with extreme carbohydrate loading. Yet we were moving away from refined, highly processed foods and the American romance with processed white sugar.

Parading through a preponderance of casseroles, grains, and baked goods, we then swung to the other end of the spectrum, embracing a raw foods diet. For a while we tossed out dairy cheese in favor of seed cheese and turned our kitchen into a mighty sprout factory. We then moved back to cooked foods, punctuating them with a weekly day of purification when we fasted on orange juice, whole fruit, or rice.

We also learned about Indian cooking from Urmila Desai, coauthor of *The Ayur-vedic Cookbook,* which presents a whole array of nutritional information and recipes based in the ancient Indian science called Ayurveda (see Bibliography).

In the early 1980s, we became acquainted with macrobiotics (a restricted diet of chiefly whole grains) and started adding miso to soups, sea vegetables and boiled salads to our lunch lines, and an impressive array of new grains and beans to our general fare.

Back and forth went the pendulum; at any given time, some of us disapproved of dairy foods, or too much cooked food, or too much raw food—imagine attending to the whims and food fancies of 300 people! Rising to this challenge in heroic measure, the Kripalu kitchen managed to evolve a cooking style that met everyone's needs and provided variety, color, and delightful gourmet eating experiences at every turn of the menu. We developed "light" and "bright" food lines, from which people could choose according to their preferences.

Over the years we were graced by wisdom brought to us by nutritional experts of every description, from Paavo Airola to Michio Kushi to Deepak Chopra. Lino Stanchich came and taught us how to chew our food seriously; before his arrival, what we considered chewing was more akin to suctioning meals down whole. Annemarie Colbin taught us the secrets of nourishing ourselves through a balance of food types. A revival of raw foods came after a visit from Rishi Prabhakar; it was nursed along by our association with Ann Wigmore and her bright-eyed raw foods devotees. Many, many others dipped their spoons into our soup and helped us to improve it.

Dietary Principles

From our many years of experimentation, we've developed principles that guide as we take on the responsibility for nourishing so many people. These principles, listed below, are reflected in all of the recipes and techniques offered in this book.

- We eat vital, whole foods that, as much as possible, are minimally processed or refined.
- We moderate the addition of fats and oils in our diet and, whenever possible, use oils that are easy to digest and assimilate. We use oils moderately when sautéing or grilling. We avoid the use of hydrogenated and partially hydrogenated oils, and we avoid deep frying.
- We moderate the use of sweeteners and choose those that are least refined and adulterated, such as pure maple syrup, honey, unsulphured molasses, and fruit juice concentrate.
- We exclude certain products that we consider unhealthy or unnecessary, among them animal flesh, alcohol (except in extracts or cooking wine), caffeine, and refined sugar.
- We provide a primarily lacto-vegetarian menu. This means a lot of fresh vegetables and fruits, along with beans, whole grains, nuts, and seeds. We use some dairy products regularly and use eggs occasionally in special dishes. Our aim is to create a diet that nourishes the body, pleases the palate, and supports our yogic lifestyle, which emphasizes moderation in all things. (For a complete description of the Kripalu lifestyle, see *Kripalu's Self Health Guide* in the Bibliography and Sources.)
- We prepare meals with an attitude of reverence, joy, equanimity, and respect, in order to promote the well-being of those cooking and serving the food as well as of those eating it.

The Basics: Getting Ready to Cook

Chapter 2

IN THIS CHAPTER, we take a closer look at kitchen organization and common, but important basic equipment, as well as the kinds of cooking methods and foods that support a healthier approach to nutrition.

KITCHEN SETUP

The kitchen is an environment that prominently displays how we nourish ourselves and our family, what we consider important tools and cooking techniques, and which foods we value having on hand. Hansaraj, a longtime Kripalu chef, shared his thoughts on setting up a kitchen, "I'm basically a creature of inertia, so I don't like to move around very much while I cook. I have arranged my kitchen so I can turn from the stove to the fridge and back again on a mere pivot of the foot." He has spices close to the stove, a vegetable scrub brush at hand, a cutting board in easy reach of both stove and sink, baskets filled with garlic and onions, and dried herbs hanging overhead.

"Hansaraj" is a Sanskrit name taken as a symbol of commitment to the spiritual path of yoga. In this book you will read about Kripalu community members and guests; many will be designated by their Sanskrit names.

You don't want to be logging a mile a day in walking back and forth preparing meals, so may we pose some ergonomically inspired questions:

- What is the most traveled area in your kitchen? Least traveled?
- Do you have to walk more than three or four steps to get from the sink to the stove? From the refrigerator to the sink?
- When cutting vegetables, how far must you walk to transfer them from the cutting board to the pots on the stove?
- Are your most used pots and utensils in easy reach?
- Are your most used appliances out on the counter for easy access?

Consider all of these questions and then think about how to make your kitchen more efficient. Though it may be impractical to move your stove or refrigerator, you can still save labor simply by moving a cutting board closer to the stove or placing a blender or food processor where it can be washed and easily put back into service. If your kitchen doesn't have a pleasing and suitable design, then you may want to reevaluate the space to have it better meet your needs.

No single detail is critical to the successful management of a kitchen. What is important, however, is the context in which we create our meals. Cooking, like any other activity, is an extension of whatever state of mind we're in. You may recall a meal prepared with not enough time and the resultant feelings of pressure or failure to perform — it's not a pleasant experience. Yet the very same meal, prepared in a relaxed manner, evokes feelings of accomplishment and satisfaction.

Our state of mind fluctuates in response to the conditions that we create in our lives. Having an attractive kitchen environment, where things are easy to access, fun to use, and simple to reassemble enhances the conditions for cooking with ease.

BASIC KITCHEN TOOLS AND EQUIPMENT

It isn't necessary to have high-tech, state-of-the-art equipment to deliver sumptuous vegetarian meals. There are, however, some important tools and implements to have on hand to complement your creativity.

A blender or food processor are very helpful, since in vegetarian cookery many sauces, fillings, soups, and stews are blended or pureed. For preparing vegetables, a large cutting surface and several knives of different sizes are useful, including a square-tipped Japanese knife and a large-pointed chef's knife (good for cutting squash and other hard-to-cut vegetables). Since browning vegetables is also an integral part of vegetarian cooking, a well-seasoned cast-iron skillet is a must.

Good vegetarian cooking draws on a range of ethnic backgrounds and styles, so consider purchasing a large-sized rack or lazy Susan to accommodate a variety of spices. A large strainer for rinsing grains is a definite time saver and so is a pressure cooker, if you prefer your grains and beans well cooked and don't want to wait for the full cooking time.

Many other tools come in handy, too. If you do a lot of cooking, several measuring cups will be useful, as will saucepans and casserole dishes in a range of sizes. If you have a busy schedule, consider using a slow cooker—just add beans, vegetables, herbs, spices, and plenty of water at 7 A.M., turn on the cooker, and at 7 P.M. you have a delicious meal ready to serve.

FOOD STORAGE AND COOKING METHODS

Just about all vegetables and fruits, except for potatoes and winter squash should be stored in the refrigerator. Air, light, and heat rob vegetables and fruits of vital nutrients. Raw vegetables, for example, kept at room temperature for 3 days lose up to 70 percent of the B vitamin folic acid, but little or no folic acid in the vegetables is lost after 2 weeks in the refrigerator.

Not only the storage, but the preparation of foods, so they keep their vital, health-giving properties, is as important to nutrition as the foods themselves. We try to prepare food so it retains its wholesome nutrients, flavor, and color as much as possible. Then the life energy (or what yogis call *prana*) in the food is easily transmitted to those who eat it.

The cooking methods commonly used at Kripalu involve either dry or moist heat. See the following:

Baking and roasting are simple methods of food preparation that use dry heat in a ventilated space to cook foods thoroughly. Baking, of course, is done in the oven, and we bake many of our casseroles, morning cereals, and pan-served vegetable dishes, such as *Baked Wakame and Vegetables.* Roasting is also generally done in the oven. (Sometimes in nice weather we roast food outside using a fire pit or charcoal.) Roasting helps to tenderize many vegetables that require long cooking times, such as potatoes, beets, squash, onions, and carrots.

When baking or roasting, place the foods in the oven and leave them alone for the full cooking time, checking only near the end for doneness. It's also particularly important when roasting vegetables not to mix or stir them in the pan, since the roasting process includes caramelizing (when the sugars in the vegetables turn brown).

Blanching is a quick-cooking method in which vegetables are submerged briefly in a pan of boiling water, then removed from the water and "shocked," that is, plunged into very cold water to stop the cooking and to preserve their nutrients and color. Blanching works well for thinly sliced vegetables, which can be used for boiled salads, vegetable platters, dipping, or blending into pâtés or terrines.

Boiling generally refers to cooking foods submerged in water that has come to a rolling boil. Some sauces and puddings need to be boiled to activate their thickeners. Root vegetables can be boiled, but most other vegetables, including corn on the cob, cook better steamed, losing fewer of their nutrients to the boiling water.

Braising means browning, then boiling or simmering foods in a skillet or saucepan. Sometimes we use a combination of oil and water as a means of cutting back on oil. Onions, mushrooms, and tofu cook up very well if braised beforehand.

Broiling and grilling entail cooking foods one side at a time on very high heat so the juices are locked inside. Grilled foods are often soaked in advance in marinades that impart distinctive flavors.

Nishime is a macrobiotic variant of steaming in which a small amount of water is placed on the bottom of a saucepan, then foods are layered on top and steamed without losing their nutrients.

Pressure cooking tenderizes grains and beans and greatly reduces their cooking time. (We recommend a good stainless steel, midsized pressure cooker for home use.) Once you've tasted pressure-cooked rice, you may be unwilling to go back to the old cooked-in-a-saucepan variety.

Sautéing is cooking foods, uncovered in a skillet, with a small amount of oil at a very high temperature. (As with braising, we sometimes use a combination of oil and water.) Sautéing takes a relatively short time, allows the flavors of the seasonings to be released, and locks the juices into the foods; it also can be used to prepare foods for the next phase of cooking. It is important when sautéing to heat the pan well before adding the oil and to heat the oil well before sautéing the foods.

Simmering is cooking foods in a saucepan on very *low* heat after they have been brought to a boil or cooked on very *high* heat. Their liquids are allowed to bubble, but not to boil. Most whole grains are cooked by simmering; when all of the water has evaporated after simmering for some time, the grains remain in a covered saucepan and then steam completes the final phase of cooking.

Steaming is cooking foods with the steam from boiling water. We use huge steamers that can cook five or six gallons of vegetables at a time, but for home use, you'll need only a small steaming basket to place inside a covered saucepan. Once the water has reached a boil, the heat is turned off and the covered food cooks in the steam.

Stir-frying is cooking foods in a wok or skillet on high heat with a moderate amount of oil. Foods are moved briskly in the pan so they are coated and cooked on all sides. Stir-frying seals in the juices, keeps the colors bright, and renders a crisp, but tender texture. It is important when using this method, as with sautéing, to heat the oil well before adding the food. We also use a no-oil variation of stir-frying, adding a dash of salt to a cast-iron skillet, instead of oil. Our *Broccoli with Tofu and Mung Bean Sprouts* cooks up perfectly using this no-oil variation.

BREAKFASTS to BRIGHTEN YOUR DAY

Chapter 3

 MORNING HAS ARRIVED. Slide back the covers and stretch, it's time to greet the day. With the sun barely peeking through the window, the key question is "What's for breakfast?"

Breakfast is certainly a time for varying tastes and appetites. At Kripalu, we're used to seeing people enjoying a variety of breakfasts: plump muffins, fresh fruit, hot cereals, golden fruit crisps, or maybe our robust *Upma Cereal.* In this chapter, you'll find an assortment of our outstanding breakfast choices, with a definite leaning toward the most popular Kripalu breakfast foods. You may want to balance some of these richer dishes with simpler foods, opting on some mornings for just fruit, yogurt, or plain-cooked grains.

On a weekend morning, you may wish to experiment with *Soysage* and *Scrambled Tofu,* a hearty, no-cholesterol version of "ye ole sausage and eggs." Devangana, one of our longtime kitchen chefs and menu planners, devised *Soysage* in a mad scramble to come up with an exciting breakfast for 300 residents who were participating in an Inner Quest Intensive, our well-known weekend growth workshop.

In Chapter 6, "Glorious Grains and Bountiful Beans," you'll also find a selection of potential breakfast dishes. If, for example, you're an oatmeal fan, try some *Almond Rice* or *Couscous with Chickpeas* for a change of pace. Or join some of us at Kripalu who eat lunch for breakfast—we dine on *White Miso-Ginger Soup* (see Chapter 4), enjoying the full-bodied flavor of miso, a fermented soybean product that has lots of protein and B vitamins, as well as minerals and digestive enzymes.

Take the opportunity to experiment with new tastes, textures, and flavors. Surprise yourself one morning with a *Spiced Yogurt Nog,* instead of the habitual coffee or tea, and you'll see how welcome a new flavor can be; or sit down to the crunch of our *Baked Granola,* an all-time favorite. Soymilk and amasake are healthful, interesting alternatives to dairy; try a serving of *Amasake French Toast* as a taste treat. Or wake up to a welcome *Almond Coffee Cake* or *Cranberry-Mandarin Muffins,* then on to the events of the day.

BAKED GRANOLA

6 cups rolled oats
3½ cups rye flakes
2 cups shredded coconut
2 cups sunflower seeds
1 cup sesame seeds
2 cups chopped almonds
¾ cup barley malt
⅔ cup canola oil
1¼ cups pure maple syrup
1 tablespoon pure vanilla extract
1 tablespoon pure almond extract
¼ teaspoon pure maple extract
½ teaspoon salt
1 cup raisins

Preheat oven to 375°F. In a large bowl, combine the oats, rye flakes, coconut, sunflower and sesame seeds, and almonds. In a separate bowl, stir together the barley malt, oil, syrup, all of the extracts, and salt. Add the wet mixture to the dry mixture and mix together well. (For granola that sticks together more, use a food processor to combine the wet and dry mixtures.)

Spread the combined mixture onto a large baking sheet and bake for 50 minutes, or until the mixture is lightly browned. Let cool for 30 minutes. (Granola will harden and darken as it cools.)

Mix in the raisins and serve immediately or store in an airtight, sealable container for future breakfasts.

**Preparation time
15 minutes.**

**Baking time
50 minutes.**

**Cooling time
30 minutes.**

Makes 1 gallon.

Always a favorite at Kripalu, this recipe supplies enough breakfast and snack granola for one week. Give a bag to someone and make a friend for life.

*This sweet, puffy
cereal is full of fiber
and protein and
tastes as indulgent
as dessert. Some of
us even make it
while camping in
the woods, soaking
it overnight and
awaking the next
morning to a deli-
cious,* haute cuisine
trail mix breakfast.

MUESLI

2 cups rolled oats
1 cup rye flakes
1 cup chopped dried dates
1 cup raisins
1 cup whole almonds
½ cup whole walnuts
½ cup sunflower seeds
1 teaspoon pure vanilla extract
¼ teaspoon ground nutmeg
½ teaspoon ground cinnamon
4 cups apple cider

In a large bowl, combine all of the ingredients, except the cider, and mix well. Place the mixture in an airtight, sealable container and stir in the cider.

Refrigerate overnight and serve in the morning. (This cereal can be stored in the refrigerator for several days.)

Millet-Carrot Cereal

Preparation and cooking time 45–60 minutes.

Serves 4.

1½ cups chopped carrots
¾ cup rinsed drained millet
3 cups water
½ teaspoon salt

Place the carrots on the bottom of a large saucepan. Add the millet. Pour 2 cups of the water gently into the saucepan, so the carrots stay on the bottom as much as possible.

Bring to a boil and add the salt. Reduce heat to low, cover, and cook for 15 minutes. Add the remaining water and cook for 30–45 minutes more. Serve hot with a dash of ghee (see page 325) or tahini, if desired.

You can start this breakfast in the morning, bring it to a simmer, then go back to bed (with your alarm set, of course) and wake up to it 45 minutes later. Millet and carrots cooked together have an incredibly sweet, earthy flavor.

*Here's a breakfast
at the other end of
the spectrum: a
bright yellow,
Indian-style hot
cereal with pota-
toes, peas, carrots,
and all manner of
spices. This dish
derives its fragrant,
spicy flavor from the
creation of a
"vagar," a ghee-
based sauce in
which hot spices are
sautéed and then
blended into the
cereal.*

UPMA CEREAL

4 tablespoons ghee (see page 325)
1 cup farina
⅓ cup diced potatoes
¼ cup diced carrots
¼ cup fresh or frozen peas
1 teaspoon black mustard seeds
½ teaspoon cumin seeds
½ teaspoon ground turmeric
Pinch cayenne pepper
Pinch ground asafetida (hing)
1⅔ cups hot water
1 teaspoon salt
⅓ cup diced green bell peppers
¼ cup raisins
¼ cup whole cashews
1 tablespoon Sucanat (granulated cane juice)
1 teaspoon fresh lemon juice
1 tablespoon chopped fresh cilantro

In a large saucepan, melt 3 tablespoons of the ghee and
sauté the farina, stirring constantly, until the farina becomes fragrant and begins to brown. Keep warm.

Meanwhile, in a medium-sized, covered saucepan with a
steamer basket, lightly steam the potatoes, carrots, and
peas in water for 5–7 minutes. Make a vagar by melting
the remaining ghee in a small saucepan on medium heat
and adding the mustard and cumin seeds. When the seeds
start to pop, stir in the turmeric, cayenne pepper, and
asafetida. Turn off heat.

Add the vagar to the farina mixture and stir well. Add the hot water and salt, whisking to break up any lumps. Add the steamed vegetables, the bell peppers, raisins, cashews, Sucanat, lemon juice, and cilantro. Stir until fluffy and serve immediately.

Preparation and
cooking time
30 minutes.

Soaking time
overnight.

Cooling time
2–4 minutes.

Serves 4–6.

*This is a nourish-
ing, yet delightfully
light, breakfast
pudding. Although
milk is called for in
the recipe, feel free
to experiment by
substituting either
rice milk or soymilk,
or try the wonderful
new almond milks
available in natural
foods stores and
specialty markets.*

BASMATI RICE PUDDING

1½ cups uncooked white basmati rice
5 cups water
1 tablespoon butter
½ teaspoon ground cinnamon
½ teaspoon ground cardamom
1¾ cups milk
½ teaspoon salt
⅓ cup raisins
¼ teaspoon pure vanilla extract
⅔ cup honey
¼ cup slivered almonds

Rinse and drain the basmati rice. In a blender or food
processor, chop the rice into small pieces and soak overnight in water to cover. Drain the rice.

In a large pot, combine the 5 cups water, drained rice,
butter, cinnamon, and cardamom and cook on medium
heat for about 20 minutes, or until the rice is soft.

Add the milk, salt, and raisins and cook to a pudding consistency, stirring frequently. Remove from heat and let
cool for 2–4 minutes. Stir in the vanilla, honey, and almonds and serve immediately.

*Heating milk can send precious calcium to
the bottom of the saucepan in the form of salts called
calcium phosphates. Stir the milk as it warms, and
the calcium will be kept in the liquid.*

RAISIN SAUCE

Method 1:
¾ cup raisins
1½ cups water

Place the raisins and water in an airtight, sealable container and refrigerate for 2 days.

In a blender or food processor, blend the raisin mixture until smooth. Serve.

Method 2:
¾ cup raisins
2 cups water
½ teaspoon ground cinnamon
¼ teaspoon pure vanilla extract
½ tablespoon kuzu dissolved in 2 tablespoons
  cold water

**Preparation time
1 hour 30 minutes.**

**Cooling time
variable.**

Makes 2 cups.

In a small saucepan, combine the raisins and water and bring to a boil. Stir in the cinnamon and vanilla. Reduce heat to simmer and cook for 1 hour.

Return the mixture to a boil. Stir in the dissolved kuzu and mix together well. Remove from heat and let cool. Serve.

Here's a wonderful breakfast topping — excellent over hot cereal or yogurt or as an accompaniment to toast, muffins, or scones.

This tofu dish is reminiscent of western or ranch-style omelettes. The good news is that you can enjoy a hearty Tex-Mex breakfast and forego the cholesterol. Try this with our Soysage (see page 33) for a full-bodied, protein-rich meal — enough energy for some mountain climbing or horseback riding!

SCRAMBLED TOFU

3 tablespoons olive oil
1½ cups diced onions
1 tablespoon finely chopped garlic
1 pound 8 ounces firm tofu, rinsed, drained, and crumbled
½ cup diced green bell peppers
½ cup sliced fresh mushrooms
1½ tablespoons prepared brown mustard
2 tablespoons white miso
2 tablespoons water
2 teaspoons curry powder
½ tablespoon dried tarragon
½ teaspoon chili powder
¼ teaspoon black pepper
½ teaspoon salt
¼ cup grated soy or dairy cheese

In a large skillet, heat the oil and sauté the onions and garlic for 3–5 minutes, or until the onions are translucent. Add the tofu, bell peppers, and mushrooms and sauté for 5 minutes more.

In a small bowl, dilute the mustard and miso in the water and pour over the tofu. Stir in the curry powder, tarragon, chili powder, black pepper, and salt and sauté the mixture for 5 minutes.

Add the cheese, cover, and allow 3 minutes for the cheese to melt. Serve immediately.

SOYSAGE

Preparation time 15 minutes.

Baking time 45 minutes.

Chilling time 2 hours or overnight.

Serves 4–6. (Makes 10–12 patties.)

1½ cups finely chopped seitan
8 ounces firm tofu, rinsed, drained, and crumbled
3 tablespoons butter
2 teaspoons dried sage
1 teaspoon dried marjoram
1 teaspoon dried basil
1 teaspoon chopped garlic
½ teaspoon salt
1 tablespoon tamari
Pinch ground anise
Pinch cayenne pepper
⅓ cup unbleached white flour

In a food processor, blend together all of the ingredients, except the flour, until slightly smooth. Place the mixture in a covered bowl and refrigerate for at least 2 hours or overnight.

Preheat oven to 375°F. Mix the flour into the chilled mixture and form into patties, using about ¼ cup mixture per patty. In a lightly oiled, large baking pan, place the patties and bake for 45 minutes, turning the patties after 20–25 minutes. Serve piping hot with *House Salsa* (see page 227) or your favorite condiment.

Soysage patties have the taste and feel of sausage, but they're made from soy protein, so they're healthier and easier to digest than those made from meat. They go well with Scrambled Tofu *or* Amasake French Toast *(see pages 32 and 34).*

Preparation and cooking time 20–25 minutes.

Serves 2–4.

Here's an easy, healthful alternative to the traditional milk-and-egg French toast. Amasake is a cultured rice drink that you can buy in different consistencies; the type that we use has the consistency of light cream. Since the amasake is naturally sweet, you won't need much maple syrup or sweetener to perk up this morning treat. (This recipe may take slightly longer to cook than traditional French toast.)

AMASAKE FRENCH TOAST

1 cup amasake
¼ teaspoon ground cinnamon
Pinch ground nutmeg
Pinch ground anise
Pinch ground cloves
6–8 slices bread (any type)
¼ cup butter

In a large mixing bowl, stir together the amasake and all of the spices. Coat each slice of bread with the amasake mixture and let stand while heating the skillet.

In a large skillet, melt the butter and generously coat the skillet with the butter. Cook the coated bread on medium heat for about 5 minutes per side. Serve immediately.

BANANA-WALNUT MUFFINS

**Preparation time
15 minutes.**

**Baking time
25–35 minutes.**

Makes approximately 18 muffins.

3 cups mashed bananas
  (approximately 6 medium bananas)
1 cup honey
½ cup canola oil
½ tablespoon pure vanilla extract
3½ cups whole-wheat pastry flour
1 teaspoon baking powder
2 teaspoons baking soda
1 cup finely chopped walnuts
1 teaspoon ground nutmeg
1 teaspoon salt

There is no way you can go wrong with these wonderful muffins; something about the sweetness of the bananas combined with the nutty flavor of the walnuts and nutmeg makes them a sure hit.

Preheat oven to 375° F. In a large bowl, stir together the bananas, honey, oil, and vanilla. In a separate bowl, combine the flour, baking powder, baking soda, walnuts, nutmeg, and salt. Add the wet mixture to the dry mixture and mix together until well blended.

Fill oiled muffin tins ⅔ full and bake for 25–35 minutes or until lightly browned on top. Cool on a wire rack or serve warm.

Variation: For a special dessert, mix 1 cup chocolate chips into the batter and serve hot out of the oven.

Here in New England, we're very fond of cranberries. These muffins blend cranberries' tartness with the sweet taste of mandarin oranges.

CRANBERRY-MANDARIN MUFFINS

2½ cups whole-wheat pastry flour
2 teaspoons baking powder
½ teaspoon salt
⅔ cup canned mandarin oranges
⅔ cup fresh orange juice
⅓ cup honey
⅔ cup rice syrup
¼ cup canola oil
¾ cup fresh or thawed frozen cranberries

Preheat oven to 375°F. In a large bowl, combine the flour, baking powder, and salt. In a separate bowl, mix together the oranges, orange juice, honey, syrup, and oil. Add the wet mixture to the dry mixture and mix together until well blended. Gently fold in the cranberries until well combined.

Fill oiled muffin tins ⅔ full and bake for 30 minutes or until golden brown on top. Cool on a wire rack or serve warm.

OATMEAL-NUT SCONES

Preparation time
15 minutes.

Baking time
15 minutes.

Makes 15–18 scones.

3½ cups unbleached white flour
1½ cups rolled oats
1 tablespoon baking powder
1 teaspoon baking soda
⅓ cup currants
⅓ cup raisins
1 cup chopped walnuts
½ cup Sucanat (granulated cane juice)
½ teaspoon salt
1¾ cups soymilk
¾ cup ghee (see page 325)
1 teaspoon pure vanilla extract

Preheat oven to 375°F. In a large bowl, combine the first nine ingredients and mix together well. Add the soymilk, vanilla, and ghee and mix together until well combined.

Shape the batter into triangles or flatten on an ungreased baking sheet. Bake for 15 minutes. Serve warm with butter and jam.

What a delightful way to start the morning! These scones were conjured up in Kripalu's bakery, and our guests and residents often count the days until they show up on the morning breakfast line.

*Since this classic
Kripalu coffee cake
stays so moist, it
can be made one
day and served the
next morning. It
has a sweet, nutty
crumb topping and
a golden cake of
almond, maple,
and vanilla flavors,
with just a hint of
orange.*

ALMOND COFFEE CAKE

Cake:
1½ cups whole-wheat pastry flour
2 cups unbleached white flour
1 tablespoon baking powder
1 teaspoon baking soda
½ teaspoon salt
1 cup water
⅔ cup rice syrup
⅓ cup pure maple syrup
⅓ cup fresh orange juice
1 teaspoon pure vanilla extract
½ teaspoon pure almond extract
½ cup canola oil

Topping:
1 cup chopped almonds
¾ cup ground pecans
⅔ cup whole-wheat pastry flour
⅓ cup rice syrup
⅓ cup pure maple syrup
½ teaspoon ground cinnamon
Zest of 1 orange

Preheat oven to 375°F. To make the cake: In a large
bowl, combine both flours, the baking powder, baking
soda, and salt. In a separate bowl, stir together the water,
both syrups, orange juice, both extracts, and oil. Add the
wet mixture to the dry mixture and mix together until
well blended. Pour the batter into an oiled 9 x 12-inch
baking pan.

To make the topping: In a medium-sized bowl, mix together all of the topping ingredients and spread on top of the batter. Bake for 35 minutes, or until a tester inserted in the center comes out clean. Cool on a wire rack or serve warm.

*A "crisp" morning
wake-up breakfast
that tastes so good
it's like starting the
day with a healthy
dessert. (This
recipe can also be
made with peaches
or other ripe fruit
in season.)*

APPLE CRISP

10 cups chopped red apples
  (approximately 8 medium apples)
3 cups apple cider
¾ cup raisins
¼ teaspoon salt
½ teaspoon ground cinnamon
4 tablespoons arrowroot
2 teaspoons pure vanilla extract

Topping:
½ cup canola oil
¾ cup rice syrup
1 cup pure maple syrup
¾ cup chopped walnuts
½ teaspoon salt
4½ cups rolled oats

Preheat oven to 375°F. Place the apples in a 9 x 12-inch baking pan.

In a medium-sized saucepan, combine 2½ cups of the apple cider, the raisins, salt, and cinnamon and bring to a boil. Dissolve the arrowroot in the remaining cider and stir the arrowroot mixture into the boiling cider mixture to thicken. Turn off heat and add the vanilla.

To make the topping: In a large bowl, stir together the oil and both syrups. Mix in the walnuts, salt, and oats. Pour the thickened cider mixture over the apples and spread on the topping. Bake, covered, for 40 minutes. Uncover and bake for 15 minutes more. Serve warm.

Apple-Banana Smoothie

2 peeled frozen bananas
4 cups apple cider
½ cup fresh or frozen fruit (optional)
¼ cup chopped walnuts or peanut butter
 (optional)

In a blender, combine the bananas, cider, fruit, and nuts and blend on high for 1 minute. Serve immediately.

Preparation time 5 minutes.

Makes 2 large smoothies.

This morning beverage can be served alone or with other breakfast dishes.

Spiced Yogurt Nog

3½ cups plain yogurt
¼ cup water
¼ cup honey
1 teaspoon ground cardamom
½ teaspoon ground cinnamon
¼ teaspoon ground nutmeg
¼ teaspoon ground ginger

In a blender or food processor, blend together all of the ingredients until smooth. Serve immediately.

Variation: Blend in 1 banana or ½ cup fresh berries.

Preparation time 5 minutes.

Makes 4 cups.

This is a cooling and refreshing yogurt drink that Indians call lassi. *It's served with spicy foods, with sweets, or as a small meal. A perfect breakfast for hot, humid mornings!*

Hot cider is a splendid way to start off the morning or a pleasant, warming treat for a cold day.

HOT MULLED CIDER

6 cups apple cider
1 cinnamon stick, or
  1 tablespoon ground cinnamon
1 teaspoon whole cloves
¼ teaspoon ground ginger, or one 3-inch length
  fresh gingerroot, peeled and grated

In a large saucepan, combine all of the ingredients and bring to a boil. Reduce heat to simmer and cook for 10 minutes (cider reduces as it cooks). Strain and serve immediately.

The flavor of this tea nicely complements sweet things, and it is also an excellent tea to drink when you feel a cold coming on.

GINGER-SAGE TEA

4 cups water
One 3-inch length fresh gingerroot, peeled
  and grated
2 tablespoons dried sage

In a medium-sized saucepan, combine all of the ingredients and bring to a boil. Reduce heat to simmer and cook for at least 20 minutes. Strain and serve piping hot.

Soups, Stews, and Sauces

Chapter 4

 THERE'S NOTHING SO WARMING AND SOOTHING as soup on a cold afternoon. At Kripalu, we've developed a vast repertoire of rich and tasty soups and stews for all occasions.

In this chapter, we share more than a dozen of our most versatile and tempting recipes, from *Tofu Stew* to *Mexican Corn Chowder* to *Split Pea Soup*. We also provide many superb sauces to adorn your pilafs, casseroles, and stir-fries.

One of the Kripalu kitchen trademarks is our effort to transmit a sense of love and wholesome nourishment to all who eat our food. We, consequently, pay attention to all of the ingredients that go into the food, adding our love through that quality of concentration to every step of preparation.

As you prepare the recipes, remember not only to cook with attention and care, but also to envision in advance the result you want, much in the way an accomplished skier might mentally rehearse moving down the course to pave the way for a successful ski run. Such concentration defines and thereby helps create the end product. Relative to this, Jayendra, one of our cooks, tells this story:

> I learned something from Hansaraj about creating foods with positive thoughts. One day, while teaching us to cook soup, he carefully chopped and sliced the different ingredients. Finally, before seasoning the soup, he closed his eyes as he held some salt in the palm of his hand. He let it get nice and warm and focused his thoughts before adding the salt to the soup. We learned the result after we served lunch that day.
>
> Since it was the middle of winter, many people were experiencing cabin fever and were wanting to get away from the cold. But that afternoon, people kept coming to the kitchen and asking what we had put in the soup, because it tasted *tropical*. Finally, Hansaraj told us that he had wanted to create a warm, Caribbean feeling, so he put that thought into the soup, and even though it was January in New England, we got it!

We've also had plenty of woeful failures, soups that fell flat or burned (although one of our cooks insists that the only way to get a truly smoky quality in pea soup is to deliberately burn it on the bottom). Sometimes, as in this story also told by Jayendra, we start out with a fiasco and turn it into a feast.

One day we were serving cream of tomato soup, and I had six gallons of whole plum tomatoes to process in our huge food processor. I poured them in, turned on the machine, and closed my eyes to meditate. I wanted to impart a sense of warmth and peace to the tomatoes that would be carried on to the soup. Suddenly, I heard a funny sound, and as I opened my eyes, the lid popped off. Tomato sauce shot into the air, flew at the walls, dripped over the counter, filled up my sneakers, and drenched my apron, shirt, and pants. I guess I hadn't fastened the lid tightly.

Everything was covered with tomato sauce, and everyone in a ten-foot radius got hit, except my supervisor. He came over wearing a smile or a frown, I'm not sure which, and said, "Jayendra, the next time you use the food processor, would you mind meditating with your eyes open?"

So much for sending good thoughts into the soup. That happened at ten o'clock, but by noon, with everyone pitching in, not only did we clean up the kitchen, but we also blended another round of plum tomatoes. We served the tomato soup after all, which was a good thing, because guests and residents always clamor for it.

Although we advocate sending positive thoughts into the foods we prepare, we definitely recommend doing it with the lid on tight!

This soup is a favorite in the fall and early winter when squash is harvested. Buttercup squash will produce a slightly thicker and sweeter result than butternut, but either makes a nutty, sweet-flavored, golden soup.

CHESTNUT-SQUASH SOUP

¾ cup shelled chestnuts
10 cups peeled chopped butternut or buttercup
  squash (approximately 2 large squash)
6 cups vegetable stock or water
2¼ teaspoons salt
Sprig fresh dill or chopped fresh chives

Preheat oven to 400°F. On a baking sheet, roast the chestnuts for 15 minutes.

In a large pot, combine the roasted chestnuts, squash, and stock and bring to a boil. Add the salt. Reduce heat to simmer and cook, stirring occasionally, for about 25 minutes, or until the squash is tender.

In a blender or food processor, puree the squash mixture until well blended. Return the mixture to the pot and reheat. Serve immediately, garnished with the dill or chives.

Carrot-Ginger Soup with Chives

Preparation and cooking time 55 minutes.

Serves 6.

Here is a delicately flavored soup that combines the spiciness of ginger with the sweetness of carrots and onions.

1 tablespoon canola oil
1½ cups sliced onions
1½ tablespoons peeled chopped fresh gingerroot
4 cups chopped carrots (5–6 large carrots)
4 cups vegetable stock or water
½ tablespoon salt
½ cup soymilk or light cream (optional)
½ teaspoon black pepper
¼ cup chopped fresh chives

In a large pot, heat the oil and sauté the onions for 3–5 minutes or until translucent. Add the ginger and sauté for 1 minute. Stir in the carrots and stock and bring to a boil. Add the salt. Reduce heat to simmer and cook, stirring occasionally, for about 40 minutes.

In a blender or food processor, puree the mixture until creamy, adding the soymilk, if desired. Return the mixture to the pot, reheat, and stir in the black pepper and chives. Serve immediately.

Variation: Add the soymilk or light cream to make a cream of carrot soup.

There's something delightful about the combination of cheddar cheese and cauliflower: The cauliflower has a certain astringency, and the cheese has a rich, robust flavor. The addition of potatoes makes this a choice autumn or winter soup.

CAULIFLOWER-CHEDDAR CHEESE SOUP

1 tablespoon butter
1 cup chopped onions
3 cups coarsely chopped cauliflower
   (approximately 1 medium head cauliflower)
1½ cups cubed potatoes
¾ cup water
½ tablespoon salt
¾ cup milk
1½ cups shredded cheddar cheese
¼ teaspoon dried dill, or
   1 teaspoon chopped fresh dill
½ teaspoon ground mustard
⅛ teaspoon white pepper
Pinch black pepper
Pinch ground nutmeg
1 cup small cauliflower florets

In a large pot, melt the butter and sauté the onions for 3–5 minutes or until translucent. Add the chopped cauliflower, potatoes, water, and salt and bring to a boil. Boil for 10 minutes, or until the potatoes are tender.

In a blender or food processor, puree the cauliflower mixture with the milk until smooth and creamy. Return the mixture to the pot and reheat. Add the cheese. Stir in the dill, mustard, white and black peppers, and nutmeg. Add the cauliflower florets and simmer for 5–10 minutes, or until the florets are tender. Serve immediately.

FRENCH ONION SOUP

**Preparation and cooking time
1 hour 25 minutes.
Serves 6.**

This is another classic soup, served for years at Kripalu and frequently requested by our guests. The secret lies in bringing out the onions' sweetness by caramelizing and long cooking.

7 cups sliced sweet Spanish onions, or
  in-season Vidalia onions (6–7 medium onions)
3 tablespoons olive oil
One 2-inch strip kombu
5 cups water
1 teaspoon salt
1½ tablespoons tamari
2¼ teaspoons onion powder
2¼ teaspoons dried tarragon, or
  1½ tablespoons chopped fresh tarragon
½ teaspoon black pepper

In a large pot, mix together the onions and oil. Cover and cook on medium heat for 30 minutes, stirring occasionally. Reduce heat to low and cook for 30 minutes more. (The onions should be well caramelized—their juices released into the oil.)

Meanwhile, in a large saucepan, combine the kombu and water and bring to a boil. Reduce heat to simmer and cook the kombu mixture until the onions are carmelized.

Combine the kombu mixture with the carmelized onions, the salt, tamari, onion powder, tarragon, and black pepper and simmer for at least 10 minutes. Serve immediately.

Variation: Pour the prepared soup in ovenproof bowls, top with cheese and croutons, and bake at 300°F until the cheese is melted.

This is a thick, rich potato soup that includes the delicate flavors of leeks, celery, thyme, and tarragon.

POTATO-LEEK SOUP

3 cups sliced leeks (3–4 leeks, well washed)
7 cups chopped potatoes
  (6–7 medium potatoes)
6 cups vegetable stock or water
3¾ teaspoons salt
1½ tablespoons canola oil
1 tablespoon chopped garlic
1 cup milk
¾ cup sliced celery
½ tablespoon dried tarragon, or
  1½ tablespoons chopped fresh tarragon
½ tablespoon dried thyme, or
  1½ tablespoons chopped fresh thyme
¼ teaspoon black pepper
Pinch ground nutmeg
Sprig fresh dill

In a large pot, layer 2 cups of the leeks and all of the potatoes. Cover with the stock and bring to a boil. Add the salt. Reduce heat to simmer and cook for 20–25 minutes, or until the potatoes are tender.

Meanwhile, in a medium-sized skillet, heat the oil and sauté the remaining leeks and the garlic for 4–6 minutes. Set aside.

When the potatoes are tender, blend together half of the potato mixture and the milk in a blender or food processor until smooth and creamy. Return the mixture to the pot and add the reserved leek mixture, the celery, herbs, and spices. Simmer for at least 10 minutes. Garnish with the dill and serve immediately.

CREAMY ZUCCHINI SOUP

This lovely nondairy zucchini soup uses oats as the thickening agent.

1½ cups sliced onions
¼ cup rolled oats
6 cups chopped zucchini
  (3–4 medium zucchini)
2½ cups water
1 teaspoon salt
1 teaspoon dried basil, or
  1 tablespoon chopped fresh basil
⅛ teaspoon black pepper
1½ tablespoons tahini
2 teaspoons umeboshi vinegar
1 tablespoon fresh lemon juice

In a large pot, layer the onions, oats, and zucchini. Cover with the water and bring to a boil. Add the salt, dried basil, and black pepper. (If using fresh basil, see below.) Reduce heat to simmer, cover, and cook, stirring occasionally, for 40 minutes.

In a blender or food processor, puree the zucchini mixture with the tahini, vinegar, lemon juice, and fresh basil until well blended. Return the mixture to the pot, reheat, and simmer for 5 minutes. Serve immediately.

*There is nothing
more comforting
than a bowl of
cream of tomato
soup; it's definitely
worth the time and
effort.*

CREAM OF TOMATO SOUP

1 tablespoon butter
2 cups sliced onions
2 tablespoons chopped garlic
1 teaspoon salt
2 cups diced carrots
6 cups canned whole plum tomatoes
  (three 16-ounce cans)
¾ cup canned tomato sauce
¼ cup canned tomato paste
½ tablespoon dried basil, or
  1½ tablespoons chopped fresh basil
½ tablespoon dried marjoram, or
  1½ tablespoons chopped fresh marjoram
¼ teaspoon black pepper
¼ teaspoon curry powder
Pinch ground nutmeg
Pinch cayenne pepper
½ cup milk
½ cup light cream

In a large pot, melt the butter and sauté the onions and garlic for 3–5 minutes, or until the onions are translucent.

Mix in the salt, carrots, all of the tomato products, dried herbs, and spices. (If using fresh herbs, see below.) Cook for about 1 hour on medium heat, stirring occasionally.

In a blender or food processor, puree the tomato mixture with the milk and cream until smooth and creamy. Return the mixture to the pot, reheat, and add the fresh herbs. Serve immediately. (This recipe can be stored overnight in the refrigerator.)

Variation: For a nondairy version, use 1 cup soymilk instead of the milk and cream.

Preparation and
cooking time
2 hours.

Soaking time
1 hour.

Serves 4–6.

*This robust black
bean soup benefits
from as much
cooking time as
possible. The soup
combines the earthy
tastes of cumin,
garlic, and sage
with the richness of
black beans.
Kombu, a sea
vegetable, provides
added nutrients,
including trace
minerals. Serve with
rice or millet.*

Black Bean Soup

2 cups dried black beans
One 2-inch strip kombu
9 cups water
1½ cups diced onions
1 tablespoon chopped garlic
1 bay leaf
2½ tablespoons tamari
1½ teaspoons ground cumin
1½ teaspoons dried sage
1 tablespoon fresh lemon juice

Wash the beans. In a large pot, combine the beans, kombu, and water and bring to a boil. Turn off heat and let soak for 1 hour.

Return the bean mixture to a boil. Reduce heat to simmer and cook, stirring occasionally, for 1 hour 30 minutes, or until the beans are soft.

After about 1 hour, add the onions, garlic, and bay leaf and continue to cook. When the bean mixture is soft, blend half of the mixture in a blender or food processor until very smooth.

Return the mixture to the pot and reheat. Stir in the tamari, cumin, and sage and simmer for 15 minutes. Add the lemon juice just before serving. Serve immediately.

WHITE BEAN-ESCAROLE SOUP

Preparation and cooking time 1 hour 45 minutes. Serves 6.

This delicately flavored soup combines the earthiness of navy beans, the sweetness of white miso, and the tang of mustard and escarole.

2 cups dried navy beans
One 2-inch strip kombu
7 cups vegetable stock or water
1 tablespoon olive oil
1½ cups sliced onions
½ teaspoon salt
3 tablespoons white miso diluted in ½ cup
  warm water
⅓ cup prepared brown mustard
2 cups chopped fresh escarole

Wash the beans. Soak overnight or use the quick-soak method (see page 128). In a large pot, combine the beans, kombu, and stock and bring to a boil. Reduce heat to medium-low and cook, stirring occasionally, for 1 hour 15 minutes, or until the beans are soft.

Meanwhile, in a medium-sized skillet, heat the oil and sauté the onions for 3–5 minutes or until translucent. Add the onions to the beans.

When the beans are soft, add the salt. Blend two-thirds of the bean mixture in a blender or food processor until very smooth. Return the mixture to the pot. Stir in the diluted miso and the mustard and simmer for 10 minutes.

If the soup is too thick, add additional stock or water. Just before serving, add the escarole and turn off heat. Let stand for 5 minutes and serve.

This is a festive, savory soup that draws on classic Italian ingredients: tomatoes, oregano, basil, garlic, and olive oil.

Italian Lentil Soup

2 cups dried green lentils
2 bay leaves
6 cups vegetable stock or water
3 tablespoons olive oil
2 cups diced onions
2 tablespoons chopped garlic
2 cups chopped fresh tomatoes
2 cups sliced zucchini
1½ tablespoons dried oregano
1½ tablespoons dried basil
2¼ teaspoons red wine vinegar
2¼ teaspoons onion powder
1 tablespoon salt
⅓ cup canned tomato paste
1 tablespoon balsamic vinegar
½ teaspoon black pepper

Wash the lentils. In a large pot, combine the lentils, bay leaves, and stock and bring to a boil. Reduce heat to medium and cook, stirring occasionally, for 30 minutes, or until the lentils are soft. In a large skillet, heat the oil and sauté the onions and garlic for 5–10 minutes, or until the onions are golden brown. Stir in the tomatoes, zucchini, oregano, basil, wine vinegar, and onion powder and sauté for 5 minutes. Set aside.

When the lentils are nearly soft, add the salt and reserved tomato mixture. Stir in the tomato paste, balsamic vinegar, and black pepper and simmer for 10–20 minutes. Remove the bay leaves and serve piping hot.

Split Pea Soup

1¾ cups dried green or yellow split peas
2 cups sliced onions
1½ cups sliced carrots
6 cups vegetable stock or water
1 teaspoon salt
¼ teaspoon fennel seeds
½ tablespoon tamari

Wash the peas. In a large pot, combine the peas, onions, carrots, and stock and bring to a boil. Reduce heat to medium-low and cook, stirring occasionally, for 35–40 minutes, or until the peas are soft and beginning to break apart.

Add the salt and fennel seeds and cook for about 10 minutes, or until the peas are mushy. Stir in the tamari and serve immediately.

Preparation and cooking time 1 hour.
Serves 4–6.

Here is one of our most popular soups. Simple ingredients and preparation make it a welcome weekend meal after a hike in the woods or a ski down a mountain. Serve with Anadama Bread, Peasant French Bread *(see Chapter 10 for bread recipes), or garlic croutons.*

Preparation and cooking time 25 minutes.

Serves 6.

Here is a Kripalu classic, a soup that makes a fine addition to a lunch or an evening meal. At Kripalu, we even eat this soup for breakfast. It's important <u>not to boil</u> the miso so its enzymes are not destroyed.

WHITE MISO-GINGER SOUP

7 cups vegetable stock or water
1 cup sliced onions
1 cup peeled cubed butternut squash
½ cup sliced carrots
½ tablespoon ginger juice
  (one 2-inch length fresh gingerroot, peeled)
2 tablespoons white miso
¾ cup small broccoli florets

In a large pot, combine the stock, onions, squash, and carrots and bring to a boil. Reduce heat to medium and cook for about 10 minutes.

Meanwhile, prepare the ginger juice by grating and squeezing the gingerroot. Dilute the miso in ¼ cup of the soup broth. Add the ginger juice, broccoli, and diluted miso to the pot and cook on low heat for 5 minutes. Serve immediately.

CHICKPEA STEW

1½ cups dried chickpeas
8 cups vegetable stock or water
One 2-inch strip kombu
1 bay leaf
2 tablespoons olive oil
1½ cups chopped onions
¾ cup sliced celery
1½ cups peeled cubed butternut squash
1 cup sliced carrots
2 tablespoons white miso diluted in ¼ cup
  warm water
1 teaspoon salt
1 teaspoon umeboshi vinegar
¼ cup chopped fresh parsley

Wash the chickpeas. In a large pot, combine the chickpeas and stock and bring to a boil. Turn off heat and let soak for 1 hour. Add the kombu and bay leaf and return to a boil. Reduce heat to simmer and cook, stirring occasionally, for about 45 minutes.

Meanwhile, in a large skillet, heat the oil and sauté the onions for 3–5 minutes or until translucent. Stir in the celery and sauté for 5 minutes more. Set aside.

After the beans have cooked for 30 minutes, add the reserved onion mixture, the squash, and carrots. Cover and cook, stirring occasionally, for 45–50 minutes, or until the beans are soft.

Add the diluted miso, salt, vinegar, and parsley and simmer for 5 minutes. Serve immediately.

**Preparation and cooking time
1 hour 45 minutes.**

**Soaking time
1 hour.**

Serves 4–6.

Chickpeas add a sweet flavor to a stew if they've been well soaked and cooked. Here they combine with onions, squash, and carrots to create an appealing autumn stew that will warm and energize you just enough to rake the remaining leaves in the yard or go for a bicycle ride.

*Here's a pleasant,
easy stew with a
two-part prepara-
tion: baking the tofu
and simmering the
stew ingredients.
The yams contribute
a slight sweetness,
the rosemary and
thyme a savory
background, and the
tahini and miso a
sweet saltiness.*

TOFU STEW

2 tablespoons olive oil
1 cup chopped onions
2 cups peeled cubed winter squash
1½ cups sliced carrots
2 cups cubed yams
4 cups vegetable stock or water
1 tablespoon salt
1 tablespoon tamari
½ tablespoon brown rice vinegar
1 pound firm tofu, rinsed, drained, and diced
1½ cups small cauliflower florets
½ cup fresh or frozen peas
2 tablespoons white miso diluted in ¼ cup
   warm water
3 tablespoons tahini
2 teaspoons umeboshi vinegar
1 teaspoon dried thyme, or
   1 tablespoon chopped fresh thyme
½ teaspoon dried rosemary, or
   ½ tablespoon chopped fresh rosemary
¼ teaspoon white pepper
¾ cup sliced celery

Preheat oven to 375°F. In a large pot, heat 1½ tablespoons of the oil and sauté the onions for 3–5 minutes or
until translucent. Add the squash, carrots, yams, and
stock and bring to a boil. Add the salt. Reduce heat to
simmer and cook for 15 minutes.

Meanwhile, in a small bowl, mix together the tamari, rice
vinegar, and remaining oil. Place the tofu on a rimmed

baking sheet and coat with the tamari mixture. Bake for 15 minutes, or until the tofu begins to firm.

Add the baked tofu, the cauliflower, and peas to the pot. Stir in the diluted miso, tahini, umeboshi vinegar, thyme, rosemary, and white pepper and simmer for 10 minutes. Add the celery and simmer for 8–10 minutes more. Serve immediately.

*Believe it or not,
this stew tastes like
the beef stew many
of us ate growing
up. It has carrots,
peas, turnips, and
chunks of sautéed
seitan, a gluten
product that mimics
meat in flavor and
texture.*

SEITAN STEW

3 tablespoons olive oil
1 cup chopped onions
1½ cups coarsely chopped seitan
1 cup coarsely chopped turnips
1 cup sliced carrots
¾ cup sliced celery
1 cup coarsely chopped parsnips or potatoes
6 cups water
¼ cup tamari
¾ cup halved fresh mushrooms
¼ cup canned crushed or pureed tomatoes
1 teaspoon dried sage
1 cup fresh or frozen peas
1 tablespoon arrowroot dissolved in ½ cup
  cold water
½ teaspoon balsamic vinegar

In a large pot, heat the oil and sauté the onions for 3–5 minutes or until translucent. Add the seitan and continue to sauté until the seitan starts to brown.

Mix in the turnips, carrots, celery, parsnips, water, and tamari and bring to a boil. Reduce heat to simmer and cook for about 25 minutes, or until the vegetables are tender. Add the mushrooms, tomatoes, sage, and peas and simmer for 10 minutes more.

Stir in the dissolved arrowroot and bring to a boil, stirring constantly. When the arrowroot is fully absorbed, reduce heat to simmer and cook, stirring occasionally, for 5–10 minutes. Add the vinegar and serve immediately.

Mexican Corn Chowder

Preparation and cooking time 30 minutes.

Serves 6.

This is a bright and spicy version of an old favorite. It cooks up in a short time to provide a festive lunch or to accompany a Mexican meal.

2 tablespoons olive oil
1½ cups diced onions
4 cups fresh or frozen corn (approximately 6–8 ears fresh, or 1 pound frozen corn)
2 teaspoons umeboshi vinegar
½ teaspoon white pepper
2 cups diced potatoes
4 cups vegetable stock or water
1 cup sliced celery
1 cup diced red bell peppers
1 teaspoon salt
2¼ teaspoons onion powder
1 teaspoon ground cumin
1 teaspoon ground paprika
⅛ teaspoon black pepper
½ tablespoon tamari
¼ cup chopped fresh cilantro

In a large pot, heat the oil and sauté the onions for 3–5 minutes or until translucent. Add the corn, vinegar, and white pepper and sauté for 5 minutes more. Stir in the potatoes and stock and bring to a boil. Reduce heat to simmer and cook for 10 minutes.

Blend one-third of the mixture in a blender or food processor. Return the blended mixture to the pot. Add the celery, bell peppers, salt, onion powder, cumin, paprika, black pepper, and tamari and simmer for 5 minutes or more. Add the cilantro just before serving. Serve.

Preparation and
cooking time
1 hour 55 minutes.
Soaking time
1 hour.
Serves 6–8.

*The combination of
kidney beans, black
beans, fresh
cilantro, and sea-
sonings that are a
little sweet, a little
sour, and very spicy
make this an un-
usual and delicious
chili. For a warm
winter meal, serve
with* Pan Corn
Bread *(see page
253).*

RED AND BLACK
BEAN CHILI

2 cups dried kidney beans
1½ cups dried black beans
14 cups boiling water or vegetable stock
2 bay leaves
¼ cup canola oil
2 cups chopped onions
2 tablespoons chopped garlic
1½ cups diced green bell peppers
3 cups chopped fresh tomatoes
    (approximately 4 medium tomatoes)
1 tablespoon dried oregano
1½ tablespoons ground cumin
1½ tablespoons ground paprika
1 teaspoon cayenne pepper
1½ tablespoons chili powder
1 teaspoon dried crushed mild chili peppers
2 tablespoons dried basil
2 teaspoons salt
1½ cups canned tomato paste
¼ cup chopped fresh cilantro
2 tablespoons fresh lemon juice

Wash the beans. Soak the beans overnight or use the
quick-soak method (see page 128), using the 14 cups
boiling water and soaking time of 1 hour.

Return the beans to a boil. Reduce heat to medium-high,
add the bay leaf, and cook, stirring occasionally, for 1
hour 45 minutes.

Meanwhile, in a large, deep skillet, heat the oil and sauté the onions and garlic for 3–5 minutes. Mix in the bell peppers, tomatoes, oregano, cumin, paprika, cayenne pepper, chili powder, chili peppers, and basil and sauté for 5 minutes more. Set aside.

After 1 hour 15 minutes, add the reserved vegetable mixture, salt, and tomato paste to the beans and cook for 30 minutes more, or until the beans are soft. Add the cilantro and lemon juice and adjust the seasonings. Serve immediately.

*This is a New
Orleans-style soup
with lots of red and
green colors (no less
than 11 cups of
chopped greens
grace this soup) and
the fire of red chili
peppers, Tabasco,
and white pepper. It
provides a powerful
nutrient "punch"
and is an excellent
way to prepare
greens for people
not used to eating
them.*

GREENS GUMBO

3 tablespoons olive oil
1 cup chopped onions
1 tablespoon chopped garlic
½ cup diced green bell peppers
½ cup diced red bell peppers
½ cup sliced celery
11 cups chopped fresh greens (any combination
  of kale, collards, spinach, Swiss chard, mustard
  greens, beet greens, watercress, or parsley)
7 cups water
One 2-inch strip kombu
2 bay leaves
½ teaspoon dried thyme
½ teaspoon dried dill
½ teaspoon dried marjoram
½ teaspoon dried sage
¼ teaspoon white pepper
¼ teaspoon dried crushed red chili peppers
1½ tablespoons salt
⅓ cup sun-dried tomatoes
1 cup hot water
1½ tablespoons kuzu dissolved in ¼ cup
  cold water
¼ teaspoon Tabasco sauce
1 tablespoon umeboshi vinegar
1 teaspoon filé powder (optional)

In a large pot, heat the oil and sauté the onions and garlic for 3–5 minutes, or until the onions are translucent.
Add both bell peppers and celery and sauté for 7–10
minutes more.

Add the greens, 7 cups water, kombu, bay leaves, herbs, white pepper, and chili peppers and bring to a boil. Add the salt. Reduce heat to medium-high and cook for 20–25 minutes.

Meanwhile, soak the sun-dried tomatoes in the hot water for 10 minutes. In a blender or food processor, blend together the tomatoes and one-third of the greens mixture. Return the blended mixture to the pot and bring to a boil.

Add the dissolved kuzu and stir until the mixture thickens just slightly. Reduce heat to low and stir in the Tabasco sauce and vinegar. Add the filé powder just before serving, if desired. Serve immediately.

*This is one of our
most popular pasta
sauces.*

SAUCE RAPHAEL

3 tablespoons olive oil
2 cups chopped onions
1½ tablespoons chopped garlic
2½ cups canned whole plum tomatoes
1¼ cups canned tomato sauce
1¼ cups canned crushed tomatoes
½ cup canned tomato paste
2 cups water
2 tablespoons dried basil, or
  ⅓ cup chopped fresh basil
½ tablespoon dried oregano, or
  1½ tablespoons chopped fresh oregano
1 teaspoon salt
¼ teaspoon whole black peppercorns
1½ cups quartered canned artichoke hearts

In a large pot, heat the oil and sauté the onions and garlic for 3–5 minutes, or until the onions are translucent. Stir in all of the tomato products, the water, herbs, salt, and peppercorns and cook on medium-high heat for 20 minutes.

Add the artichoke hearts and cook for at least 20 minutes more, stirring occasionally. Serve with your favorite pasta.

TOFU ALFREDO SAUCE

Preparation and cooking time 30 minutes.

Serves 6.

Here's a nondairy, low-calorie version of Alfredo sauce that livens up fettuccine and other pasta dishes.

¼ cup olive oil
1½ cups diced onions
1 tablespoon chopped garlic
2 cups chopped cauliflower
1 pound 12 ounces firm tofu, rinsed, drained, and cubed
1 cup whole cashews
1 cup water
½ cup soymilk
1½ tablespoons white miso
2¼ teaspoons umeboshi paste
2¼ teaspoons brown rice vinegar
1 teaspoon balsamic vinegar
Pinch white pepper
Pinch black pepper
Pinch ground nutmeg

In a medium-sized skillet, heat the oil and sauté the onions and garlic for 3–5 minutes, or until the onions are translucent. In a large, covered saucepan with a steamer basket, steam the cauliflower and tofu in water for about 10 minutes, or until the cauliflower is tender.

In a food processor, process the cashews to a paste. Continue processing and slowly add the water to create a very thick sauce. Add the steamed cauliflower and tofu, the onion mixture, and all of the remaining ingredients and blend until smooth. Pour the blended mixture in a large saucepan and heat on low heat. Serve with your favorite pasta.

Preparation and cooking time 2–3 hours or longer. Serves 8–10.

Mark, one of our cooks, had just returned from his Uncle Pasquale's funeral feeling downcast at having lost such a free-wheeling spirit, a man who smoked a mean stogie and cooked a great tomato sauce. It so happened that the Kripalu marinara sauce had gone through several incarnations, being at times too thick, too bitter, or too sour. So, on spaghetti day, everyone gathered round and thought of Uncle

Uncle Pasquale's Marinara Sauce

2½ cups canned tomato puree
3¼ cups canned crushed tomatoes
4 cups canned whole plum tomatoes
⅔ cup canned tomato paste
1½ cups diced carrots
2 bay leaves
1 tablespoon dried oregano, or
  3 tablespoons chopped fresh oregano
1 tablespoon dried basil, or
  3 tablespoons chopped fresh basil
1 tablespoon dried parsley
1 teaspoon dried marjoram
1 teaspoon fennel seeds
½ teaspoon dried crushed red chili peppers
1 tablespoon salt
½ cup extra-virgin olive oil
2 cups diced onions
¼ cup chopped garlic
1½ cups sliced celery

In a large pot, combine all of the tomato products, the carrots, bay leaves, dried herbs, chili peppers, and salt and bring to a boil. (If using fresh herbs, see below.) Reduce heat to medium and cook, stirring frequently, for 1 hour.

Meanwhile, in a large skillet, heat the oil and sauté the onions and garlic for 3–5 minutes, or until the onions are translucent. Add the celery and sauté for 5 minutes more.

Add the celery mixture to the tomato mixture and cook, stirring occasionally, for at least 1 hour (preferably 2–3 hours).

Add the fresh herbs 10 minutes before serving. Serve with your favorite pasta.

Pasquale; sure enough, help came through. Mark got the idea to add carrots for sweetness, then olive oil right at the end to smooth out the flavors. He added the final touch after a conversation with his grandmother, who said to him, "What, you have no sausage in your tomato sauce? At least add some fennel!"

**Preparation and
cooking time
35 minutes.

Serves 4–6.**

*This sauce is quick
and easy and is
delicious with
Broccoli-Walnut
Polenta (see page
87) and with simple
rice or couscous
dishes.*

Tomato-Basil Sauce

1½ tablespoons olive oil
2 cups diced onions
1½ tablespoons chopped garlic
4 cups canned tomato sauce or puree
4 cups canned whole plum tomatoes
1 teaspoon salt
½ cup chopped fresh basil

In a large pot, heat the oil and sauté the onions and garlic for 3–5 minutes, or until the onions are translucent. Stir in the tomato sauce. Crush the tomatoes by hand and add to the pot. Add the salt and simmer for 20 minutes.

Add the basil and simmer for 5 minutes more. Serve with your favorite pasta.

CREAMY MUSHROOM SAUCE

Here's a sauce for rice, vegetables, or tofu. It tastes delicious, yet takes little time to prepare.

2 tablespoons butter
5 cups sliced fresh mushrooms
  (12–16 ounces mushrooms)
3 cups milk
1 cup cream
¼ cup chopped scallions
1 teaspoon salt
1 teaspoon garlic powder
1 teaspoon dried tarragon, or
  1 tablespoon chopped fresh tarragon
¼ teaspoon black pepper
½ cup unbleached white flour

In a large skillet, melt the butter and sauté the mushrooms for 10 minutes.

Mix in the milk, cream, scallions, salt, garlic powder, tarragon, and black pepper. Heat until warm, then slowly whisk in the flour, stirring constantly until the mixture becomes thick and creamy. Serve.

**Preparation and
cooking time
40 minutes.
Serves 4–6.**

*This is the perfect
sauce to serve with
Grilled Tempeh
with Broccoli (see
page 96) or with
rice or stir-fry
dishes.*

ALMOND-
MUSTARD SAUCE

1 ½ cups slivered almonds
3 ½ cups water
2 tablespoons prepared brown mustard
1 teaspoon salt
1 teaspoon umeboshi vinegar
½ teaspoon onion powder
½ teaspoon dried tarragon, or
    1 ½ teaspoons chopped fresh tarragon
½ teaspoon mirin
⅛ teaspoon ground paprika
⅛ teaspoon black pepper
⅛ teaspoon white pepper
Pinch ground nutmeg

In a blender or food processor, process the almonds until
well ground. Gradually add the water and mustard and
blend well.

Pour the almond mixture into a medium-sized saucepan
and fold in the remaining ingredients. (If using fresh tarragon, see below.) Cook on low heat, stirring frequently,
for 20–25 minutes, or until the sauce thickens to the
desired consistency.

Add the fresh tarragon 5–10 minutes before serving.
Serve.

Spiced Peanut Sauce

Preparation and cooking time 15 minutes.

Serves 4–6.

This sauce was created to accompany Pad Thai Noodles (see pages 104– 105) or for dishes that need spicing up. (Use peanut butter that is free of salt, sugar, and additives.)

2½ tablespoons sesame oil
1 tablespoon ground cumin
½ tablespoon dried crushed mild chili peppers
1 teaspoon ground coriander
Pinch cayenne pepper
1½ cups natural peanut butter
2½ tablespoons tamari
1 teaspoon salt
½ teaspoon black pepper
2 cups water

In a small skillet, heat the oil and sauté the cumin, chili peppers, coriander, and cayenne pepper for 1–2 minutes.

In a blender or food processor, slowly blend together the cumin mixture, peanut butter, tamari, salt, and black pepper, adding the water while blending, until desired thickness.

In a medium-sized saucepan, heat the mixture on low heat until warm. Serve.

*This sauce is rich
and sweet, with a
hint of sour. It
complements
sautéed vegetables
and tofu, soba
noodles, rice, or
stir-fry.*

PLUM SAUCE

1 tablespoon sesame oil
1¾ cups sliced red onions
½ cup canned crushed pineapple
½ teaspoon dried crushed mild chili peppers
¾ cup diced prunes
2½ cups apple cider
3 tablespoons canned tomato paste
1 cup canned tomato sauce
1 tablespoon cider vinegar
2¼ teaspoons salt
½ tablespoon fresh lemon juice
¼ teaspoon black pepper

In a large saucepan, heat the oil and sauté the onions for
3–5 minutes or until translucent. Add the pineapple and
chili peppers and continue to sauté on low heat.

Meanwhile, in a blender or food processor, blend together the prunes, cider, and tomato paste. Add the
prune mixture to the onion mixture and mix together
well.

Stir in the tomato sauce, vinegar, salt, lemon juice, and
black pepper and simmer for 10 minutes. Serve.

Lemon Tahini Sauce

1 cup tahini
¾ cup water
2 tablespoons tamari
3 tablespoons fresh lemon juice

In a blender or with a fork, blend all of the ingredients until smooth. Serve. (This sauce can be stored in the refrigerator for several days.)

**Preparation time
5 minutes.**

Serves 6–8.

This simple sauce goes well over Hummus Among Us (see page 201) or with couscous dishes.

Sweet Mustard Sauce

2½ cups water
⅓ cup tamari
2 cups rice syrup
⅓ cup prepared brown mustard

In a large saucepan, mix together the water and tamari and bring to a boil. Reduce heat to simmer and cook for 3–5 minutes.

Add the syrup and return to a boil. Turn off heat and add the mustard, whisking the sauce to a smooth consistency. Serve.

**Preparation and
cooking time
10 minutes.**

Serves 6.

This is a tasty dipping sauce for stir-fry, grilled tofu, or tempeh.

*Here's another rich-
tasting, nondairy,
low-calorie sauce;
use it like any dairy
hollandaise sauce.
It's especially good
over fresh spring
asparagus or veg-
etables and rice.*

Tofu Hollandaise Sauce

1 cup cooked oatmeal
1 pound soft tofu, rinsed and drained
3 tablespoons fresh lemon juice
2½ tablespoons tahini
2¼ teaspoons prepared brown mustard
2¼ teaspoons umeboshi vinegar
1 teaspoon salt
1 teaspoon dried tarragon, or
  1 tablespoon chopped fresh tarragon
¼ teaspoon ground turmeric
⅛ teaspoon black pepper

In a blender or food processor, blend together all of the
ingredients until smooth. (May need to add ½ cup or
more water, depending on the consistency of the oatmeal.)

In a medium-sized saucepan, heat the oatmeal mixture
on low heat, stirring constantly, until evenly warm. Serve.

TOFU SOUR CREAM

1 pound soft tofu, rinsed and drained
¼ cup chopped scallions
1 tablespoon umeboshi vinegar
1 tablespoon fresh lemon juice
½ teaspoon salt
1 tablespoon chopped fresh chives (optional)
2 tablespoons olive oil

In a blender or food processor, blend together all of the ingredients, except the oil.

While blending, slowly pour in the oil and blend until smooth. Serve at room temperature or chill and serve later. (This topping can be stored in the refrigerator for 2–3 days.)

Preparation time 10 minutes.

Makes 1½ cups.

Try this healthy topping with potatoes, tacos, or enchiladas.

Here's a simple brown gravy that will perk up mashed potatoes or millet. Nutritional yeast boosts the flavor and adds B vitamins. The secret to this recipe is to cook the onions thoroughly.

AUTUMN GRAVY

¼ cup corn or canola oil
4 cups diced onions (3–4 medium onions)
1¾ cups water
2 tablespoons tamari
3 tablespoons nutritional yeast
2 teaspoons dried sage
¼ teaspoon black pepper

In a large skillet, heat the oil and sauté the onions for 10–12 minutes or until browned.

When the onions begin to caramelize, slowly add the water, about ½ cup at a time, stirring constantly. Add the tamari, yeast, sage, and black pepper and simmer for 5 minutes.

In a blender or food processor, blend the mixture thoroughly. Return the mixture to the skillet and reheat. Serve.

ENTICING ENTRÉES

Chapter 5

MANY PEOPLE ASK how we manage to come up with the impressive array of dishes that we serve at Kripalu. In two words: bold experimentation. To satisfy a multitude of visiting guests and live-in residents, we have experimented through the years with a wide range of cooking methods and have adapted recipes to suit our evergrowing clientele. Creating tasty meals that please a variety of palates is a challenge, especially combined with the logistics of serving so many people, but our cook's team always rises to the challenge.

For example, when Balavant, one of our bakers, had the inspiration to add white pizza to the menu, he visited every restaurant in the Berkshires that had white pizza; he also had some varieties of white pizza delivered to our bakery, where he consumed them with the kitchen purchasing agent and the baking chef. Then for "Pizza Monday," our famous pizza day, Balavant promised to deliver twenty white pizzas to the serving line. Huddled in the kitchen, with help and advice from good friends and up to his ears in cheddar, mozzarella, and ricotta cheeses, he finally emerged with the quintessential *Kripalu White Pizza.*

Similarly, Lokesh, a longtime Kripalu cook, wanted to create a veggie burger that would knock our socks off. We had had many varieties through the years—some with tofu, some with lentils, some that crumbled, and some that challenged Plymouth Rock for hardness. But he wanted a recipe that called out, "This is it!"—the Big Mac of vegetarian circles. Lokesh experimented with all manner of ingredients from rice to cheese to tofu to seitan and finally came up with our *Cheese-Nut Burger,* a burger that will knock your shoes off, too.

Our entrées draw on diverse national and ethnic heritages. We have *Southern-Fried Tofu, Pad Thai Noodles, Seitan Stroganoff,* and many dishes inspired by Italian, Greek, and Indian cuisine. It's fun trying your hand at something different, if only to break through resistance to the unknown. Try seitan or tempeh, for instance, if you haven't already; you'll find quite a few artful recipes for them in this chapter, with excellent instructions so you can serve them with pride.

If you're looking for a light variation, a main dish that truly nourishes, while holding the line on fat and calories, turn to Chapter 13 for our low-fat alternatives.

See what happens when you adapt these recipes to suit your taste and available time. Most of our cooks have at one time or another had a hand in adjusting old recipes, while creating new ones to surprise us all. In fact, the beauty of our kitchen is the quality of spaciousness and open-ended play that allows the cooks to turn cooking into creation, while attending to the logistics of serving meals on time. The amazing thing is that most of us are not professionally trained cooks, at least not at the beginning. Our cooks have chosen to live the Kripalu spiritual lifestyle, which includes the yogic practice of *seva,* or service. *Seva* means service not just to others, but also to the undiscovered, potential parts of ourselves.

If you have the idea that you're not much of a cook, here's the chance to dismiss that thought and start on a new path. Sometimes breakthrough occurs; for me, it happened years ago when I worked on Chandrakant's paint crew. We were on the second floor of a meditation building "slinging mud," that is, applying thick coats of joint compound to the drywall to prepare it for painting; I had never "slung mud" before. But Chandrakant said, and I can still hear his voice ringing out to me, "Just put it up like you know what you're doing." In the same spirit of adventure, I invite you to enter your kitchen and create along with us—just cook it as if you know what you're doing! You'll surprise yourself with some dazzling feasts.

*This Greek-style
casserole combines
the nutty, aromatic
flavor of white
basmati rice with
the savory tastes of
feta, spinach, and
dill and the sweet-
ness of raisins. The
longer preparation
and cooking time is
worth the effort,
and the flavors
deepen when refrig-
erated and reheated.*

SPINACH-FETA CASSEROLE

Rice Layer:
1 tablespoon olive oil
$1\frac{1}{2}$ cups sliced onions
$\frac{1}{2}$ tablespoon chopped garlic
$2\frac{1}{2}$ cups water
1 cup white basmati rice
$\frac{1}{2}$ teaspoon salt
$\frac{1}{8}$ teaspoon black pepper
$\frac{1}{2}$ cup raisins
$\frac{1}{3}$ cup slivered almonds
1 teaspoon dried dill
1 tablespoon chopped fresh dill

Spinach Layer:
1 tablespoon olive oil
$1\frac{1}{2}$ cups sliced onions
$\frac{1}{2}$ tablespoon chopped garlic
1 pound 8 ounces frozen spinach, thawed
$1\frac{2}{3}$ cups diced fresh tomatoes
$1\frac{1}{2}$ tablespoons fresh lemon juice
$\frac{1}{2}$ teaspoon salt
$\frac{1}{8}$ teaspoon black pepper
$\frac{2}{3}$ pound feta cheese, crumbled
1 medium tomato, sliced

To make the rice layer: In a large skillet, heat the oil and
sauté the onions and garlic for 3–5 minutes, or until the
onions are translucent. Add the water, rice, salt, black
pepper, raisins, almonds, and dried dill. Cover and cook
on medium heat for 15–20 minutes, or until the rice is

soft and the water is absorbed. Add the fresh dill and set aside.

To make the spinach layer: In a separate large skillet, heat the oil and sauté the onions and garlic for 3–5 minutes, or until the onions are translucent. Stir in the spinach, diced tomatoes, lemon juice, salt, and black pepper and mix thoroughly. Heat the mixture until warm. Turn off heat and add the cheese.

Preheat oven to 350°F. In a 9 x 12-inch baking pan, spread the rice mixture on the bottom and layer the spinach mixture on top. Garnish with the sliced tomato and warm in the oven for 10 minutes. Serve immediately.

This elegant pasta dish combines the richness of eggplant with the earthy tones of mushrooms, olives, and artichokes. It's delicious served hot or cold.

To wash mushrooms: In a plastic bag, place the mushrooms and add water. Gently shake the bag several times and change the water, if needed. Drain the mushrooms in a colander. Lay the mushrooms on a clean towel and pat dry.

EGGPLANT PROVENÇAL

12 ounces dried fettuccine pasta
½ cup olive oil
2 tablespoons chopped garlic
4 cups peeled cubed eggplant
  (approximately 1 pound eggplant)
½ cup halved fresh mushrooms
1 cup sliced red onions
½ cup diced red bell peppers
½ cup chopped fresh basil
1 teaspoon salt
¼ teaspoon black pepper
1 cup canned artichoke hearts
1½ cups chopped fresh tomatoes
1 cup pitted whole small black olives
½ tablespoon balsamic vinegar
½ cup grated Parmesan cheese (optional)

In a large saucepan, cook the pasta in boiling water until tender but still firm. Drain and rinse. Set aside and keep warm.

Meanwhile, in a large skillet, heat the oil and sauté the garlic for 3 minutes. Add the eggplant and sauté for 5–10 minutes, or until the eggplant is tender. Stir in the mushrooms, onions, and bell peppers and sauté for 2 minutes more. After 1 minute, add the basil, salt, and black pepper. Turn off heat.

Add the reserved noodles, artichoke hearts, tomatoes, olives, and vinegar to the eggplant mixture. Top with the cheese, if desired, and serve immediately.

BROCCOLI-WALNUT POLENTA

2 tablespoons olive oil
2 tablespoons chopped garlic
2½ cups grated broccoli including stems
5¾ cups water
2¼ teaspoons salt
1¾ cups yellow cornmeal
1 cup cold water
1¼ cups chopped walnuts
2 cups diced red bell peppers
⅓ cup chopped fresh parsley
2¼ teaspoons umeboshi vinegar
2¼ teaspoons black pepper

In a large skillet, heat the oil and sauté the garlic for 3 minutes. Add the broccoli and sauté for 10 minutes more. Set aside and keep warm.

In a large pot, bring the water to a boil. Add the salt. In a blender or food processor, mix together the cornmeal and cold water to make a slurry. Slowly stir the slurry into the boiling water. Reduce heat to medium and continue stirring until the mixture begins to thicken. Add the reserved broccoli mixture, the walnuts, bell peppers, parsley, vinegar, and black pepper and cook, stirring frequently, for about 30 minutes.

To test for doneness, take a spoonful of the hot mixture and let cool. It should hold together well. Pour the mixture into a lightly oiled 9 x 12-inch baking pan and let cool for 30 minutes or longer before slicing. Serve.

Preparation and cooking time 45 minutes.

Cooling time 30 minutes.

Serves 6–8.

The inclusion of broccoli and walnuts turns this polenta into a hearty main dish. Wonderful by itself or served with Tomato-Basil Sauce or Vegetable Creole (see pages 72 and 150–151).

Here is one of our richer concoctions, a delicious Stroganoff without the beef. This creamy dish of seitan, mushrooms, peas, and noodles is a real company-pleaser, and it can be prepared quickly so you can mingle with your guests.

SEITAN STROGANOFF

½ pound dried ribbon egg noodles
¼ cup butter
1½ cups sliced onions
2 cups cubed seitan
  (approximately 1 pound seitan)
3 cups sliced fresh mushrooms
  (8–12 ounces mushrooms)
1 tablespoon dried tarragon
1½ cups milk
⅓ cup unbleached white flour
2 cups light cream
1 cup cooked peas
½ tablespoon salt
½ teaspoon ground nutmeg

In a medium-sized saucepan, cook the noodles until tender but still firm. Drain and rinse. Set aside.

In a large, deep skillet, melt the butter and sauté the onions for 3–5 minutes. Add the seitan and sauté for 5 minutes. Add the mushrooms and sauté for 5 minutes more. Stir in the tarragon and turn off heat.

In a medium-sized saucepan, heat the milk and whisk in the flour until smooth and well blended. Stir in the cream and blend well. Add the reserved noodles, cream mixture, peas, salt, and nutmeg to the seitan mixture. Reheat until hot and well combined. Serve immediately.

SPECIAL TOFU MARINADES

The following three tofu recipes make use of marinades that can be prepared the night before so you're off to a running start the next day. A delightful and easy way to serve tofu, each dish combines well with any of our grain dishes or with *Light and Lively Stir-Fry with Tofu* (see pages 344–345).

GRILLED TOFU CUBES

1 pound firm tofu, rinsed, drained, and patted dry
1 tablespoon ginger juice (one 1½-inch length fresh gingerroot, peeled)
½ cup tamari
½ tablespoon brown rice vinegar or fresh lemon juice
½ cup water
¼ cup canola oil
½ teaspoon chopped fresh basil

Cut the tofu into cubes and place in a large, shallow bowl.

Prepare the ginger juice by grating and squeezing the gingerroot. In a small bowl, blend together the ginger juice, tamari, vinegar, and water and pour over the tofu. Marinate for at least 1 hour at room temperature or cover and marinate overnight in the refrigerator, turning the tofu at least once.

In a medium-sized skillet, heat the oil and grill the tofu on medium-high heat until the outsides are crispy. Stir in the basil just before serving. Serve.

Variation: Slice the tofu, instead of cubing, to make tofu sandwiches.

Preparation and cooking time 20 minutes. Marinating time 1 hour or overnight. Serves 4.

GOLDEN BROWN TOFU

1 pound firm tofu, rinsed and
    drained

Marinade:
1½ cups water
2 tablespoons peeled grated
    fresh gingerroot
2 tablespoons fresh lemon juice

Sauce:
1 tablespoon olive oil
1 cup sliced red onions
1 tablespoon chopped garlic
2 tablespoons unsulphured
    molasses
2 tablespoons fresh orange juice
2 tablespoons fresh lemon juice
½ tablespoon canned tomato
    paste
2 teaspoons salt
½ teaspoon yellow mustard
    seeds
¼ teaspoon black pepper
¼ teaspoon white pepper
⅛ teaspoon cayenne pepper
Sprig fresh parsley

Cut the tofu into 8–10 slices and place
in a large, shallow bowl.

To make the marinade: In a small

bowl, mix together all of the marinade
ingredients and pour over the tofu.
Marinate for at least 1 hour at room
temperature or cover and marinate
overnight in the refrigerator, turning
the tofu at least once.

Preheat oven to 375°F. To make the
sauce: In a medium-sized skillet, heat the
oil and sauté the onions and garlic for
6–8 minutes, or until the onions begin
to brown. Stir in the remaining sauce
ingredients, except the parsley, and
simmer for 3–5 minutes.

Place the tofu in an oiled 9 x 9-inch
baking pan and cover with the sauce.
Bake for 20–25 minutes or until piping
hot. Garnish with the parsley and serve
immediately.

**Preparation 20 minutes. Baking
time 20–25 minutes. Marinating
time 1 hour or overnight. Serves 4.**

SOUTHERN-FRIED TOFU

2 pounds firm tofu, rinsed,
    drained, and patted dry

Marinade:
2½ cups warm water
¼ cup white miso
1 teaspoon salt
1 tablespoon dried thyme
1 tablespoon dried sage
¼ teaspoon black pepper

Breading:
⅓ cup nutritional yeast
1⅔ cups crushed unsweetened
    cornflakes
1 tablespoon onion powder
1 tablespoon garlic powder
2 teaspoons dried oregano
1 teaspoon dried basil
1 teaspoon ground paprika
½ teaspoon celery seeds
½ teaspoon chili powder
½ teaspoon black pepper
½ teaspoon ground mustard
¼ teaspoon ground cloves

Cut each pound of tofu into 8–10 slices
and place in a large, shallow bowl.

To make the marinade: In a small bowl,
mix together all of the marinade ingredients and pour over the tofu. Marinate for 2 hours at room temperature or cover and marinate overnight
in the refrigerator, turning the tofu
at least once.

Preheat oven to 400°F. To make the
breading: In a large bowl, combine
all of the breading ingredients and
mix together well.

Lightly coat each tofu slice with the
breading. Place the slices on a well-
oiled baking sheet and bake for 20–
25 minutes or until crinkly and
browned. Serve immediately.

**Preparation and baking time
30 minutes. Marinating time
2 hours or overnight. Serves 4.**

*An orange and
pepper glaze com-
bine with a spicy
marinade to make
this sweet and tangy
dish. It's a deli-
cious, unusual, and
quick entrée for a
main meal. Serve
over brown rice or
with your favorite
pasta.*

TOFU IN ORANGE PEPPER SAUCE

1 pound firm tofu, rinsed and drained

Marinade:
1½ tablespoons sesame oil
2¼ teaspoons chopped garlic
2¼ teaspoons peeled finely chopped fresh
  gingerroot
¾ cup fresh orange juice
1 teaspoon Tabasco sauce
¼ cup apple cider
1 teaspoon chili powder
½ teaspoon dried crushed mild chili peppers
1 teaspoon ground paprika
1 tablespoon fresh lemon juice
1½ tablespoons tamari
½ tablespoon salt
⅛ teaspoon ground anise

Glaze:
1 tablespoon orange zest
2¼ teaspoons kuzu dissolved in ⅛ cup cold
  water
2 tablespoons fresh orange juice
½ cup diced red bell peppers
1 tablespoon pure maple syrup
⅛ teaspoon black pepper
Pinch cayenne pepper
¼ cup chopped fresh parsley

Preheat oven to 350°F. Cut the tofu into 8 slices, then
cut into triangles. Set aside.

To make the marinade: In a medium-sized saucepan, heat the oil and sauté the garlic and gingerroot for 3–5 minutes. Add the remaining marinade ingredients and mix together well.

In a lightly oiled 9 x 9-inch baking pan, place the reserved tofu and cover with three-fourths of the marinade. Bake for about 15 minutes or until lightly browned.

To make the glaze: Peel and finely chop some of the outer skin of 1 orange to make the zest. (Do not include the white membrane.)

In a small saucepan, bring to a boil the remaining marinade. Reduce heat to medium and stir in the dissolved kuzu. Add the remaining glaze ingredients, except the parsley, and cook, stirring constantly, until a thick and cloudy glaze forms. Pour the glaze over the baked tofu and garnish with the parsley. Serve immediately.

*This delightful,
easy-to-make tofu
dish needs only 15
minutes of hands-on
time, yet it tastes
like a gourmet
offering. Its rich
flavor is brightened
with the tang of
ginger and scallions.*

Baked Tofu with Mushrooms and Scallions

2 pounds firm tofu, rinsed and drained
1 tablespoon ginger juice
  (one 2-inch length fresh gingerroot, peeled)
¾ cup water or vegetable stock
¼ cup tamari
¼ cup brown rice vinegar
⅔ cup chopped scallions
1½ tablespoons kuzu dissolved in ¼ cup cold
  water
3½ cups sliced fresh mushrooms
  (8–12 ounces mushrooms)

Squeeze out excess water in the tofu with a clean towel.
Cut each pound into 8–9 slices. Place the tofu in an oiled
9 x 12-inch baking pan. Prepare the ginger juice by grating and squeezing the gingerroot.

Preheat oven to 375°F. In a large saucepan, combine the
water, tamari, vinegar, prepared ginger juice, and ⅓ cup
of the scallions and bring to a boil. Add the dissolved
kuzu, stirring constantly, until the mixture thickens. Turn
off heat.

Stir in the mushrooms and pour the mixture over the
tofu. Bake for about 30 minutes, or until the tofu is hot.
Garnish with the remaining scallions. Serve immediately.

Variation: Use 2 cups dried shiitake mushrooms, soaked,
trimmed, and sliced, instead of white mushrooms.

TOFU YUNG

1 tablespoon canola oil
¾ cup sliced fresh mushrooms
¾ cup chopped scallions
¾ cup frozen peas
1 cup sliced canned water chestnuts
1 pound soft tofu, rinsed and drained
2 tablespoons tamari
1½ cups fresh mung bean sprouts
½ teaspoon salt

Preheat oven to 325°F. In a large skillet, heat the oil and sauté the mushrooms, scallions, peas, and water chestnuts for 5 minutes.

In a medium-sized bowl, blend together the tofu and tamari until smooth. Add the tofu mixture, bean sprouts, and salt to the mushroom mixture.

Scoop the mixture onto an oiled baking sheet and form flat patties. Bake for 20 minutes, or until the patties are firm and slightly brown. Serve immediately.

Adapted from *Tofu Cookery* by Louise Hagler. 1991. Reprinted by permission of The Book Publishing Company. (See Bibliography.)

**Preparation time
15 minutes.**

**Baking time
20 minutes.**

**Serves 4–6. (Makes
8–10 patties.)**

This is a latter-day and much-revised version of a recipe from Louise Hagler's Tofu Cookery. *The patties have a burgerlike texture and flavor and make excellent lunch-box-fillers. For the best results, use soft tofu and serve with* Almond-Mustard Sauce *(see page 74) and rice.*

Preparation and
cooking time
30 minutes.

Marinating time
2 hours.

Serves 4.

*By blending the
light flavors of
broccoli and basil
with the nutty,
substantial flavor of
tempeh, this grilled
tempeh dish be-
comes a classic.
Don't be frightened
away by tempeh: It
marinates just like
fish filets or firm
tofu and can be
successfully grilled,
baked, or fried.*

GRILLED TEMPEH WITH BROCCOLI

8 ounces tempeh, cut into 1–1½-inch cubes
   or triangles
½ cup tamari
½ cup apple cider
½ cup water
1 tablespoon brown rice vinegar
⅓ cup arrowroot
1 tablespoon dried basil
¼ teaspoon black pepper
3 tablespoons canola oil
4 cups broccoli spears
   (approximately 2 stalks broccoli)
1½ cups fresh mung bean sprouts
2 tablespoons water
1 tablespoon tamari
½ tablespoon umeboshi vinegar

Place the tempeh in a large, shallow bowl. In a small
bowl, mix together the ½ cup tamari, the cider, ½ cup
water, and rice vinegar to make a marinade. Pour over the
tempeh and marinate for at least 2 hours.

In a quart-sized, sealable plastic bag, combine the arrowroot, basil, and black pepper. Place half of the the tempeh
in the bag and shake until well coated. Remove and repeat with the remaining tempeh. Set aside.

In a large skillet, heat the oil and grill the tempeh on
medium-high heat until brown on each side. Drain on
paper towels and set aside.

Add the broccoli and bean sprouts to the same skillet and sauté for 2 minutes. Stir in the 2 tablespoons water, 1 tablespoon tamari, and umeboshi vinegar. Cover and cook until the broccoli is bright green and tender-crisp. Mix in the reserved tempeh and serve immediately.

Here's a pleasant tempeh variant with peanuts, dried chili peppers, green bell peppers, and garlic. With a mildly piquant flavor and a personality all its own, this dish is excellent with your favorite pasta or served over brown rice.

KUNG PAO TEMPEH

6 tablespoons canola oil
Pinch salt
8 ounces tempeh, cut into 1-inch squares
1½ cups diced onions
1 tablespoon chopped garlic
1 tablespoon peeled grated fresh gingerroot
½ teaspoon dried crushed mild chili peppers
1½ cups small broccoli florets
½ cup diced carrots
½ cup diced green bell peppers
½ cup unsalted dry roasted peanuts
2½ tablespoons tamari
1½ teaspoons sesame oil

In a large skillet, heat 4 tablespoons of the canola oil and the salt and grill the tempeh on medium-high heat until golden brown and crispy. Drain on papers towels and set aside.

In a separate, large skillet, heat the remaining canola oil and sauté the onions and garlic for 3–5 minutes, or until the onions are translucent. Stir in the gingerroot, chili peppers, broccoli, carrots, bell peppers, and peanuts and sauté for 5–7 minutes more, or until the vegetables are tender-crisp.

Add the reserved tempeh, the tamari, and sesame oil and simmer for 5–10 minutes. Serve immediately.

TEMPEH BARBECUE

3 tablespoons canola oil
8 ounces tempeh, cut into $2\frac{1}{2}$ x $\frac{1}{2}$-inch pieces
$1\frac{1}{2}$ teaspoons salt
1 teaspoon garlic powder
$\frac{3}{4}$ teaspoon black pepper
1 cup sliced onions
$\frac{1}{2}$ cup sliced fresh mushrooms
$\frac{1}{2}$ cup canned tomato sauce
1–2 tablespoons canned tomato paste
2 tablespoons unsulphured molasses
2 tablespoons fresh lemon juice
1 tablespoon red wine vinegar
1 tablespoon prepared brown mustard
$\frac{1}{2}$ teaspoon ground mustard
$2\frac{1}{4}$ teaspoons tamari

In a medium-sized skillet, heat 2 tablespoons of the oil and grill the tempeh on medium-high heat until brown on both sides, adding 1 teaspoon of the salt, the garlic powder, and $\frac{1}{4}$ teaspoon of the black pepper. Drain on paper towels and set aside.

In a large skillet, heat the remaining oil and sauté the onions and mushrooms for 3–5 minutes, or until the onions are translucent.

Add the tomato sauce and paste, molasses, lemon juice, vinegar, prepared and ground mustards, tamari, remaining black pepper and salt and bring to a boil. Reduce heat to simmer, add the reserved tempeh, and cook for at least 15 minutes. Serve immediately.

Preparation and cooking time 30 minutes.

Serves 2–4.

The thick "meatiness" of the tempeh lends itself well to a barbecue. Here's a delicious, protein-rich meal, ready in just 30 minutes. Serve over rice or in whole-wheat buns.

Preparation time 45 minutes.

Baking time 35–45 minutes.

Serves 6–8.

Here is a classic lasagna that combines spinach and mushrooms for flavor and color. Use canned tomato sauce or, if you have time, prepare one of the homemade tomato sauces in Chapter 4. Children (and others) will not have to be told to eat their spinach when you serve this meal.

SPINACH-CHEESE LASAGNA

2 tablespoons olive oil
1½ cups chopped onions
1 tablespoon chopped garlic
1½ cups sliced fresh mushrooms
6 cups washed chopped fresh spinach
   (approximately 1 pound spinach, loosely
   packed)
1 teaspoon salt
¼ teaspoon black pepper
2 eggs, beaten
2 cups ricotta cheese
½ tablespoon dried oregano
1½ cups grated mozzarella cheese
3 cups canned tomato sauce
1 pound dried lasagna pasta, cooked, drained,
   and rinsed, or 3 sheets fresh lasagna pasta,
   cooked, drained, and rinsed
⅓ cup grated Parmesan cheese

Preheat oven to 375°F. In a large skillet, heat the oil and sauté the onions and garlic for 3–5 minutes, or until the onions are translucent.

Add the mushrooms to the onion mixture and sauté for 5 minutes. Add the spinach, salt, and black pepper and sauté for 3–5 minutes, or until the spinach wilts. Turn off heat and stir in the eggs, ricotta cheese, oregano, and mozzarella cheese.

In an oiled 9 x 12-inch baking pan, make alternating layers of the tomato sauce, cooked pasta, and cheese mixture, ending with the tomato sauce. (Make sure the pasta is well covered with the sauce so it remains soft and moist while cooking.)

Top with the Parmesan cheese and bake for 35–45 minutes, or until the sauce is bubbly and the cheese is melted. Let stand for 5 minutes before serving. Serve.

*Kuntal, our chief
recipe tester, devel-
oped this recipe
using grated soy
cheese, which can be
found in many
natural foods stores
and specialty mar-
kets. She likes the
idea that you can
have a nondairy
lasagna that's as
rich and satisfying
as a traditional
lasagna without all
of the fat and
calories. Plus, this
lasagna tastes just
as good reheated, so
you can serve deli-
cious leftovers.*

TOFU-BASIL
LASAGNA

1 pound soft tofu, rinsed, drained, and mashed
2 cups finely chopped onions
3 tablespoons umeboshi vinegar
½ teaspoon black pepper
1 teaspoon onion powder
1 tablespoon dried oregano
4 cups washed chopped fresh spinach
   (approximately 12 ounces spinach, loosely
   packed)
1½ cups chopped fresh basil
½ cup olive oil
1 tablespoon chopped garlic
⅓ cup chopped walnuts
1½ teaspoons salt
2½ cups grated soy cheese
1½ cups *Tomato-Basil Sauce* (see page 72) or
   canned tomato sauce
1 pound dried lasagna pasta, cooked, drained,
   and rinsed, or 3 sheets fresh lasagna pasta,
   cooked, drained, and rinsed

In a large bowl, mix together the tofu, onions, vinegar,
black pepper, onion powder, oregano, and spinach and
set aside.

In a blender or food processor, blend together the basil,
oil, garlic, walnuts, and salt. Add the basil mixture to the
reserved tofu mixture and stir together well. Mix in 1½
cups of the cheese.

Preheat oven to 375°F. In an oiled 9 x 12-inch baking pan, make alternating layers of the *Tomato-Basil Sauce,* cooked pasta, and the combined tofu mixture, ending with the tomato sauce. (Make sure the pasta is well covered with the sauce so it remains soft and moist while cooking.)

Top with the remaining cheese and bake for 35–45 minutes, or until the sauce is bubbly and the cheese is melted. Let stand for 5 minutes before serving. Serve.

Preparation and
cooking time
45 minutes.

Marinating time
1 hour.

Serves 4.

*This spicy tempeh
and noodle dish
evokes an Oriental
mood. It is no
wonder, because a
young chef named
Justis spent many
hours in our
kitchen, pondering
how to create a
combination of
tangy, peanutty,
and spicy qualities
and aroma. After
much sampling,
adjusting, tasting,
and thinking, he hit
upon just the right
blend. Try this dish
with* Spiced Peanut
Sauce *(see page
75).*

Pad Thai Noodles

8 ounces tempeh, cut into ¼ x ½-inch
   rectangles
¼ cup tamari
¼ cup brown rice vinegar
1 cup water
½ cup arrowroot
¼ cup canola oil
⅔ pound dried ¼-inch wide rice noodles
2 tablespoons sesame oil
2 tablespoons chopped garlic
¾ cup chopped unsalted peanuts
¾ cup chopped scallions
1¼ cups fresh mung bean sprouts

Sauce:
½ cup water
½ cup rice syrup
¼ cup cider vinegar
1 teaspoon ground paprika
1½ tablespoons tamari
1 teaspoon dried crushed red chili peppers

Place the tempeh in a medium-sized bowl. In a small
saucepan, stir together the tamari, vinegar, and water and
bring to a boil. Pour the mixture over the tempeh and
marinate for at least 1 hour.

Drain the tempeh and coat with the arrowroot. In a medium-sized skillet, heat the canola oil and grill the
tempeh on high heat. Remove and drain on paper towels.

Set aside and keep warm.

Meanwhile, in a large bowl, soak the noodles in the warm water for about 15 minutes or until tender but still firm. Drain and rinse. Set aside and keep warm.

To make the sauce: In a small bowl, combine all of the sauce ingredients and set aside.

In a large skillet, heat the sesame oil and sauté the garlic for 3–5 minutes. Add the sauce and simmer for 2–3 minutes. Stir in the reserved noodles and coat well with the sauce. Mix in the reserved tempeh, the peanuts, scallions, and bean sprouts. Serve immediately.

*A longtime favorite
of Kripalu resi-
dents, perhaps
because it reminds
us of childhood,
this dish is a hearty
version of the old
standard, with a
tasteful blend of
broccoli, mush-
rooms, and cheddar
and Parmesan
cheeses.*

BAKED MACARONI AND CHEESE CASSEROLE

12 ounces dried elbow macaroni pasta
1½ cups small broccoli florets
1½ cups sliced fresh mushrooms
5 tablespoons butter
1½ cups milk
2 tablespoons unbleached white flour
1 teaspoon salt
¼ teaspoon ground nutmeg
1½ teaspoons ground mustard
½ teaspoon white pepper
1¾ cups grated sharp cheddar cheese
1 cup dried whole-grain bread crumbs
1½ tablespoons grated Parmesan cheese

In a large saucepan, cook the pasta until tender but still firm, adding the broccoli and mushrooms at the end of the cooking time to parboil them. Drain, rinse, and set aside.

Preheat oven to 400°F. In a separate saucepan, melt the butter. Reserve 1 tablespoon melted butter and set aside.

Add the milk to the saucepan and warm the mixture on low heat. Whisk in the flour, salt, nutmeg, mustard, white pepper, and cheddar cheese until well blended. Turn off heat.

In a large bowl, combine the reserved pasta mixture and the cheese mixture and place in an oiled 9 x 12-inch baking pan. In a small bowl, mix together the bread crumbs, Parmesan cheese, and the reserved melted butter. Top the casserole with the bread crumb mixture and bake for 40–45 minutes. Serve immediately.

Preparation time
30 minutes.

Baking time
20 minutes.

Serves 4–6.

Kuntal, our chief recipe tester, developed this recipe years ago when she was looking for a nondairy alternative to our macaroni and cheese casserole. It has since become very popular in its own right. It's a colorful dish — the macaroni is faintly dyed the color of the squash. Also, children seem to like this dish and don't mind forgoing the cheese for the appetizing blend of tahini, squash, and miso.

SQUASHARONI

12 ounces dried elbow macaroni pasta
2½ tablespoons olive oil
1½ cups sliced onions
5 cups peeled cubed butternut or buttercup
  squash (approximately 1 large squash)
½ cup water
1 teaspoon salt, divided
⅓ cup tahini
1 tablespoon white miso
1 tablespoon umeboshi vinegar
1 teaspoon tamari
⅓ cup chopped walnuts
½ tablespoon dried parsley
½ tablespoon dried oregano
¾ cup dried whole-grain bread crumbs

In a large saucepan, cook the pasta in boiling water until tender but still firm. Drain, rinse, and set aside. In a large, deep ovenproof skillet, heat 1½ tablespoons of the oil and sauté the onions for 3–5 minutes or until translucent. Add the squash and water and bring to a boil. Add ½ teaspoon of the salt. Reduce heat to medium, cover, and cook for 15–20 minutes, or until the squash is soft.

Preheat oven to 375°F. In a small bowl, stir together the tahini, miso, vinegar, tamari, and remaining salt. Add the tahini mixture to the squash and mix together until creamy. Add the reserved pasta, remaining oil, the walnuts, parsley, and oregano. Top with the bread crumbs and bake for 20 minutes. Serve immediately.

Fettuccine with Sun-Dried Tomatoes and Feta Cheese

Preparation and cooking time 30 minutes.

Serves 4–6.

1 pound 4 ounces dried fettuccine pasta
2 cups sun-dried tomatoes
½ cup extra-virgin olive oil
1½ tablespoons chopped garlic
¼ cup chopped fresh basil
½ tablespoon salt
1 teaspoon black pepper
12 ounces feta cheese, crumbled
1 cup pitted whole black olives

In a large pot, cook the pasta in boiling water until tender but still firm. While the pasta is cooking, slice the tomatoes. In a small bowl, soak the slices in the oil for 15 minutes.

In a medium-sized skillet, heat 1 tablespoon of the soaking oil and sauté the garlic for 3–5 minutes. Turn off heat and add the soaked tomato mixture. Stir in the basil, salt, and black pepper.

Drain and rinse the cooked pasta and place the pasta in a serving bowl. Add the tomato mixture, cheese, and olives and mix together well. Serve immediately.

The key to cooking dried pasta is to keep the water boiling continuously until the pasta tests tender but still firm to the bite.

This highly acclaimed fettuccine was developed in our kitchen over several years. This dish is even better if you soak the sun-dried tomatoes overnight in the mixture of olive oil, garlic, and basil. Double these ingredients and keep the flavored oil in the refrigerator; then heat the oil anytime for another quick, delicious pasta meal.

BERKSHIRE PIE

Preparation time
30 minutes.

Baking time
40 minutes.

Cooling time
5–10 minutes.

Serves 6.

Here is a rich, delightful broccoli and cheddar cheese pie that will warm up everyone on a wintry evening or will be a show-stopper at your holiday buffet.

1 recipe *Basic Pie Crust* (see pages 265 or 266)

Filling:
2 tablespoons olive oil
4 cups cubed onions (4–5 medium onions)
1½ cups chopped green cabbage
2¼ teaspoons salt
2 teaspoons dried basil
2 teaspoons dried thyme
2 teaspoons dried tarragon
1 teaspoon freshly ground black pepper
2½ cups small broccoli florets
2 cups grated mild cheddar cheese
1½ cups ricotta cheese
½ cup sour cream
¾ cup grated carrots
⅓ cup unbleached white flour

Prepare *Basic Pie Crust* and place in a 9-inch pie pan. Pre-heat oven to 375°F.

To make the filling: In a large, deep skillet, heat the oil and sauté the onions for 3–5 minutes or until translucent. Add the cabbage, salt, basil, thyme, tarragon, and black pepper and sauté on medium heat for 5–10 minutes. Turn off heat. Add the broccoli, cheddar and ricotta cheeses, sour cream, carrots, and flour and mix together well.

Pour the mixture into the prepared pie shell and bake for 40 minutes. Let cool for 5–10 minutes. Serve.

Noodle Pie

8 ounces dried ribbon egg noodles
1 tablespoon butter
1 tablespoon chopped garlic
1½ cups sliced fresh mushrooms
½ tablespoon dried marjoram
½ tablespoon dried basil, or
  1½ tablespoons chopped fresh basil
½ tablespoon dried oregano, or
  1½ tablespoons chopped fresh oregano
1 teaspoon salt
½ teaspoon black pepper
1 cup chopped fresh tomatoes
1 cup medium broccoli florets
¾ cup milk
3 tablespoons unbleached white flour
1¾ cups grated mild cheddar cheese

In a large saucepan, cook the noodles in boiling water until tender but still firm. Drain, rinse, and set aside. In a large, deep skillet, melt the butter and sauté the garlic for 3–5 minutes. Add the mushrooms and sauté for 5 minutes more. Stir in the marjoram, basil, oregano, salt, and black pepper. Turn off heat. Mix in the tomatoes and broccoli.

Preheat oven to 375°F. In a large saucepan, heat the milk on low heat and sift in the flour, whisking until a thick roux forms. Add the reserved noodles, the mushroom mixture, and three-fourths of the cheese and blend well. Place the mixture in a buttered 9-inch pie pan and top with the remaining cheese. Bake for 15 minutes, or until the cheese is melted. Let cool for 5–10 minutes. Serve.

Preparation time
30 minutes.

Baking time
15 minutes.

Cooling time
5–10 minutes.

Serves 6.

This egg noodle pie is seasoned with basil, marjoram, and oregano and filled with mushrooms, broccoli, and fresh tomatoes and looks as good as it tastes.

Preparation time
50 minutes.

Baking time
35 minutes.

Cooling time
5–10 minutes.

Serves 6–8.

*There's something
warm and homey
about a pot pie. This
one has the sweet
flavor of carrots and
the hearty flavor of
squash. Add a salad
and you have a
complete meal.*

TOFU POT PIE

2½ cups peeled cubed butternut or buttercup
  squash
2½ cups chopped cauliflower
1 cup water
1 teaspoon salt, divided
¼ cup tahini
¼ cup soymilk
2 teaspoons umeboshi vinegar
1 teaspoon brown rice vinegar
1 teaspoon white miso
¼ teaspoon black pepper
1 teaspoon mirin
2 tablespoons olive oil
3 cups diced onions
2 cups diced potatoes
1 cup diced carrots
Pinch salt
1 pound firm tofu, rinsed, drained, and diced
⅔ cup diced celery
⅔ cup frozen peas
½ cup corn kernels

Topping:
2¼ cups whole-wheat pastry flour
½ teaspoon salt
2 teaspoons baking powder
1 teaspoon baking soda
3 tablespoons canola oil
1¼ cups soymilk

In a large saucepan, boil the squash and cauliflower in the
water and ½ teaspoon of the salt for 10–15 minutes.

In a blender or food processor, combine the squash mixture, tahini, soymilk, both vinegars, miso, remaining salt, black pepper, and mirin until smooth and well blended.

While the squash and cauliflower are cooking, in a large, deep skillet, heat the oil and sauté the onions for 3–5 minutes or until translucent. Stir in the potatoes, carrots, and pinch of salt. Cover and simmer for 15 minutes.

Add the pureed squash mixture, tofu, celery, peas, and corn to the onion mixture and mix together well. Place the combined mixture in an oiled 9 x 12-inch baking pan.

Preheat oven to 375°F. To make the topping: In a medium-sized bowl, stir together the flour, salt, baking powder, and baking soda. Add the oil and soymilk and blend together until smooth.

Pour the mixture on top of the tofu-vegetable mixture and bake for 35 minutes, or until the top is golden. Let cool for 5–10 minutes. Serve.

Variation: If you prefer a pie crust topping, first prepare *Basic Pie Crust* (see pages 265 or 266). Prebake the bottom crust for 5 minutes before adding the tofu-vegetable mixture, then top with the crust. Bake at 375°F for 35 minutes, or until the crust is golden.

Preparation time
30 minutes.

Baking time
30 minutes.

Cooling time
5–10 minutes.

Serves 6.

Highlighted by the colors of fresh mushrooms, spinach, and red Swiss chard, this quiche delights the eye as well as the palate.

Tofu-Spinach Quiche

1 recipe *Basic Pie Crust* (see pages 265 or 266)
2 tablespoons olive oil
2 cups sliced onions
2 cups sliced fresh mushrooms
½ teaspoon salt
5 cups chopped fresh spinach
  (approximately 14 ounces spinach, loosely
  packed)
5 cups chopped red Swiss chard
  (approximately 1 pound chard, loosely
  packed)
⅓ cup uncooked couscous
1 pound soft tofu, rinsed and drained
1 tablespoon white miso
1 tablespoon umeboshi paste
3¾ teaspoons prepared brown mustard
3¾ teaspoons kuzu
¾ cup slivered almonds

Prepare *Basic Pie Crust.*

In a large, deep skillet, heat the oil and sauté the onions for 3–5 minutes or until translucent. Add the mushrooms and salt and sauté for 5 minutes more. Add the spinach and Swiss chard and cook until the greens are soft, adding small amounts at a time.

Preheat oven to 425°F. When both greens are soft, stir in the couscous and turn off heat. Cover and let stand for 10 minutes.

Meanwhile, in a blender or food processor, mix together the tofu, miso, umeboshi paste, mustard, and kuzu. Combine the tofu mixture with the greens mixture and mix together well. Stir in the almonds.

Place the combined mixture in the prepared pie shell and bake for 30 minutes. Let cool for 5–10 minutes. Serve.

*This is a spicy
seitan dish laced
with many striking
flavors and colors,
including the sweet
tastes of fennel and
cinnamon and the
earthy flavors of
onions, garlic, and
mushrooms. It can
be served in pita
pockets, on whole-
wheat buns, or with
Wild Rice Pilaf
(see page 133) and
a salad for a grati-
fying meal.*

SEITAN PITA FILLING

¼ cup canola oil
2 cups diced onions
1 tablespoon chopped garlic
2½ cups cubed or shredded seitan
1 tablespoon garlic powder
½ tablespoon salt
2¼ teaspoons dried basil
½ tablespoon dried oregano
2¼ teaspoons ground paprika
½ teaspoon ground cinnamon
1 teaspoon fennel seeds
1 teaspoon black pepper
2 cups sliced fresh mushrooms
2 cups sliced red bell peppers
3 cups chopped fresh spinach (approximately
   10 ounces spinach, loosely packed)
2 tablespoons fresh lemon juice

In a large skillet, heat the oil and sauté the onions and
garlic for 3–5 minutes, or until the onions are translucent. Stir in the seitan and sauté until the seitan begins to
brown.

Meanwhile, in a small bowl, mix together the garlic powder, salt, basil, oregano, paprika, cinnamon, fennel seeds,
and black pepper. Sprinkle some of this seasoning on the
seitan as it cooks. Add the mushrooms, bell peppers, and
spinach, and continue to cook, adding the remaining seasoning, for 15 minutes. Stir in the lemon juice and serve
immediately.

CHEESE-NUT BURGERS

2 tablespoons olive oil
2 cups chopped onions
1 tablespoon chopped garlic
1½ cups chopped seitan
2 cups sliced fresh mushrooms
1 teaspoon salt
2 teaspoons tamari
1 teaspoon dried thyme
1 teaspoon dried marjoram
¼ teaspoon black pepper
1 cup cooked brown rice
1 cup grated mild cheddar cheese
1 cup chopped walnuts

In a large, deep skillet, heat the oil and sauté the onions and garlic for 3–5 minutes, or until the onions are translucent. Mix in the seitan, mushrooms, and salt and sauté for 5–10 minutes, or until the juices are absorbed.

Stir in the tamari, thyme, marjoram, and black pepper and sauté for 5 minutes. Turn off heat. Mix in the rice and cheese, cover, and let stand for 5 minutes. Add the walnuts. In a blender or food processor, blend the mixture together and shape into patties. Refrigerate the patties for at least 30 minutes.

In a large skillet, grill the patties for 3–5 minutes per side on medium-high heat. Serve immediately.

Preparation time
45 minutes.

Grilling time
10 minutes.

Chilling time
30 minutes.

Serves 4–6.
(Makes 10 burgers.)

Here is a sensational veggie burger with a nutty, smoky flavor. These burgers can be made in a large batch: Cook a few and freeze the remaining patties with wax paper between each patty in a sealable, airtight container. Grill later for a quick, delicious meal.

TOFU REUBEN

**Preparation time
10 minutes.**

**Baking time
20 minutes or
grilling time
5 minutes.**

**Marinating time
at least 2 hours
or overnight
(optional).**

Serves 6–8.

*Originally developed
for tempeh, this
recipe is also good
with tofu. Either
way you have a
luscious, thickly
stacked, open-faced
sandwich. If you
choose to marinate,
the longer you
marinate the better,
particularly if you
use tempeh. The
marinade imparts a
salty, garlic flavor
that contrasts nicely
with the sauerkraut
and sweet sauce.*

1 pound firm tofu, rinsed and drained, or
    8 ounces tempeh

Marinade:
½ cup tamari
½ cup water
1 tablespoon mirin
½ tablespoon cider vinegar
2 tablespoons peeled finely chopped fresh
    gingerroot
2 tablespoons finely chopped garlic
⅛ teaspoon dried crushed red chili peppers

Sauce:
1½ cups canola mayonnaise or low-fat
    mayonnaise
1 tablespoon ketchup or tomato paste
⅛ cup pickle relish
Dash salt
Dash black pepper
¼ teaspoon cider vinegar

Sandwich:
1 cup sliced zucchini
2 cups canned sauerkraut
6–8 slices rye bread
8 ounces Swiss or soy cheese, sliced

Cut the tofu into small cutlets and lay the tofu flat in a
large, shallow bowl.

To make the marinade: In a small saucepan, mix together
all of the marinade ingredients and bring to a boil. Re-

serve 6 tablespoons of the marinade. Pour the remaining marinade over the tofu and set aside, or cover and refrigerate overnight.

To make the sauce: In a small bowl, mix together all of the sauce ingredients and set aside.

Preheat oven to 400°F. To make the sandwiches: In a small skillet, heat 2 tablespoons of the reserved marinade and grill the zucchini on medium-high heat for 3–5 minutes. In a separate skillet, heat the remaining reserved marinade and grill the sauerkraut on medium-high heat for 2–4 minutes.

In an oiled 12 x 15-inch baking pan, place the bread slices and spread 1 tablespoon of the reserved sauce on each slice. Layer the marinated tofu, zucchini, sauerkraut, and cheese on each slice. Bake for about 20 minutes or grill under the broiler for 5 minutes. Serve hot.

PIZZA MAGIC

For many years Kripalu has been known for its outstanding vegetarian pizza. Some people have even asked us to package and sell it. Its origins lie in the experiments of a long-ago Kripalu cook named Narendra, a former Italian chef. Legend has it that Narendra would stand at the back door of the kitchen and beckon to residents to taste his latest creation. Narendra's humor and his pizza delightfully kept us from taking our diet too seriously. Since his departure, our cooks have experimented with many different textures and toppings, and our legendary pizza continues to improve.

BASIC PIZZA DOUGH

1 teaspoon active dry yeast
½ cup warm water
2 tablespoons honey or barley malt
3 cups high-gluten flour
1½ cups unbleached white flour
2 tablespoons olive oil
½ tablespoon salt

In a large bowl, combine the yeast, water, and honey. Let stand for 2 minutes. Add both flours, oil, and salt and mix together well, but do not over knead. Put the dough in an oiled bowl, cover, and place in a warm place. Let rise for 1 hour.

Punch down the dough and divide in half. Form each half into a ball and wrap in wax paper. Refrigerate overnight. The next day let the dough stand at room temperature for 2 hours.

Preheat oven to 500°F. Roll or flip the dough into desired shape on a large baking sheet and bake for 2–5 minutes. Add the prepared sauce and toppings and bake according to the directions in the following pizza recipes.

(Prepare the day before serving.) Preparation time 3 hours 10 minutes. Chilling time overnight. Baking time 2–5 minutes. Makes two 9 x 12-inch pizzas.

Tomato Pizza Sauce

¼ cup olive oil
2 tablespoons chopped garlic
1 tablespoon dried oregano
1 tablespoon dried basil
½ tablespoon dried marjoram
½ teaspoon black pepper
¼ teaspoon dried crushed
  mild chili peppers
3 cups canned tomato puree
  (one 28-ounce can puree)
3 cups canned crushed tomatoes
  (one 28-ounce can tomatoes)
½ cup canned tomato paste
1 teaspoon salt

In a large pot, heat the oil and sauté the garlic for 3–5 minutes. Stir in the oregano, basil, marjoram, black pepper, and chili peppers. Add all of the tomato products and salt and mix together well. Bring the mixture to a boil, stirring frequently. Reduce heat to simmer and cook, stirring occasionally, for at least 20 minutes. Let cool. Use immediately or store, covered, in the refrigerator until ready to use.

Preparation and cooking time 30–35 minutes. Cooling time variable. Makes sauce for two 9 x 12-inch pizzas.

Kripalu's Famous Tomato-Cheese Pizza

1 recipe *Tomato Pizza Sauce*
  (see page 121)
1 recipe *Basic Pizza Dough*
  (see page 120)
¼ cup chopped onions
¼ cup sliced fresh mushrooms
¼ cup chopped green bell
  peppers
¼ cup pitted sliced black olives
¾ cup shredded mozzarella
  cheese
¾ cup shredded cheddar cheese

Prepare the first two recipes. Preheat oven to 500°F. Spread the prepared sauce on the baked crust. Add all of the vegetables and the olives and top with both cheeses. Bake for 15 minutes, or until both cheeses are completely melted. Slice and serve immediately.

**Preparation time variable.
Baking time 15 minutes.
Makes one 9 x 12-inch pizza.**

KRIPALU'S WHITE PIZZA

1 recipe *Basic Pizza Dough*
  (see page 120)
2 tablespoons olive oil
¼ teaspoon black pepper
1 tablespoon chopped garlic
2 cups sliced fresh tomatoes
¾ cup sliced fresh mushrooms
¾ cup grated cheddar cheese
¾ cup grated mozzarella cheese
1 cup canned artichoke hearts
¼ cup chopped fresh basil

Topping:
2 cups ricotta cheese
1½ cups chopped fresh basil
½ cup grated Parmesan cheese
2½ tablespoons olive oil
½ teaspoon salt
⅛ teaspoon black pepper
⅛ teaspoon ground nutmeg

Prepare *Basic Pizza Dough.*

Preheat oven to 500°F. On the baked crust, brush a thin layer of the oil. Sprinkle on the black pepper and garlic and spread half of the tomatoes and half of the mushrooms over the top.

To make the topping: In a medium-sized bowl, mix together all of the top-ping ingredients and spread over the tomato-mushroom layer. Sprinkle on the cheddar and mozzarella cheeses, patting them down.

Add the artichoke hearts, remaining tomatoes and mushrooms, and the basil. Bake for 20 minutes, or until the topping is hot and the cheeses are completely melted. Slice and serve immediately.

Preparation time variable.
Baking time 20 minutes.
Makes one 9 x 12-inch pizza.

BROCCOLI-PESTO PIZZA

1 recipe *Tomato Pizza Sauce*
  (see page 121)
1 recipe *Basic Pizza Dough*
  (see page 120)

Topping:
¼ cup olive oil
1 cup diced onions
1 tablespoon chopped garlic
2¼ cups grated broccoli
  including stems

½ cup chopped fresh basil
½ cup whole green olives
¼ cup grated Parmesan cheese
1 teaspoon salt
¼ teaspoon black pepper
¼ cup chopped fresh parsley
1½ cups grated mozzarella or
  cheddar cheese

Prepare the first two recipes.

Preheat oven to 500°F. To make the topping: In a large skillet, heat the oil and sauté the onions and garlic for 3–5 minutes. Stir in the broccoli and sauté for 5 minutes more.

In a blender or food processor, blend together the broccoli mixture and the remaining topping ingredients, except the mozzarella cheese, for 1 minute.

Spread the prepared sauce on the baked crust. Spread on the topping mixture, add any desired chopped vegetables, and top with the cheese. Bake for 15 minutes, or until the cheese is completely melted. Slice and serve immediately.

Preparation time variable.
Baking time 15 minutes.
Makes one 9 x 12-inch pizza.

TOFU PIZZA

1 recipe *Tomato Pizza Sauce*
  (see page 121)
1 recipe *Basic Pizza Dough*
  (see page 120)

Topping:
1 pound firm tofu, rinsed,
  drained, and mashed
1 tablespoon white miso
1 tablespoon nutritional yeast
½ tablespoon tahini
½ teaspoon salt
1 teaspoon dried basil
1 teaspoon dried oregano
½ teaspoon fresh lemon juice
¼ teaspoon black pepper
¼ teaspoon ground mustard
Pinch ground nutmeg
1½ cups grated soy cheese

Prepare the first two recipes.

Preheat oven to 500°F. To make the topping: In a medium-sized bowl, mix together all of the topping ingredients, except the cheese.

Spread the prepared sauce on the baked crust. Sprinkle the tofu mixture on top, add any desired chopped vegetables, and top with the cheese. Bake for 15 minutes, or until the cheese is completely melted. Slice and serve immediately.

Preparation time variable.
Baking time 15 minutes.
Makes one 9 x 12-inch pizza.

GLORIOUS GRAINS AND BOUNTIFUL BEANS

Chapter 6

GRAINS

High in carbohydrates, grains offer the advantage that, as they're digested, their starch converts to glucose much more slowly than do simple or concentrated sugars; thus, they provide energy and a feeling of satisfaction over a longer period of time. Whole grains, which have not gone through excessive milling or refinement, contain valuable inner germ and outer bran layers. Whole grains are important sources of dietary fiber, zinc, copper, iron, and vitamins A, B, and E.

At Kripalu, our favorite grain is brown rice. We serve it as a side dish everyday at one or two meals, and often people will pass up dried cereal or fruit in the morning in favor of a hearty bowl of brown rice with aduki beans or tamari. Because brown rice has its bran coat and germ intact, it takes longer to cook than white rice, but it has more B vitamins, protein, and fiber.

Other grains that we especially enjoy are millet, a tiny yellow grain that warms the body; bulgur, a form of cracked wheat with a nutty, earthy flavor; and couscous, a precooked form of durum semolina wheat that cooks up very quickly. For variation in our rice dishes, we use white or brown basmati rice, which has an aromatic and distinctive flavor amenable to Asian and Indian dishes, and sweet rice, which is a short-grained hybrid cultivated for its sweet flavor.

BEANS

In addition to protein, beans have a variety of nutrients, including iron, thiamine, niacin, riboflavin, and folic acid, as well as calcium, phosphorus, magnesium, sulfur, and potassium. We most frequently use mung beans, lima beans, black beans, pinto beans, soybeans, aduki beans, chickpeas, split peas, and lentils.

Many different grains and beans can be simply prepared to make up or round out a meal—so many that we find it handy to keep cooking charts at hand. The charts in this chapter summarize all that you'll need to know about preparation, cooking times, and yields. Following the charts are some of our most popular grain and bean recipes.

Cooking Grains

GRAIN (1 CUP)	COOKING WATER	COOKING TIME	YIELD
Amaranth	3 cups	25–30 min.	3½ cups
Barley	2½ cups	1¼ hours	3 cups
Basmati rice, brown	2 cups	30–40 min.	4 cups
Basmati rice, white	2 cups	20–25 min.	4 cups
Brown rice	2 cups	45–50 min.	4 cups
Buckwheat groats	2 cups	20–30 min.	2½ cups
Bulgur*	1¾ cups	15 min.	2½ cups
Cornmeal*	4 cups	25 min.	4 cups
Couscous*	1½ cups	5–10 min.	3 cups
Millet	2 cups	40 min.	3½ cups
Oats, rolled*	2 cups	20–30 min.	2 cups
Oats, whole	3 cups	1¼ hours	3 cups
Quinoa	2 cups	20–25 min.	3½ cups

These grain products do not need to be washed and drained.

Wash the grain thoroughly in a colander under cold running water and drain well. In a saucepan, combine the grain with the required amount of water and bring to a boil. Reduce heat to simmer and cook, covered, for the required time. Do not uncover or stir the grain. (Barley and whole oats may be soaked in water to cover for several hours or overnight to reduce cooking time.)

Cooking Pasta

To cook dried pasta: For each 1 cup of pasta, use 3–4 cups of water. Bring the water to a boil and add the pasta. Return to a boil and cook for a minimum of 15–20 minutes, stirring frequently. Dried pasta should be cooked until tender but still firm to the bite. Drain and rinse the pasta under hot water. The yield will be approximately 2½ times the dry measure. (Lasagna and heavier noodles, such as soba noodles, take longer to cook—follow package directions.)

Cooking Beans

BEAN (1 CUP)	COOKING WATER	COOKING TIME	YIELD
Aduki beans	4 cups	1¾ hours	3 cups
Black beans	4 cups	2½ hours	2½ cups
Chickpeas	6 cups	3–4 hours	3 cups
Kidney beans	4 cups	2 hours	2¼ cups
Lentils, green, brown	3 cups	1 hour	3 cups
Lentils, red	3 cups	30–40 min.	3 cups
Lima beans	3 cups	1¾ hours	2½ cups
Mung beans	4 cups	1¼ hours	3 cups
Navy beans	4 cups	3 hours	2½ cups
Pinto beans	3 cups	2½ hours	2¼ cups
Soybeans	4 cups	4–5 hours	2½ cups
Split peas, green, yellow	3 cups	2½ hours	3½ cups

Wash the beans thoroughly in a colander under cold running water and drain well. In a pot, combine the beans with the required amount of cooking water and bring to a boil. Reduce heat to simmer and cook for the required time, stirring occasionally. Add more water, if needed, and add any salt, if desired, *after* the beans have cooked and are nearly soft; otherwise, the beans will take a very long time to cook and may never become soft.

Cooking times are for beans that have been soaked, either by soaking overnight in water to cover or by using the quick-soak method (see below). If soaking is eliminated, cook the beans two to three times the cooking time required. (Lentils and split peas do not need to be soaked before cooking.)

Quick-Soak Method: Place the beans in a pot of boiling water to cover and cook for 10–15 minutes. Turn off heat and let soak, covered, for 1–2 hours. Drain. This is equivalent to as much as 10–12 hours soaking time.

HERBED BROWN BASMATI RICE

Preparation and cooking time 45 minutes.

Serves 4–6.

2 cups uncooked brown basmati rice
3½ cups water
2 teaspoons dried thyme, or
  2 tablespoons chopped fresh thyme
1½ teaspoons dried marjoram, or
  1½ tablespoons chopped fresh marjoram
½ teaspoon salt
⅓ cup pine nuts
¼ cup chopped fresh parsley

Here's a simple rice dish to accompany Vegetable Creole, Baked Wakame and Vegetables (see pages 150–151 and 153), or your favorite steamed vegetables.

Wash and drain the rice. In a medium-sized saucepan, combine the rice, water, and both dried herbs and bring to a boil. (If using fresh herbs, add after the rice has cooked for 20 minutes.) Add the salt. Reduce heat to simmer and cook, covered, for about 35 minutes, or until the rice is soft and the water is absorbed.

Fluff the rice with a fork and stir in the pine nuts and parsley. Serve immediately.

*Asapao literally
means "in the
soup." In many
Latin American
countries, rice is
served fluffy white in
a bowl of soup
stock, thick with
potatoes, carrots,
and spices. Our
version uses white
basmati rice and
combines peas,
tomatoes, red bell
peppers, garlic, and
onions. For a
slightly more moist
version, add more
stock or water
toward the very end
of cooking.*

ASAPAO RICE

1½ cups uncooked white basmati rice
3 tablespoons olive oil
½ cup chopped onions
1 tablespoon chopped garlic
1 teaspoon ground cumin
¼ teaspoon black pepper
Pinch cayenne pepper
2½ cups vegetable stock or water
1 teaspoon salt
½ cup diced green bell peppers
½ cup diced red bell peppers
½ cup chopped fresh tomatoes
½ cup frozen peas
¾ teaspoon dried oregano, or
  2 tablespoons chopped fresh oregano

Wash and drain the rice. In a large, hot skillet, dry roast the rice, stirring constantly, for about 5 minutes, or until the rice is slightly golden. Remove the rice and set aside.

In the same skillet, heat the oil and sauté the onions and garlic for 3–5 minutes, or until the onions are translucent. Stir in the cumin, black pepper, cayenne pepper, and reserved rice. Add the stock and bring to a boil. Add the salt. Reduce heat to simmer and cook, covered, for 10–12 minutes.

Add both bell peppers, the tomatoes, peas, and oregano. Cover and simmer for 5–7 minutes more, or until the rice is soft and the water is absorbed. Serve immediately.

Jambalaya Rice

1¼ cups uncooked white basmati rice
2 tablespoons olive oil
¾ cup chopped onions
1½ tablespoons chopped garlic
¾ cup sliced fresh mushrooms
2¼ cups water
½ tablespoon dried thyme
½ tablespoon ground cumin
1 teaspoon ground mustard
¼ teaspoon dried crushed red chili peppers
⅛ teaspoon Tabasco sauce
½ teaspoon salt
¾ cup sliced celery
¾ cup diced carrots
½ cup fresh or frozen peas
⅓ cup diced red bell peppers
¼ cup chopped fresh cilantro

Wash and drain the rice. Set aside. In a large, deep skillet, heat the oil and sauté the onions and garlic for 3–5 minutes, or until the onions are translucent.

Stir in the mushrooms and sauté for 5 minutes more. Add the next six ingredients and the reserved rice and bring to a boil. Add the salt. Reduce heat to simmer and cook, covered, for 5 minutes.

Add the celery, carrots, peas, and bell peppers and cook, covered, for 15 minutes, or until the rice is soft and the water is absorbed.

Fluff the rice with a fork and stir in the cilantro. Serve.

Preparation and cooking time 40–45 minutes. Serves 4–6.

This festive New Orleans rice dish is surprisingly easy to prepare and has a variety of tasty ingredients, including red bell peppers, celery, carrots, fresh cilantro, and hot seasonings.

In this aromatic mixed rice and vegetable dish, roasted almonds add crunch and flavor to the versatile white basmati rice. Carrots, zucchini, green beans, and green bell peppers add color and make this practically a complete meal. Cooking the spices in ghee or olive oil helps unlock their flavors.

ALMOND RICE

1 ¼ cups uncooked white basmati rice
2 cups water
½ cup diced carrots
½ cup diced zucchini
½ cup ½-inch cut green beans
½ cup diced green bell peppers
½ teaspoon salt
2 tablespoons ghee (see page 325) or olive oil
½ tablespoon cumin seeds
⅛ teaspoon black pepper
Pinch ground nutmeg
Pinch ground cinnamon
½ cup chopped roasted almonds
¾ cup chopped fresh parsley

Wash and drain the rice. In a medium-sized saucepan, combine the rice, water, carrots, zucchini, green beans, and bell peppers and bring to a boil. Add the salt. Reduce heat to simmer and cook, covered, for about 20 minutes, or until the rice is soft and the water is absorbed.

In a small skillet, melt the ghee and sauté the seeds for 30 seconds. Stir in the black pepper, nutmeg, and cinnamon. Set aside.

Add the reserved spice mixture to the cooked rice and mix together with a fork. Stir in the almonds and parsley and serve immediately.

To roast almonds: Preheat oven to 350 °F. In a small baking pan, place the almonds and bake for 5–7 minutes or until golden, stirring frequently.

WILD RICE PILAF

¹⁄₃ cup uncooked wild rice
1 cup uncooked long-grain brown rice or
  brown basmati rice
2¾ cups water
¼ teaspoon salt
1 tablespoon canola oil
½ cup julienned carrots
1 cup sliced fresh mushrooms
½ cup sliced celery
½ tablespoon tamari
1 teaspoon sesame oil
¹⁄₃ cup whole almonds
¹⁄₃ cup chopped fresh parsley

Wash and drain the wild and basmati rice separately. In a medium-sized saucepan, combine the wild rice and water and bring to a boil. Reduce heat to simmer and cook, covered, for 10 minutes. Add the basmati rice and return to a boil. Add the salt. Reduce heat to simmer and cook, covered, for 25 minutes, or until the rice is soft and the water is absorbed.

Meanwhile, in a medium-sized skillet, heat the canola oil and sauté the carrots, mushrooms, and celery for 5 minutes. Stir in the tamari and sesame oil and set aside.

Preheat oven to 350°F. In a small baking pan, roast the almonds in the oven for 5 minutes, stirring frequently. Let cool. Chop the cooled almonds into large pieces and set aside. Add the reserved carrot mixture and reserved almonds to the cooked rice and stir together with a fork. Add the parsley and serve immediately.

Preparation and cooking time 40 minutes.

Cooling time variable.

Serves 4–6.

Try this delicious blend of wild rice, brown rice, carrots, mushrooms, and almonds with Baked Onions or Collards with Brown Rice Vinegar and Tamari (see pages 156 and 167).

Preparation and
cooking time
40 minutes.

Soaking time
overnight.

Serves 6.

*This is a lovely
winter rice dish that
combines the aro-
matic flavor of the
sweet rice (a hybrid
brown rice) with the
crunch of chestnuts.*

SWEET RICE AND CHESTNUTS

½ cup shelled dried chestnuts
4½ cups water
1½ cups uncooked sweet brown rice*
½ teaspoon salt

In a small bowl, combine the chestnuts and 2 cups of the
water and soak overnight. Drain the chestnuts and set
aside.

Wash and drain the rice. In a medium-sized saucepan,
combine the rice, remaining water, and reserved chestnuts and bring to a boil. Add the salt. Reduce heat to
medium-low and cook, covered, for 30–35 minutes, or
until the rice and chestnuts are soft and the water is absorbed. Serve immediately.

*Sweet brown rice is available in natural foods stores and specialty
markets.

BULGUR-WALNUT LOAF

1⅓ cups water
¾ cup uncooked bulgur
2 tablespoons olive oil
1 cup chopped onions
1 tablespoon chopped garlic
1½ cups finely chopped carrots
⅓ cup barley miso diluted in ¼ cup warm water
2¼ teaspoons dried thyme, or
  2 tablespoons chopped fresh thyme
½ cup chopped walnuts
¼ cup dried sunflower seeds
¼ cup whole-wheat flour
¼ cup unbleached white flour

In a small saucepan, bring the water to a boil. Add the bulgur. Reduce heat to simmer and cook, covered, for 10 minutes, or until the water is absorbed.

In a medium-sized skillet, heat the oil and sauté the onions and garlic for 3–5 minutes, or until the onions are translucent. Add the carrots and simmer for 3 minutes. Stir in the diluted miso and add the thyme. In a blender or food processor, grind the walnuts and seeds to a medium pulp.

Preheat oven to 350°F. In a large bowl, combine the cooked bulgur, carrot mixture, ground walnuts and seeds, and both flours and mix together well. Pat the mixture into an oiled 9-inch loaf pan and bake for 1 hour. Cool before slicing. Serve.

Preparation time 20 minutes.

Baking time 1 hour.

Cooling time variable.

Serves 4.

This recipe combines the robust flavors of barley miso, garlic, onions, and thyme to complement the nuttiness of the bulgur and walnuts. Slice the loaf and serve with Veg- etable Masamba or Cajun Turnips and Greens (see pages 152 and 166).

Preparation and cooking time 50 minutes.

Serves 4–6. (Makes 12 croquettes.)

It's easy to make these tasty croquettes, which come out of the oven golden yellow. Topped with Beet-Horseradish Sauce, *they provide an excellent source of vitamins and minerals, as well as being very colorful. Serve with* Umeboshi Cabbage Wedges *or* Confetti Kale *(see pages 158 and 168) for a lovely, healthful meal.*

MILLET CROQUETTES WITH BEET-HORSERADISH SAUCE

Croquettes:
1 cup uncooked millet
1 tablespoon olive oil
¾ cup sliced onions
2 teaspoons chopped garlic
1¼ cups diced yams
3¼ cups water
½ cup uncooked couscous
1 teaspoon crushed dried rosemary
¼ teaspoon black pepper
5 teaspoons tahini
1 tablespoon white miso
1 teaspoon salt

Wash and drain the millet. In a medium-sized skillet, dry roast the millet on medium heat, stirring constantly, for about 5–7 minutes, or until the millet begins to brown slightly. Remove from heat and set aside.

In a large skillet, heat the oil and sauté the onions and garlic for 3–5 minutes, or until the onions are translucent. Add the reserved roasted millet, the yams, water, couscous, rosemary, black pepper, and tahini and bring to a boil. Reduce heat to simmer and add the miso and salt. Cook, covered, for 15 minutes.

Prepare the *Beet-Horseradish Sauce.*

Turn off heat and let the millet mixture stand, covered, for 10 minutes. (Form the croquettes immediately after the standing time or the millet will stiffen and become difficult to mold.)

Preheat oven to 350°F. Using an ice cream scoop or a large spoon, form the croquettes, approximately 2½ inch round, on an oiled baking sheet. Top with the *Beet-Horseradish Sauce* and bake for 15 minutes, or until the croquettes turn golden and crusty. Serve immediately.

BEET-HORSERADISH SAUCE

Makes about 1¼ cups.

1 cup scrubbed chopped fresh beets
1 cup water
Pinch salt
1½ teaspoons prepared horseradish
2¼ teaspoons red wine vinegar
2¼ teaspoons umeboshi vinegar

In a small saucepan, combine the beets and water and bring to a boil. Add the salt. Reduce heat to medium and cook for about 20 minutes, or until the beets are tender.

In a blender or food processor, blend together the cooked beets, horseradish, and both vinegars. Spread the sauce over the croquettes.

Couscous is a light golden grain that cooks very quickly. If you prepare the chickpeas in advance, this dish takes only minutes. Serve hot or cold with stir-fried vegetables or a fresh garden salad.

Couscous with Chickpeas

¾ cup dried chickpeas
5¼ cups water
1 teaspoon salt
2 tablespoons olive oil
2 teaspoons umeboshi vinegar
¼ cup fresh lemon juice
1½ cups uncooked couscous
¼ cup chopped fresh parsley

Wash the chickpeas. Soak overnight or use the quick-soak method (see page 128), soaking for 1 hour.

In a large saucepan, combine the soaked chickpeas and 3½ cups of the water and bring to a boil. Reduce heat to medium and cook for 1 hour 30 minutes.

Add the salt and more water, if needed, and cook for about 30 minutes more, or until the chickpeas are very tender. Drain and set side.

In a separate saucepan, combine the remaining water, the oil, vinegar, and lemon juice and bring to a boil. Turn off heat and mix in the couscous. Cover and let stand for 12–15 minutes, or until the water is absorbed. Mix in the reserved chickpeas and parsley. Serve immediately.

LENTILS AND BULGUR

¾ cup dried green lentils
2¼ cups water
½ teaspoon salt
1½ tablespoons olive oil
1 cup diced onions
1 cup uncooked bulgur
1½ tablespoons tamari

Wash the lentils. In a medium-sized saucepan, combine the lentils and 1¼ cups of the water and bring to a boil. Reduce heat to medium and cook for 20 minutes. Add the salt and cook for 5 minutes more. (Lentils should be cooked but not mushy.)

Meanwhile, in a medium-sized skillet, heat the oil and sauté the onions for about 20 minutes or until caramelized.

Add the remaining water, carmelized onions, bulgur, and tamari to the cooked lentils and return to a boil. Turn off heat. Let stand, covered, for 30 minutes, or until the water is absorbed. Serve immediately.

**Preparation and cooking time
1 hour.
Serves 4–6.**

This combination of grains and beans, seasoned with onions and a touch of tamari, offer complete protein. Serve with Grilled Vegetable Medley *or* Arame with Spinach *(see pages 149 and 169).*

Preparation time
50 minutes.

Baking time
35 minutes.

Cooling time 5
minutes.

Serves 8.

*Garnished with
fresh parsley, red
bell peppers, and
toasted bread
crumbs, this pâté
looks stately and
pleases diverse
palates. It has a
down-to-earth
richness from the
long-cooked lentils,
onions, and season-
ings, and it tastes
wonderful on crusty
sourdough bread
(see Chapter 10 for
bread recipes) or
with soup and
crackers.*

RED LENTIL PÂTÉ

5½ cups dried red lentils
9 cups water or vegetable stock
2¼ teaspoons salt
⅓ cup olive oil
7 cups thinly sliced onions
  (6–7 medium onions)
3½ tablespoons chopped garlic
1½ tablespoons dried basil
2¼ teaspoons dried oregano
2¼ teaspoons dried thyme
2 cups sliced celery
¼ cup dried parsley
3 cups toasted whole-wheat bread crumbs
1 tablespoon umeboshi vinegar
1 teaspoon black pepper
1½ cups pitted sliced black olives
½ cup chopped fresh parsley
½ cup chopped red bell peppers

Wash the lentils. In a large pot, combine the lentils and
water and bring to a boil. Reduce heat to medium-low
and cook, stirring occasionally, for about 40 minutes, or
until the lentils are soft and the water is absorbed. Add
the salt and keep warm.

Meanwhile, in a large, deep skillet, heat the oil and sauté
the onions and garlic for 10–15 minutes. When the onions start to caramelize, stir in the basil, oregano, thyme,
celery, and dried parsley. Turn off heat.

Preheat oven to 375°F. Heavily coat the bottom of an
oiled 9 x 12-inch, deep-dish baking pan with 1 cup of the

bread crumbs. Add the onion mixture, remaining bread crumbs, the vinegar, black pepper, and olives to the cooked lentils and mix together well.

Pour the mixture into the baking pan and bake for about 35 minutes, or until the mixture is set. Let cool for 5 minutes. Turn onto a serving tray and garnish with the fresh parsley and bell peppers. Serve.

To make toasted bread crumbs: Toast slices of whole-wheat bread. Finely chop the toasted bread, in small quantities, in a blender or food processor. Store the crumbs in an airtight container.

Adapted from *The Natural Gourmet* by Annemarie Colbin. © 1989 by Annemarie Colbin. Reprinted by permission of Ballantine Books, a division of Random House, Inc. (See Bibliography.)

*Here's a delightful
lentil and vegetable
dish, tinted bright
yellow from the
turmeric and curry
powder. It has a
spicy tang, reminis-
cent of Indian
curries, and goes
well with basmati
rice dishes, a spin-
ach salad, or cooked
greens.*

SAMBHAR

2 cups dried red lentils
1 cup cubed carrots
3 cups water
1 ½ cups coarsely chopped potatoes
1 ½ teaspoons salt
1 tablespoon olive oil
1 teaspoon black mustard seeds
1 ½ teaspoons ground coriander
½ teaspoon ground cumin
¼ teaspoon ground turmeric
¼ teaspoon dried crushed mild chili peppers
½ teaspoon curry powder
1 tablespoon fresh lemon juice

Wash the lentils. In a large saucepan, combine the lentils, carrots, and water and bring to a boil. Reduce heat to medium-low and cook for 20 minutes. Add the potatoes and salt and cook for 15–20 minutes more, or until the potatoes are soft.

Meanwhile, in a small skillet, heat the oil to medium heat and stir in the seeds. Wait for 1 minute. Stir in the coriander, cumin, turmeric, chili peppers, and curry powder and sauté for 1 minute. Set aside.

Add the reserved spice mixture to the soft potato mixture and stir in the lemon juice. Serve immediately.

ADUKI BEANS AND SQUASH

1 cup dried aduki beans
One 3-inch strip kombu, cut into ⅛-inch
  wide strips
4 cups peeled cubed buttercup or butternut
  squash (approximately 1 medium squash)
½ teaspoon salt
½ tablespoon tamari

Wash the beans. Soak overnight or use the quick-soak method (see page 128), soaking for 1 hour.

In a large saucepan, layer the kombu strips, squash, and soaked beans. Cover with water to barely cover the beans (about 4 cups, depending on the type of saucepan) and bring to a boil. Reduce heat to medium-low and cook for about 1 hour 30 minutes.

Add the salt and cook for about 30 minutes more, or until the beans are soft, adding more water if needed to prevent burning on the bottom. Stir in the tamari and serve immediately.

Preparation and cooking time 2 hours.

Soaking time overnight.

Serves 4–6.

Aduki beans and squash, a pleasing fall or winter dish, seem to belong together, contributing complementary flavors, colors, and textures.

Preparation time
1 hour.

Baking time
35 minutes.

Soaking time
overnight.

Serves 4–6.

*Delicious, warming,
and mildly sweet,
these beans are
simple to prepare
and child-friendly.*

HOME-STYLE BAKED BEANS

1¾ cups dried navy beans
4 cups water
½ teaspoon salt
¾ cup sun-dried tomatoes
⅓ cup hot water
⅓ cup barley malt
2 tablespoons tamari
1 tablespoon prepared brown mustard
1½ tablespoons olive oil
1 tablespoon chopped garlic
½ teaspoon chili powder
¼ teaspoon onion powder
¼ teaspoon crushed dried rosemary
   or 1 teaspoon chopped fresh rosemary
¼ teaspoon dried thyme
1 cup chopped onions

Wash the beans. Soak overnight or use the quick-soak method (see page 128).

In a large saucepan, combine the soaked beans and the 4 cups water and bring to a boil. Reduce heat to medium-low and cook for about 45 minutes. Add the salt and cook for about 15 minutes more, or until the beans are soft.

Meanwhile, in a small bowl, soak the tomatoes in the ⅓ cup hot water for 15 minutes.

In a blender or food processor, blend the tomatoes and

soaking water until pasty. Add the barley malt, tamari, mustard, oil, garlic, chili and onion powders, rosemary, and thyme and blend until well combined.

Preheat oven to 375°F. In a lightly oiled baking pan, combine the soft beans, tomato mixture, and onions and bake for 35 minutes. Serve immediately.

Preparation and cooking time 1 hour.

Soaking time overnight.

Serves 4–6.

Serve this dish with a salad or Greens Gumbo *(see pages 66–67) and you will have a balance of flavors, plus many much-needed vita-mins and minerals.*

KIDNEY BEANS WITH YAMS

1½ cups dried kidney beans
3½ cups water
2½ cups chopped yams
½ teaspoon salt
1 tablespoon red miso or barley miso diluted in
  2 tablespoons warm water

Wash the beans. Soak overnight or use the quick-soak method (see page 128), soaking for 1 hour.

In a large saucepan, combine the soaked beans and water and bring to a boil. Reduce heat to medium-low and cook for about 30 minutes.

Add the yams and return to a boil. Add the salt. Reduce heat to medium and cook for 20 minutes, or until the beans are soft. Stir in the diluted miso and cook for 5 minutes more. Serve immediately.

From Land and Sea: Vegetable Side Dishes

Chapter 7

THE WORD *vegetable* comes from the Latin word *vegere,* which means *to enliven.* That's appropriate, since this multicolored, diverse group of good-tasting foods gives life to our menus as well as to our bodies.

Vegetables are powerhouses of important nutrients. Carrots, corn, and squash have liberal doses of vitamin A. Chicory, endive, and celery provide B as well as A vitamins. Broccoli, cauliflower, cabbage, leafy greens, parsley, tomatoes, and red bell peppers are rich in both vitamins A and C. Almost all leafy greens are rich in calcium, and broccoli and the remaining cruciferous family have recently been found to contain anticancer agents.

But it's the flavor of vegetables that is the real attraction to gourmets. For every entrée, there can be a vegetable side dish that provides the perfect complement or contrast in taste. In many cases, the best vegetable is a simple one; for example, nothing is more versatile than steamed fresh corn, especially if it's straight from a summer garden. Freshly picked (or even purchased fresh) broccoli or Swiss chard needs little more than a steaming to bring its unique flavors to life. Even simple, baked winter squash can be perfected by a touch of honey and cinnamon.

This chapter features vegetables from the sea as well as from land, for at Kripalu we have come to love the inimitable flavors contributed by sea vegetables, such as hiziki, arame, wakame, dulse, and kombu. We also appreciate the hard-to-get nutrients that they provide, including iron, calcium, iodine, and vitamin B_{12}.

Let vegetables live up to their healthful potential as they please your plate and palette with a savory bouquet of colors, flavors, and aromas.

GRILLED VEGETABLE MEDLEY

Preparation and cooking time 30 minutes.

Serves 4–6.

Colorful and simple, this delightful vegetable medley livens up a quiche or tofu entrée, yet takes almost no time to prepare.

2 tablespoons olive oil
2 cups julienned carrots
1½ cups sliced onions
3 cups diagonally sliced zucchini
  (approximately 2 medium zucchini)
1 cup diagonally sliced celery
1½ teaspoons salt

In a large skillet, heat the oil and sauté the carrots for 7–10 minutes. Add the onions and sauté for 5 minutes. Add the zucchini and sauté for 2–3 minutes.

Add the celery and salt and cook, stirring occasionally, for 5–7 minutes, or until the vegetables are tender-crisp and just beginning to brown. Serve immediately.

*A takeoff of New
Orleans cuisine,
this vegetable dish
combines classic
creole seasonings
with eggplant,
tomatoes, cabbage,
potatoes, and green
bell peppers. It's
excellent served with
Jambalaya Rice
and New Orleans
Greens Salad
(see pages 131
and 173).*

VEGETABLE CREOLE

2 cups unpeeled cubed eggplant
1½ cups cubed potatoes
1½ cups sliced green cabbage
2 cups water
2 tablespoons olive oil
1 tablespoon unbleached white flour
⅔ cup sliced onions
1 tablespoon chopped garlic
⅔ cup sliced green bell peppers
¾ cup sliced fresh mushrooms
1 cup chopped fresh tomatoes
¾ cup canned crushed or pureed tomatoes
1 teaspoon salt
1 bay leaf
2 teaspoons dried basil
2 teaspoons dried thyme
2 teaspoons ground paprika
1 teaspoon dried oregano
¼ teaspoon black pepper
¼ teaspoon white pepper
¼ teaspoon cayenne pepper
½ cup sliced celery
¾ cup frozen peas
1 tablespoon fresh lemon juice

In a large, covered saucepan with a steamer basket, steam
the eggplant, potatoes, and cabbage in the 2 cups water
for 15 minutes.

Meanwhile, in a large, deep skillet, combine the oil and flour and heat on medium-low, stirring constantly, for 5 minutes. Add the onions and garlic and sauté for 5 minutes. Add the bell peppers and mushrooms and sauté for 5 minutes. Add all of the tomatoes, the salt, and all of the seasonings and sauté for 5 minutes.

Stir in the steamed vegetables and sauté for 15 minutes. Add the celery and peas and sauté for 10 minutes more. Add the lemon juice and serve immediately.

*In this African-
inspired dish, kale's
flavor is contrasted
with the peanuts,
tomatoes, onions,
and special season-
ings. Serve with
Wild Rice Pilaf or
Couscous with
Chickpeas (see
pages 133 and
138).*

VEGETABLE MASAMBA

2 tablespoons ghee (see page 325) or
  unsalted butter
1 cup diced onions
1 teaspoon ground coriander
¾ teaspoon ground cumin
Pinch ground nutmeg
Pinch ground cloves
Pinch ground paprika
Pinch ground cinnamon
Pinch black pepper
9 cups washed, dried, and chopped fresh kale
  (10–12 ounces kale)
½ teaspoon salt
½ cup diced fresh tomatoes
⅔ cup unsalted peanuts

In a large skillet, melt the ghee and sauté the onions for
3–5 minutes or until translucent. Stir in the next seven
ingredients and sauté for 1 minute. Add the kale, stirring
to coat thoroughly with the spices. Add the salt and fold
into the mixture.

Reduce heat to medium-low and cook, covered, for 15
minutes, stirring every 3–4 minutes. Turn off heat. Add
the tomatoes and peanuts, cover, and let stand for 5 minutes before serving. Serve.

BAKED WAKAME AND VEGETABLES

Preparation and cooking time 35 minutes.

Baking time 50 minutes.

Serves 6.

The nutritional content and unique taste of this sea vegetable dish make it well worth the preparation time. The combination of tahini and wakame flavors is rich and satisfying.

2 ounces dried wakame, well rinsed in cold
  water and drained
2 cups cold water
1 tablespoon canola oil
2 cups sliced onions
2 cups grated carrots
1½ cups sliced green cabbage
⅔ cup tahini
1 tablespoon tamari
2 cups water
¼ cup white sesame seeds

In a medium-sized, covered bowl, soak the wakame in the 2 cups cold water for 20 minutes.

Meanwhile, in a large skillet, heat the oil and sauté the onions, carrots, and cabbage for 5 minutes. Drain the wakame when soft and cut into 2-inch lengths, cutting out the center vein. Set aside.

Preheat oven to 350°F. In a large bowl, stir together the tahini, tamari, and the 2 cups water. Mix in the reserved wakame and the onion mixture.

In an oiled 9 x 12-inch baking pan, place the mixture and sprinkle the seeds on top. Bake, covered, for 50 minutes. Serve immediately.

Preparation and cooking time 40 minutes.

Serves 4.

This is a tasteful, elegant side dish for any evening meal and requires very little preparation. The secret ingredient is miso, brushed on liberally.

BAKED CAULIFLOWER

1 medium head cauliflower, washed and cut into large florets
¼ cup barley miso or red miso diluted in ¾ cup warm water
½ cup water
1½ tablespoons chopped fresh parsley

Preheat oven to 425°F. Place the cauliflower in a baking pan. Spread the diluted miso over the cauliflower with a pastry brush. Add the water to the bottom of the pan.

Cover and bake for 25 minutes. Uncover and bake for 5–10 minutes more. Sprinkle the parsley over the top and serve immediately.

RED ONIONS AND DULSE

Preparation and cooking time 25 minutes.

Serves 6.

Here's an easy-to-make, highly nutritious side dish that can be served warm or cold.

6 cups sliced red onions (4–5 medium onions)
3 tablespoons dried dulse flakes, or
  ¼ cup chopped dried dulse
1 tablespoon brown rice vinegar
1 tablespoon umeboshi vinegar

In a large, covered saucepan with a steamer basket, steam the onions in water for 4–5 minutes.

Place the onions in a serving bowl and add the dulse flakes. (If using dried dulse, soak for 2–3 minutes; drain and chop into small pieces, then add to the onions.)

Add the vinegars and mix well. Let stand for at least 10 minutes before serving. Serve warm or cold.

*This dish goes well
with many different
entrées. Try it with
Pasta Primavera
Salad (see pages
194–195).*

BAKED ONIONS

4 cups quartered sweet Spanish onions
  (approximately 3 medium onions)
2 tablespoons olive oil
3 tablespoons barley miso or red miso
3 tablespoons water
1 teaspoon dried thyme, or
  1 tablespoon chopped fresh thyme

Preheat oven to 425°F. Place the onions in a baking pan.

In a small bowl, stir together the oil, miso, water, and
thyme and pour over the onions. Cover and bake for
about 35 minutes, or until the onions are soft. Serve immediately.

Beet Nishime

4 cups scrubbed coarsely chopped fresh beets
  (approximately 3 medium beets)
1 cup water
2 teaspoons umeboshi vinegar

In a large saucepan, combine the beets and water and
bring to a boil. Reduce heat to simmer and cook for 45
minutes. (Check water level occasionally to prevent
scorching.)

Add the vinegar and simmer for 15 minutes more, or
until the beets are tender. Serve immediately.

**Preparation and
cooking time
1 hour 10 minutes.
Serves 4.**

*Nishime is a steam-
ing method that
uses a little water to
slowly tenderize
vegetables. This
dish is tasty and
satisfying, even
though it's ex-
tremely simple and
requires little
hands-on time.*

Preparation and cooking time 30 minutes.

Serves 4–6.

Simple to prepare, with few ingredients, this cabbage dish is very tasty. Serve with Almond Rice *(see page 132) for a hearty lunch or evening meal.*

UMEBOSHI CABBAGE WEDGES

1 large head green cabbage, washed and cut
  into large wedges
1 tablespoon umeboshi paste diluted in
  $\frac{1}{3}$ cup water
$\frac{1}{2}$ cup water

In a large saucepan, arrange the cabbage in a circular pattern and pour the diluted paste over the cabbage. Add the water to the bottom of the pan. Cover and bring to a boil.

Reduce heat to simmer and cook for 20 minutes, or until the cabbage is tender. Serve immediately.

Roasted Rosemary Red Potatoes

12 small red potatoes, washed and unpeeled
2 tablespoons olive oil
1 teaspoon dried rosemary, or 1½ tablespoons
  chopped fresh rosemary
½ teaspoon salt
⅛ teaspoon black pepper

Preheat oven to 425°F. In a large bowl, mix together the potatoes, oil, rosemary, salt, and black pepper. Place the mixture on a rimmed baking sheet and bake for about 40 minutes, or until the potatoes are soft on the inside.

Check the potatoes occasionally for browning. Turn very carefully, if at all, to keep from breaking apart. Serve immediately.

**Preparation time
10 minutes.**

**Baking time
40 minutes.**

Serves 4.

Here's a quick and easy roasted potato dish that complements anything from a casual lunch to an elegant dinner party.

*Here's a classic we
couldn't pass by. A
nondairy version
can be made by
substituting soymilk
and soy cheese for
the milk and ched-
dar cheese. Soymilk
and soy cheese can
be found in natural
foods stores and
specialty markets.*

SCALLOPED POTATOES

8 cups sliced potatoes (4–5 medium potatoes)
3–4 cups water
¼ cup butter
⅓ cup unbleached white flour
1¼ cups milk
1 teaspoon salt
2 teaspoons ground mustard
¼ teaspoon ground paprika
2¼ cups grated sharp cheddar cheese

In a large, covered pot with a steamer basket, steam the potatoes in the water for 20 minutes or until cooked but still firm.

Preheat oven to 350°F. In a small saucepan, melt the butter and sprinkle in the flour. Simmer for 2–3 minutes, stirring constantly. Add the milk, salt, mustard, and paprika and stir together well. Turn off heat.

In a baking pan, layer the cooked potatoes and pour the milk mixture over the potatoes. Sprinkle the cheese over the top, cover, and bake for 45 minutes. Uncover and bake for 15–20 minutes more. Serve immediately.

Sweet Potato Tsimmes

Preparation and cooking time 55 minutes.

Serves 4.

A variation on a traditional dish, this recipe combines wonderfully different flavors — prunes, barley miso, carrots, and sweet potatoes or yams — to make a rich, nutritious dish suitable for holidays or special occasions.

3 cups thickly sliced carrots
  (5–6 medium carrots)
3 cups sliced sweet potatoes or yams
  (2–3 medium sweet potatoes)
$\frac{1}{3}$ cup chopped prunes
$\frac{1}{4}$ cup butter
1 tablespoon Sucanat (granulated cane juice)
1 teaspoon ground cinnamon
1 teaspoon barley miso
$\frac{1}{2}$ teaspoon salt
$\frac{1}{4}$ teaspoon ground ginger

In a large, covered saucepan with a steamer basket, steam the carrots and potatoes in water for 15 minutes.

Meanwhile, in a small bowl, soak the prunes for 5 minutes in water to cover. Drain and set aside.

Preheat oven to 400°F. In a small saucepan, melt the butter and stir in the Sucanat, cinnamon, miso, salt, and ginger and mix together well. Place the steamed vegetables in a baking pan and pour the butter mixture over the vegetables. Mix in the reserved prunes. Bake, covered, for 25 minutes. Serve immediately.

Sweet yams and salty hiziki, brightened with the zing of ginger, make a tasty and colorful side dish.

YAMS AND HIZIKI

½ ounce dried hiziki, well rinsed in cold water
  and drained
2 cups cold water
2½ cups water
10 cups peeled cubed yams (6–7 medium yams)
1 teaspoon salt
1 tablespoon canola oil
1 tablespoon tamari
1 tablespoon ginger juice
  (one 2-inch length fresh gingerroot, peeled)
¼ cup tahini
2 tablespoons chopped fresh parsley
⅓ cup chopped scallions

In a large, covered bowl, soak the drained hiziki in the 2 cups cold water for 30 minutes.

Meanwhile, in a large saucepan, combine the yams and 1 cup of the water and bring to a boil. Add the salt. Reduce heat to simmer and cook for 20 minutes or until soft. (Check water level occasionally to prevent scorching.)

When the hiziki has soaked, drain and rinse again. In a large skillet, combine the hiziki, 1 cup of the water, and the oil and cook, covered, on medium heat for 45 minutes. After 20 minutes, add the tamari. (Water should be fully evaporated after 45 minutes.)

Meanwhile, preheat oven to 350°F. Prepare the ginger juice by grating and squeezing the gingerroot. In a blender or food processor, blend together the cooked yams and ginger juice until creamy. In an oiled 9 x 12-inch baking pan, place half of the blended yams and layer the cooked hiziki. Top with the remaining yams.

In a small bowl, whisk together the tahini and remaining water and drizzle the mixture on top of the yams. Sprinkle with the parsley and scallions and bake, covered, for 20 minutes. Serve immediately.

Preparation and
cooking time
35 minutes.

Cooling time
10 minutes

Serves 4–6.

*What could be
better than a crisp,
sweet yam dish to go
with a soup and
salad or to brighten
a holiday meal?*

CANDIED YAMS

4 large yams, washed and unpeeled
¼ cup butter
¼ cup Sucanat (granulated cane juice)
1 tablespoon pure maple syrup

In a large, covered pot, boil the yams whole in water to cover. Cook for about 20 minutes or until firm but not soft. Drain and let cool for 10 minutes. Peel the yams and slice *each* yam lengthwise into 3–4 slices.

In a large skillet, melt ⅛ cup of the butter and add half of the yams. Sprinkle with ⅛ cup of the Sucanat and cook for 4–5 minutes or until brown, then flip over. Pour ½ tablespoon of the syrup over the yams and cook until both sides are brown. Remove from heat and keep warm.

Repeat the procedure with the remaining yams and ingredients. Combine the reserved yams with the remaining yams and serve immediately.

PARSNIP-SQUASH NISHIME

2 cups quartered onions
3 cups peeled coarsely chopped winter squash
  (approximately 1 medium squash)
3 cups coarsely chopped parsnips
  (3–4 medium parsnips)
2 cups water
½ teaspoon salt, or 2 tablespoons white miso
  diluted in ¼ cup warm water

In a large saucepan, layer the onions, squash, and parsnips. Add the water and bring to a boil.

Add the salt. Reduce heat to medium-low and cook, covered, for about 25 minutes, or until the vegetables are tender. (Check water level occasionally to prevent scorching.) Serve immediately.

Preparation and cooking time 35 minutes.

Serves 4.

This nishime turns the often unheralded parsnip into a star vegetable in a sweet, succulent combination of parsnips, squash, and onions.

*Turnips get a
chance to shine in
this combination of
turnips, mustard
greens, collards,
and spicy ingredi-
ents. Suddenly,
eating greens is fun!*

CAJUN TURNIPS AND GREENS

2½ cups cubed turnips
2 tablespoons olive oil
2½ cups sliced onions
1 teaspoon ground paprika
1 teaspoon diced garlic
¼ teaspoon black pepper
½ tablespoon salt
4 cups washed, dried, and chopped fresh collard
   greens (approximately 5 ounces greens)
3 cups washed, dried, and chopped fresh mustard greens (approximately 4 ounces greens)
½ cup water
1 tablespoon red wine vinegar

In a medium-sized, covered saucepan with a steamer basket, steam the turnips in water for 10 minutes. Drain.

In a large skillet, heat the oil and sauté the turnips and
onions on high heat for 5 minutes, stirring frequently.
Stir in the paprika, garlic, black pepper, and salt and
sauté on high heat for 10 minutes more, stirring frequently.

Add both greens and the water. Cover and steam for 5
minutes. Uncover and cook on high heat until the water
is evaporated. Add the vinegar and serve immediately.

COLLARDS WITH BROWN RICE VINEGAR AND TAMARI

Preparation and cooking time 30 minutes.

Serves 4–6.

Brown rice vinegar and tamari lend unusual flavor and character to these collard greens, which can be served hot or cold.

1 cup water
8 cups washed, dried, and sliced fresh collard
   greens (approximately 10 ounces greens)
1 tablespoon tamari
2¼ teaspoons brown rice vinegar
⅓ cup roasted sunflower seeds

In a large, deep skillet, heat the water and sauté the greens for about 20 minutes or until tender. Turn off heat.

Add the tamari, vinegar, and seeds and mix together well. Serve hot or cold.

To roast sunflower seeds: Preheat oven to 275 °F. In a small baking pan, place the seeds and bake for 4–6 minutes or until golden, stirring frequently.

*Kale, corn, and red
bell peppers make
this a colorful and
nutritionally bal-
anced dish.*

CONFETTI KALE

2 tablespoons olive oil
6 cups washed, dried, and chopped fresh kale
  (6–7 ounces kale)
¾ cup corn kernels
½ cup chopped red bell peppers
½ teaspoon salt
½ teaspoon black pepper

In a large skillet, heat the oil and sauté the kale on medium heat for 10 minutes, stirring constantly.

Mix in the corn, bell peppers, salt, and black pepper and
cook for 10 minutes. Serve immediately.

ARAME WITH SPINACH

½ cup water
1½ cups sliced onions
1 ounce dried arame, well rinsed in cold water
  and drained
2 cups cold water
¼ cup tahini
2 tablespoons tamari
3 cups chopped fresh spinach (approximately
  10 ounces spinach, loosely packed)

In a large skillet, heat ¼ cup of the water and sauté the onions for 3–5 minutes or until translucent. In a small, covered bowl, soak the arame in the 2 cups cold water for 5 minutes. Drain and rinse again.

Add the tahini, tamari, remaining water, and arame to the cooked onions and sauté for 10 minutes. Stir in the spinach and mix thoroughly. Turn off heat. Cover and let stand for 10 minutes. Serve.

Preparation and cooking time 40 minutes.
Serves 4.

Here is super nutrition in a side dish — a whopping dose of iron, calcium, and trace minerals, plus excellent flavor and color. Serve with Millet Croquettes with Beet-Horseradish Sauce or Couscous with Chickpeas (see pages 136–137 and 138) for a balanced, delicious meal.

Soba (buckwheat) noodles and arame, a thin, dark, succulent sea vegetable, make a very nutritious food combination and go well with stir-fried vegetables. This is a good dish to introduce sea vegetables to children, since they usually like anything combined with noodles.

Soba Noodles with Arame

8 ounces dried soba noodles
1 ounce dried arame, well rinsed in cold water
  and drained
2 cups cold water
2 tablespoons canola oil
1 cup fresh mung bean sprouts
2 tablespoons tamari
1 tablespoon brown rice vinegar
1 cup 1-inch cut scallions

In a large saucepan, cook the noodles in boiling water until tender but still firm. Drain and keep warm.

In a small, covered bowl, soak the arame for 5 minutes in the 2 cups cold water. Drain.

In a large skillet, heat the oil and sauté the arame for 10 minutes. Add the bean sprouts, tamari, and vinegar and sauté for 5 minutes more. Add the scallions and reserved noodles. Mix together and heat through. Serve immediately.

Live Foods Feasts: Salads and Raw Juices

Chapter 8

WHATEVER THE TIME of year, there is something wholesome and invigorating about fresh, raw vegetables. Since they are still full of nutrients, those nutrients are easily and quickly assimilated by the body. So raw (or slightly cooked) vegetable dishes are perfect for a quick burst of energy or a nourishing meal.

At Kripalu, we've created a number of salad recipes that we think of as "live foods feasts" that provide many vitamins and minerals, including vitamins A, C, and E, sodium, potassium, magnesium, silicon, iron, and much-needed fiber. We also make frequent use of vegetable and fruit juices to add supplementary nutrients to our standard diet or to provide an opportunity for a temporary purification diet. (One of Kripalu Center's most popular programs is "Raw Juice Fasting," in which participants take part in a five-day, body-cleansing juice fast.)

We incorporate fresh vegetable salads into our menu throughout the year, but especially in the summer, when a salad may be the main course. Besides the feelings of energy and lightness that we get from eating such foods, we also enjoy the bright colors and flavors that they add to all kinds of meals.

Salads are also great for entertaining. There are many recipes in this chapter that are excellent and easy additions to dinners or weekend parties; your family and friends will thank you for providing a combination of fresh flavors and fewer calories.

So get out your cutting board and a good sharp knife and let's begin.

New Orleans Greens Salad

This salad, tossed with lemon juice, garlic, and olive oil, nicely complements rice and beans, Vegetable Creole, *or* Red and Black Bean Chili *with* Pan Corn Bread *(see pages 150–151, 64–65, and 253).*

2 cups washed, dried, and chopped fresh romaine lettuce

2 cups washed, dried, and chopped fresh Boston lettuce

2 cups washed, dried, and chopped fresh green leaf lettuce

½ cup washed, dried, and chopped fresh chicory

½ cup washed, dried, and sliced fresh Chinese (napa) cabbage

2 tablespoons olive oil

1 tablespoon fresh lemon juice

2 tablespoons chopped fresh parsley

1 teaspoon white wine vinegar

1 teaspoon chopped garlic

1 teaspoon Dijon-style mustard

1 teaspoon rice syrup

½ teaspoon salt

Pinch white pepper

In a large bowl, combine all of the greens. In a small bowl, whisk together the remaining ingredients and pour over the greens. Toss well and serve immediately.

The combination of juicy cherry tomatoes, savory feta cheese, ripe black olives, and garlic-drenched lettuce makes this salad a big favorite. Serve with Hummus Among Us *(see page 201), stuffed thickly into pita pockets.*

GREEK SALAD

6 cups washed, dried, and chopped fresh
  romaine lettuce (1–2 medium heads lettuce)
¾ cup halved fresh cherry tomatoes
½ cup thinly sliced red onions
½ cup sliced cucumbers
8 ounces feta cheese, crumbled
½ cup pitted whole black olives
2 tablespoons chopped scallions
¾ cup olive oil
2 tablespoons red wine vinegar
½ tablespoon dried basil
½ tablespoon chopped garlic
1 teaspoon dried thyme
½ teaspoon salt
¼ teaspoon black pepper

In a large bowl, combine the lettuce, tomatoes, onions, cucumbers, cheese, olives, and scallions.

In a small bowl, whisk together the remaining ingredients and pour over the vegetables. Toss well and serve immediately.

Vegetarian Caesar Salad

1 cup prepared croutons
½ cup canola oil
3 tablespoons fresh lemon juice
1 teaspoon chopped garlic
¼ teaspoon salt
Pinch black pepper
¾ cup grated Parmesan cheese
7 cups washed, dried, and chopped fresh
  romaine lettuce (7–8 ounces lettuce)

*(If you don't have prepared croutons, cut your favorite bread into
cubes and toast until brown and crunchy.)*

In a small bowl, whisk together the oil, lemon juice, garlic, salt, black pepper, and ¼ cup of the cheese until well
combined.

In a large bowl, place the lettuce and pour the dressing
over the lettuce. Add the croutons and remaining cheese
and toss well. Serve immediately.

*Here's a light
version of Caesar
salad: no eggs, no
anchovies, no heavy
oils. Garlic and
croutons, however,
do give this salad
that specific
Caesar-salad taste.
Although we use
canola oil for its
lightness, substitute
extra-virgin olive oil
if a richer dressing
is desired.*

*This dish provides a
satisfying yet light
meal on a summer's
day. For variation,
use fresh grapefruit
slices or pineapple
chunks.*

Mixed Greens and Orange Salad

1 cup prepared croutons
4 cups washed, dried, and chopped fresh
   romaine lettuce (5–6 ounces lettuce)
1 cup washed, dried, and chopped fresh red leaf
   lettuce
1½ cups washed, dried, and chopped fresh
   watercress
¾ cup sliced canned mandarin oranges
¾ cup diced or sliced apples

*(If you don't have prepared croutons, cut your favorite bread into
cubes and toast until brown and crunchy.)*

In a large bowl, combine all of the ingredients and toss
well with *Carrot-Ginger Dressing, Creamy Italian Dressing,* or
Balsamic Vinaigrette (see Chapter 9 for dressings). Serve
immediately.

SPINACH, RADICCHIO, AND WATERCRESS SALAD

**Preparation time
15 minutes.**

Serves 4–6.

*This salad combines
the peppery flavors
of watercress and
radicchio with the
earthy flavor of
spinach. (The* Tofu
Cheese *should be
made in advance.)*

2 cups washed, dried, and chopped fresh
  romaine lettuce
2 cups washed, dried, and chopped fresh
  spinach
½ cup washed, dried, and chopped fresh
  radicchio
1 cup washed, dried, and chopped fresh
  watercress
1 cup sliced cucumbers
⅔ cup olive oil
1 tablespoon white wine vinegar
2 tablespoons fresh lemon juice
1 teaspoon salt
¼ teaspoon black pepper
½ cup thinly sliced red bell peppers
½ cup chopped walnuts
¼ cup sliced red onions
2 tablespoons finely chopped fresh chives
8 ounces *Tofu Cheese* (see page 198)

In a large bowl, combine all of the greens and the cucumbers. In a medium-sized bowl, whisk together the oil, vinegar, lemon juice, salt, and black pepper. Stir in the bell peppers, walnuts, onions, and chives and marinate for 5 minutes.

Pour the mixture over the greens and toss well. Crumble the cheese on top and serve immediately.

*This salad, which
combines the nutty
taste of sesame with
the peppery taste of
chicory, makes a
versatile side dish
that goes well with
almost any meal.*

CHICORY SALAD WITH SESAME DRESSING

¾ cup roasted sesame seeds
¾ cup water
2¼ teaspoons brown rice vinegar
1½ tablespoons tamari
½ tablespoon barley malt
8 cups washed, dried, and chopped fresh
   chicory or endive (10–12 ounces chicory, or
   1 large head endive)

In a blender or food processor, process the seeds until
well crushed. Add the water, vinegar, tamari, and barley
malt and blend until well combined.

In a large bowl, place the chicory and pour the dressing
over the chicory. Toss well and serve immediately.

*To roast sesame seeds: In a small skillet, dry roast
the seeds on medium heat, stirring constantly, for about
5 minutes or until begin to brown.*

CUCUMBER-DULSE SALAD

2½ cups sliced cucumbers
¼ cup sliced red onions
¼ cup washed, dried, and chopped fresh
  watercress
3¾ teaspoons umeboshi vinegar
1 tablespoon dried dulse flakes

In a medium-sized bowl, combine all of the ingredients and toss well. Serve. (This salad can be stored in the refrigerator for 2–3 days.)

Preparation time 10 minutes.

Serves 2.

Easy to make and cool and salty to the taste, this salad reminds us of the seashore because the dulse provides vitamins, iodine, and other trace minerals from the sea.

Preparation and
cooking time
20 minutes.

Cooling time
variable.

Serves 4.

*This salad provides a
delightful blend of
colors, flavors, and
textures. It has four
different vegetables
and a dressing of
vagar — a sauce in
which spices have
been sautéed. For a
live foods feast, serve
with* Cucumber-
Dulse Salad *and*
Carrot-Beet Salad
*(see pages 179 and
182).*

BROCCOLI-AVOCADO SALAD

Salad:
½ cup diced potatoes
2 cups finely chopped broccoli
1 ripe avocado, peeled and diced
¾ cup diced fresh tomatoes
½ cup chopped walnuts
2 tablespoons shredded coconut
½ tablespoon fresh lemon juice
½ teaspoon salt
1 tablespoon chopped fresh cilantro

Vagar:
2¼ teaspoons canola oil
½ teaspoon black mustard seeds
½ teaspoon cumin seeds
½ teaspoon ground turmeric
⅛ teaspoon garam masala

To make the salad: In a small, covered saucepan with a
steamer basket, steam the potatoes in water for about 10
minutes or until soft. Set aside and let cool.

In a blender or food processor, process half of the
chopped broccoli until smooth. In a medium-sized bowl,
combine the reserved potatoes, all of the broccoli, and
remaining salad ingredients.

To make the vagar: In a small saucepan or skillet, heat the
oil to medium heat and add the mustard and cumin
seeds, stirring constantly for 30 seconds. Add the tur-

meric and garam masala, stirring briefly to combine with oil. Turn off heat.

Pour the vagar over the vegetables and gently mix together. Serve immediately.

Preparation and cooking time 30 minutes.

Cooling time variable.

Serves 4.

This salad has unusual ingredients, including dates, apples, and sweet potatoes, that provide flavor, color, and texture and complement each other very well. Try it as a side dish for a picnic of New Orleans Greens Salad *and* Pasta Primavera Salad *(see pages 173 and 194–195).*

CARROT-BEET SALAD

½ cup diced sweet potatoes
4 cups water
½ cup chopped dried dates
½ cup chopped almonds
½ cup raisins
2 cups grated carrots
1 cup scrubbed grated fresh beets
1 cup diced apples
½ cup shredded coconut
¼ cup fresh lemon juice
½ teaspoon salt

In a small, covered saucepan with a steamer basket, steam the potatoes in 2 cups of the water for about 10 minutes or until soft. Set aside and let cool.

In a small bowl, combine the dates, almonds, raisins, and remaining water and soak for at least 10–15 minutes. Drain thoroughly.

In a medium-sized bowl, combine the reserved potatoes, raisin mixture, and remaining ingredients and gently mix together. Serve.

CARROT-CURRANT SALAD

Preparation time 15 minutes.

Serves 4–6.

This colorful salad has the sweet taste of currants and the richness of tahini.

1 cup currants or raisins
1½ cups warm water
3 tablespoons tahini
1½ tablespoons rice syrup
2 tablespoons fresh lemon juice
⅛ teaspoon ground cinnamon
5½ cups grated or shredded carrots
(8–9 medium carrots)

In a small bowl, soak the currants in the water for 5 minutes. Drain and reserve ½ cup of the soak water.

In a small bowl, whisk together the reserved soak water, the tahini, syrup, lemon juice, and cinnamon. In a large bowl, place the carrots and pour the dressing over the carrots. Add the soaked currants and mix together with a fork. Serve.

**Preparation time
20 minutes.**

**Chilling time
2 hours or over-
night.**

Serves 4–6.

*One day Mama D,
otherwise known as
Devangana, our
kitchen coordinator,
wanted to serve a
bright and lively
salad. The kitchen
had lots of cabbage
on hand, so she
dreamed up this
recipe, which has
hints of good old
"mayo" coleslaw
and a touch of
nouveau-style
vinaigrette.*

MAMA D'S COLESLAW

7 cups sliced green cabbage
  (approximately 1 large head cabbage)
1 cup grated carrots
⅓ cup currants or golden raisins
2 tablespoons brown rice vinegar
2 tablespoons umeboshi vinegar
5 tablespoons mayonnaise
1 tablespoon mirin
1 tablespoon pure maple syrup
3 tablespoons water
1 teaspoon fresh lemon juice

In a large bowl, combine the cabbage, carrots, and currants. In a blender or food processor, blend together the
remaining ingredients until creamy smooth.

Pour the mixture over the cabbage mixture and mix together with a wooden spoon until well combined. Cover
and refrigerate for at least 2 hours or overnight. Serve.

MARDI GRAS SLAW

2 cups sliced green cabbage
½ cup sliced red cabbage
½ cup grated cucumbers
½ cup grated carrots
½ cup chopped fresh parsley
¼ cup diced red onions
½ cup sliced radishes
2 tablespoons chopped fresh cilantro
1 tablespoon dried dill, or
  ¼ cup chopped fresh dill
2 tablespoons olive oil
1½ tablespoons brown rice vinegar
1 tablespoon fresh lemon juice
1½ teaspoons rice syrup
1 teaspoon salt
Pinch white pepper

In a large bowl, combine both cabbages, the cucumbers, carrots, parsley, onions, radishes, cilantro, and dill.

In a small bowl, whisk together the remaining ingredients. Pour the mixture over the cabbage mixture and mix together with a fork until well combined. Chill for at least 1 hour. Serve.

**Preparation time
25 minutes.**

**Chilling time
1 hour.**

Serves 4–6.

This is a superb holiday dish — a colorful slaw of green and red cabbages, carrots, fresh parsley, and radishes, tossed with brown rice vinegar and lemon juice.

Preparation and
cooking time
2 hours.

Soaking time
overnight.

Cooling time
variable.

Makes about 6
cups.

*So named because it
reminds us of tuna
salad, this tasty
spread is perfect on
Sunday morning
bagels or as a
dinner party dip for
crudités.*

CHICKPEA OF THE SEA

2 cups dried chickpeas
6 cups water
4 teaspoons salt
⅔ cup mayonnaise
1½ tablespoons canola oil
1½ tablespoons prepared brown mustard
1 tablespoon cider vinegar
1½ tablespoons umeboshi vinegar
1½ tablespoons nutritional yeast
1 tablespoon celery seeds
¼ teaspoon black pepper
⅛ teaspoon cayenne pepper
1 cup sliced celery
¼ cup chopped scallions

Wash the chickpeas. Soak overnight or use the quick-soak method (see page 128).

In a large saucepan, combine the soaked chickpeas and water and bring to a boil. Reduce heat to medium and cook for 1 hour 15 minutes or until soft. Add 3 teaspoons of the salt and cook for 20–30 minutes more. Drain and save cooking water. Let the chickpeas cool.

In a food processor, combine two-thirds of the cooled chickpeas, 1 cup of the cooking water, the mayonnaise, oil, mustard, both vinegars, yeast, celery seeds, remaining salt, and black and cayenne peppers and blend until well combined but *not* totally smooth. Add the celery and scallions and blend for 30 seconds more.

Add the remaining chickpeas whole, for a smooth and chunky consistency. (If a totally smooth consistency is desired, blend remaining chickpeas when the celery and scallions are added.) Serve on crackers, in sandwiches, or with crudités.

Preparation and
cooking time
2 hours (or 30
minutes, if canned
chickpeas are
used).

Soaking time
overnight.

Cooling time
variable.

Makes 3–4 cups.

*This variation of
Chickpea of the
Sea is lower in
fat because it uses
tofu instead of
mayonnaise. In
this version, the
chickpeas are not
blended, but
chopped with celery
and spices, and a
tofu blend is poured
over the top, which
makes an interest-
ing contrast of
texture and flavor.*

CHICKPEA OF
THE SEA LIGHT

⅓ cup dried chickpeas, or
 1 cup well-rinsed canned chickpeas
2 cups water
½ teaspoon salt
½ cup finely chopped celery
8 ounces soft tofu, rinsed and drained
1 tablespoon water
¼ cup chopped scallions
½ teaspoon Spike seasoning or seasoned salt
1 teaspoon olive oil
1 teaspoon Dijon-style mustard
1 teaspoon umeboshi vinegar
½ teaspoon brown rice vinegar
¼ teaspoon celery seeds
1 teaspoon nutritional yeast
Dash cayenne pepper
Dash freshly ground black pepper
Dash fresh lime juice
Salt to taste

*(If canned chickpeas are used, skip the cooking part of this
recipe.)*

Wash the chickpeas. Soak overnight or use the quick-soak
method (see page 128).

In a small saucepan, combine the soaked chickpeas and
the 2 cups water and bring to a boil. Reduce heat to medium and cook for 1 hour 15 minutes or until soft. Add

the salt and cook for 20–30 minutes more. Drain and let the chickpeas cool.

In a medium-sized bowl, chop or crush the cooled chickpeas and add the celery. In a blender or food processor, briefly blend together the tofu and the 1 tablespoon water. Add the remaining ingredients and blend until creamy.

Pour the tofu mixture over the chickpea mixture and mix together well. Adjust the seasonings and serve.

One of the tricks to a good potato salad is to blend the vegetables and seasonings while the potatoes are still hot. If you can serve the salad warm, so much the better. If not, the flavors blend well chilling overnight in the refrigerator.

POTATO SALAD

6 cups chopped potatoes
  (4–5 medium potatoes)
¾ cup sliced celery
¼ cup chopped scallions
2 tablespoons chopped fresh chives
½ cup mayonnaise
1½ tablespoons prepared brown mustard
1 tablespoon red wine vinegar
½ teaspoon celery seeds
½ teaspoon salt
¼ teaspoon black pepper
¼ teaspoon ground paprika

In a large, covered saucepan with a steamer basket, steam the potatoes for about 20 minutes or until soft (do not overcook).

In a large bowl, combine the cooked potatoes, celery, scallions, and chives. In a small bowl, mix together the remaining ingredients and pour over the potato mixture. Gently mix together and serve immediately.

TABOULI

¾ cup water
½ cup uncooked bulgur
4 cups chopped fresh parsley
   (approximately 1 large bunch parsley)
1 cup diced fresh tomatoes
¼ cup chopped fresh mint
½ cup fresh lemon juice
¼ cup olive oil
2 teaspoons salt
¼ teaspoon black pepper

In a small saucepan, bring the water to a boil. Add the bulgar and boil for about 1 minute. Turn off heat. Cover and steam-cook for about 5 minutes, or until the water is absorbed. Uncover and let cool.

In a medium-sized bowl, stir together the parsley, tomatoes, mint, lemon juice, oil, salt, and black pepper. Stir in the cooled bulgur and serve.

Preparation and cooking time 25 minutes.

Cooling time variable.

Makes about 6 cups.

With oil, garlic, fresh parsley, and a touch of fresh mint, this salad hints of the Middle East. It's easy to put together since the bulgur cooks so quickly.

Preparation and cooking time 40 minutes.

Cooling time variable.

Serves 4–6.

Here's a sweet, succulent rice salad laced with orange juice and currants, with green bell peppers, carrots, and cashews adding a delightful crunch.

INDONESIAN RICE SALAD

1 ½ cups uncooked long-grain brown rice
2 ¼ cups water
½ teaspoon salt
1 cup grated carrots
1 cup fresh mung bean sprouts
¾ cup chopped unsalted cashews
¾ cup diced green bell peppers
¼ cup chopped scallions
¼ cup fresh orange juice
¼ cup canola oil
1 ½ tablespoons tamari
1 ½ tablespoons mirin
2 ¼ teaspoons fresh lemon juice
½ teaspoon ground cumin
½ teaspoon ground ginger
½ teaspoon balsamic vinegar
¼ teaspoon black pepper

Wash and drain the rice. In a medium-sized, covered saucepan, combine the rice and water and bring to a boil. Add the salt. Reduce heat to simmer and cook for 20 minutes, or until the rice is soft and the water is absorbed. Fluff the rice with a fork and place in a medium-sized bowl. Let cool.

Stir in the carrots, sprouts, cashews, bell peppers, and scallions. In a small bowl, whisk together the remaining ingredients and pour over the rice mixture. Mix together well and serve.

RICE AND WHEAT BERRY SALAD

⅓ cup wheat berries
1 cup uncooked long-grain brown rice
2¼ cups water
½ teaspoon salt
½ cup currants or raisins
½ cup chopped walnuts
½ cup grated carrots
¼ cup chopped scallions
2 tablespoons chopped fresh parsley
2 tablespoons tamari
1 teaspoon sesame oil
1 tablespoon fresh lemon juice

Wash the wheat berries. Soak for 1 hour or overnight in water to cover. Drain and set aside.

Wash and drain the rice. In a medium-sized, covered saucepan, combine the reserved wheat berries, rice, and water and bring to a boil. Add the salt. Reduce heat to simmer and cook for 25 minutes, or until the wheat berries and rice are soft and the water is absorbed.

Fluff the wheat berries and rice with a fork and place in a medium-sized bowl. Let cool.

Stir in the currants, walnuts, carrots, scallions, and parsley. In a small bowl, whisk together the tamari, oil, and lemon juice and pour over the rice mixture. Mix together well and serve.

Preparation and cooking time 50 minutes.

Soaking time 1 hour or overnight.

Cooling time variable.

Serves 4–6.

Unusual ingredients make this a delightfully different salad.

Preparation and cooking time 25 minutes.

Cooling time variable.

Serves 4.

The secret to a good Pasta Primavera Salad is to prepare the dressing the day before so the herbs and spices marinate overnight.

PASTA PRIMAVERA SALAD

Dressing:
¼ cup olive oil
½ tablespoon chopped garlic
½ tablespoon salt
1 teaspoon dried basil
1 teaspoon balsamic vinegar
¼ teaspoon black pepper

Salad:
12 ounces dried fettuccine pasta or your
 favorite pasta
2–3 tablespoons water
1½ cups small broccoli spears
1½ cups halved small fresh mushrooms
1½ cups sliced red bell peppers
1½ cups canned artichoke hearts
1 cup pitted whole black olives
¼ cup chopped fresh basil

(If time permits, prepare the dressing the day before serving and marinate overnight.)

To make the salad: In a large saucepan, cook the pasta in boiling water until tender but still firm. Drain and rinse in cold water. Set aside and let cool.

Meanwhile, in a large, deep skillet, heat the water and sauté the broccoli, mushrooms, and bell peppers for about 5 minutes or until tender-crisp. Remove and rinse in cold water. Set aside and let cool.

(If the dressing has not been prepared, prepare now.) In a large bowl, mix together the reserved pasta and vegetables and pour the dressing over the top. Add the artichoke hearts, olives, and basil and mix together thoroughly. Serve immediately or chill for 1–2 hours, if desired.

On a picnic, serve these noodles to complement salads. Or, toss the noodles with a little sesame dressing, some scallions, and other finely diced vegetables, and you have a complete meal.

COLD SESAME NOODLES

8 ounces dried noodles (udon or soba)
6 cups boiling water
1 teaspoon ginger juice
  (one 1-inch length fresh gingerroot, peeled)
½ cup unsalted unsweetened natural peanut
  butter
¼ cup tahini
2½ tablespoons tamari
1 tablespoon sesame oil
Pinch cayenne pepper
Pinch mild chili powder
¾ cup water
1 cup peeled julienned cucumbers
½ cup roasted sesame seeds (see page 178)

In a large saucepan, cook the noodles in the boiling water until tender but still firm. Drain and rinse in cold water. Set aside and let cool.

Prepare the ginger juice by grating and squeezing the gingerroot. In a blender or food processor, combine the ginger juice and the next seven ingredients and blend together well.

In a large bowl, combine the reserved noodles, peanut butter sauce, cucumbers, and seeds and gently mix together. Serve immediately or refrigerate and serve the next day.

MARINATED TOFU

1 pound firm tofu, rinsed and drained

Marinade:
½ cup water
¼ cup olive oil
¼ cup red wine vinegar
¼ cup tamari
1½ tablespoons mirin
1 teaspoon dried oregano
1 teaspoon whole cloves
½ teaspoon dried marjoram
1 teaspoon chopped garlic
¼ teaspoon salt
Pinch black pepper

Wrap the tofu in a clean towel and place on a plate. Top with a heavy object and press out excess water for 10 minutes.

To make the marinade: In a small saucepan, combine all of the marinade ingredients and bring to a boil. Reduce heat to simmer and cook for 5 minutes.

Cut the pressed tofu into small cubes or large slices and place in a large bowl. Cover the tofu with the marinade and marinate for a least 1 hour or overnight. Serve in a mixed greens salad or as an appetizer at a family gathering.

Preparation time 15 minutes.

Marinating time 1 hour or overnight.

Makes 30–45 bite-sized pieces or 8–10 large slices.

These tasty tofu cubes, marinated in red wine vinegar, tamari, and cloves, add flavor and protein to almost any salad. Our first test of this recipe was eaten so fast that we hardly had any left to taste; even non–tofu eaters will devour these with gusto.

*Here's a great
alternative to dairy
cheese, with less fat
and no cholesterol.
Use* Tofu Cheese *as
you would any soft
cheese: crumbled in
salads, melted on
pizza or pasta, or
spread on* Peasant
French Bread *(see
page 248) with
garlic and a dab of
olive oil.*

TOFU CHEESE

1 pound firm or extra-firm tofu, rinsed and
  drained
3 tablespoons white miso

Wrap the tofu in a clean towel and place on a plate. Top
with a heavy object and press out excess water for at least
15 minutes.

Remove towel and spread the miso evenly around the
entire block of tofu, covering completely. Let stand, uncovered, at room temperature for at least 1½–2 days or
refrigerate the tofu for a minimum of 3 days. (Refrigera-
tion slows the fermentation process.)

After fermenting for the chosen time, scrape the miso off
the tofu (the miso can be used in soup or stew or dis-
carded) and use the cheese as desired.

ANTIPASTO

½ cup dried chickpeas
1½ cups water
½ teaspoon salt
1½ cups chopped cauliflower
1 cup halved fresh tomatoes
¾ cup pitted sliced black olives, or
   1 cup pitted whole black olives
1 cup julienned carrots
1 cup halved small fresh mushrooms
½ cup olive oil
¼ cup chopped fresh basil
1 tablespoon water
½ tablespoon chopped garlic
2 tablespoons red wine vinegar
2¼ teaspoons fresh lemon juice
½ teaspoon salt
¼ teaspoon black pepper

Wash the chickpeas. Soak overnight or use the quick-soak method (see page 128).

In a small saucepan, combine the soaked chickpeas and water and bring to a boil. Reduce heat to medium and cook for about 50 minutes or until soft. Add the salt and cook for 15 minutes more. Drain and let the chickpeas cool.

In a large bowl, combine the cauliflower, tomatoes, olives, carrots, and mushrooms. In a small bowl, whisk together the remaining ingredients and pour over the vegetables. Mix together well and stir in the cooled chickpeas. Serve immediately.

Preparation and cooking time 1 hour 30 minutes.

Soaking time overnight.

Cooling time variable.

Serves 4–6.

Serve this antipasto with Spinach-Cheese Lasagna *(see page 100–101) or your favorite pasta. The vegetables taste almost pickled if left in the marinade overnight.*

Preparation time 5–10 minutes.

Makes about 1½ cups.

Here's a saucy version, made with our House Salsa, *of a perennial favorite.*

GUACAMOLE

2 very ripe avocados, peeled and seeded
2 tablespoons *House Salsa* (see page 227)
1 tablespoon olive oil
1 tablespoon fresh lemon juice
1 teaspoon chopped garlic
½ teaspoon umeboshi paste

In a small bowl, mash the avocados. Stir in the remaining ingredients and blend well with a fork.

Serve with crackers or tortilla chips. (This recipe can be increased to any desired amount and can be frozen for up to 2 weeks.)

HUMMUS AMONG US

2 cups dried chickpeas
6 cups water
3½ teaspoons salt
2 tablespoons olive oil
2 tablespoons chopped fresh parsley
1½ tablespoons chopped garlic
⅔ cup fresh lemon juice
¼ cup tahini
½ teaspoon ground cumin

Wash the chickpeas. Soak overnight or use the quick-soak method (see page 128).

In a large saucepan, combine the soaked chickpeas and water and bring to a boil. Reduce heat to medium and cook for 1 hour 15 minutes or until soft. Add 3 teaspoons of the salt and cook for 20–30 minutes more. Drain and reserve the cooking water. Let the chickpeas cool.

In a food processor or by hand with a potato masher, combine the cooled chickpeas with 1 cup of the cooking water, remaining salt, and remaining ingredients. Blend or mash until completely smooth. Serve with crackers or pita bread.

Preparation and cooking time 1 hour 55 minutes.

Soaking time overnight.

Cooling time variable.

Makes about 6 cups.

I used to think that the only place you could get a decent hummus was in a certain deli in Philadelphia — now I know better. This hummus is just right: not too much garlic, not too many spices, not too much parsley — just the right amount of everything.

Carrots and cashews: what a terrific blend of flavors! This tasty spread can be served with dipping vegetables, croutons, or on bread for a late-night snack.

CARROT-CASHEW SPREAD

4 cups chopped carrots
  (approximately 7 medium carrots)
5 cups water
1 tablespoon salt
½ cup unsalted cashews

In a large saucepan, combine the carrots and water and bring to a boil. Add the salt. Reduce heat to simmer and cook for about 20 minutes or until very soft. Drain and reserve the cooking water. Let the carrots cool.

In a blender or food processor, blend together the cooled carrots and cashews. (Check the consistency and add up to ½ cup of the cooking water, if a lighter consistency is desired.) Serve with crackers, pita bread, or crudités.

TOFU, OLIVE, AND SCALLION SPREAD

**Preparation time
15 minutes.**

Makes about 4 cups.

1 pound firm tofu, rinsed and drained
2 tablespoons umeboshi vinegar
1 tablespoon brown rice vinegar
2 tablespoons fresh lemon juice
1½ tablespoons rice syrup
½ teaspoon dried dill, or
   1 tablespoon chopped fresh dill
½ teaspoon salt
½ teaspoon ground paprika
¼ cup olive oil
¼ cup chopped scallions
⅓ cup pitted sliced black olives

Press out excess water in the tofu with a clean towel. In a blender or food processor, place the tofu, both vinegars, lemon juice, syrup, dill, salt, and paprika and blend together, slowly adding the oil until creamy (similar to cream cheese).

In a medium-sized bowl, stir together the tofu mixture, scallions, and olives. Serve with crackers or crudités.

What an excellent substitute for cream cheese! This is a delicious, healthy tofu spread with a touch of mayonnaise, onions, and fresh parsley. If desired, add some fresh dill or red bell peppers to give it color.

Raw Vegetable and Fruit Juices

The following raw juice combinations provide vitamins A, C, and E, as well as many trace minerals. To promote general health and healthy digestive systems, we drink these juices periodically as part of a purification diet.

Tips for Juice Making
- Use a high-quality vegetable and fruit juicer.
- Use fresh, organically grown produce to maximize nutrients and minimize pesticides.
- Wash all unpeeled vegetables and fruits well. (Do not need to peel organic carrots.)
- For each recipe, wash, chop, and blend the listed ingredients.
- For each recipe, the yield is 2 cups juice, which takes 5–10 minutes to prepare. Any recipe can be increased to any desired amount.

Carrot-Beet Juice with Ginger

6 medium carrots
2 large fresh beets
One ½-inch length fresh
  gingerroot, peeled

Carrot-Cucumber Juice

6 medium carrots
⅔ medium cucumber, peeled

CARROT, CELERY, AND APPLE JUICE

5 medium carrots
3 stalks celery
3 small apples, cored

CARROT-GINGER JUICE

8 medium carrots
One 2-inch length fresh
  gingerroot, peeled

CARROT-PARSLEY JUICE

7 medium carrots
½ cup chopped fresh parsley

TOMATO-CELERY JUICE

3 large fresh tomatoes
3 stalks celery

CANTALOUPE-HONEYDEW JUICE

½ medium cantaloupe,
  peeled
½ medium honeydew melon,
  peeled

PINEAPPLE-GRAPEFRUIT JUICE

1 whole pineapple, peeled
  and cored
1 medium grapefruit, peeled

At Kripalu, we often drink Potassium Broth, *a rich, long-cooked brew made from onions, potatoes, beets, and carrots, to replenish not only our bodies' potassium, but also to replace many other trace minerals and nutrients. This broth provides a feeling of well-being and is especially useful for someone on a temporary purification diet or for someone who is ill and needs some robust, easy-to-digest liquid nour-ishment.*

POTASSIUM BROTH

4 cups grated potatoes (2–3 medium potatoes)
1½ cups grated carrots
1 cup sliced onions
¾ cup scrubbed grated fresh beets
2 stalks celery, halved
¼ cup chopped fresh parsley
1 bay leaf
10 cups water

In a large pot, combine all of the ingredients and bring to a boil. Reduce heat to simmer and cook for at least 1 hour, preferably for 2–3 hours.

Add more water as the vegetables cook, if needed. Strain the vegetables and discard. Reserve the clear broth. Serve hot. (This broth can be stored in the refrigerator for 1–2 days and reheated before serving.)

SALAD DRESSINGS AND CONDIMENTS

Chapter 9

PERHAPS ONE OF THE true tests of a cook is in the blending together of herbs, spices, and oils to perfectly complement a salad. At Kripalu, we've created hundreds of dressings over the years, and they tend to fall into three categories that fit the different dietary choices of our diners:

1. Simple dressings, which contain no oil or dairy products and can be refrigerated for 1–2 days; we're particularly proud of our simple dressings, made mostly from blended fresh vegetables, because they deliver great taste with lots of nutrients and few calories.

2. Oil dressings, which contain oil but no dairy and can be refrigerated for 1 week.

3. Dairy dressings, the richest of all, which contain both oil and dairy and can be refrigerated for 7–10 days.

In this chapter are eighteen recipes for our best dressings and also recipes for the various condiments that we serve with every meal to accent and contrast the flavors of different foods. Some of these—gomasio, goma-wakame, pumpkin seed-dulse—are excellent, lower sodium substitutes for salt.

COOL CUCUMBER DRESSING

**Preparation time
10 minutes.**

Makes 2 cups.

1 cup peeled cubed cucumber
4 ounces soft tofu, rinsed and drained
¼ cup water
½ teaspoon dried dill, or
  2 teaspoons chopped fresh dill
1 teaspoon umeboshi vinegar
1 teaspoon tahini
½ teaspoon salt

In a blender or food processor, combine all of the ingredients and blend until smooth.

Serve immediately or refrigerate until ready to use. (This dressing can be stored, covered, in the refrigerator for 1–2 days.)

Add a touch of umeboshi vinegar, tofu, and tahini to the delicious combination of cucumber and dill, and you have a classic cucumber dressing.

**Preparation time
25 minutes.**

**Cooling time
5 minutes.**

Makes 2 cups.

*Here's a zesty,
bright dressing that
has the perfect blend
of sweet, pungent,
and salty flavors.
Fresh gingerroot can
be used instead of
ground ginger, just
double the quantity.
In this recipe,
however, the ground
ginger gives the
dressing a dry,
piquant taste.*

CARROT-GINGER DRESSING

1 cup coarsely chopped carrots
1 cup water
2 tablespoons chopped fresh parsley
1 tablespoon tahini
1 teaspoon umeboshi vinegar
½ teaspoon salt
¼ teaspoon ground ginger

In a small saucepan, combine the carrots and water and bring to a boil. Reduce heat to simmer and cook for 10–15 minutes, or until the carrots are tender. Drain the cooking water into a measuring cup and add enough water to bring amount to 1 cup. Let the carrots cool for 5 minutes.

In a blender or food processor, combine the cooled carrots, the 1 cup cooking water, and remaining ingredients and blend until smooth.

Serve immediately or refrigerate until ready to use. (This dressing can be stored, covered, in the refrigerator for 1–2 days.)

Umeboshi Beet Dressing

1¼ cups scrubbed chopped fresh beets
1 cup water
4 ounces soft tofu, rinsed and drained
1 tablespoon umeboshi vinegar
½ tablespoon tahini
¼ teaspoon salt
¾ cup water

In a medium-sized, covered saucepan with a steamer basket, steam the beets in the 1 cup water for about 25 minutes or until tender. Drain and let cool for 5 minutes.

In a blender or food processor, combine the cooled beets and remaining ingredients and blend until smooth.

Serve immediately or refrigerate until ready to use. (This dressing can be stored, covered, in the refrigerator for 1–2 days.)

Preparation time
30 minutes.

Cooling time
5 minutes.

Makes 2 cups.

Here's a bright, fuchsia-colored dressing with the sweetness of beets, the saltiness of umeboshi, and the richness of tahini.

*Tofu and scallions,
always a great taste
combination, create
a light and flavorful
dressing.*

Tofu-Scallion Dressing

8 ounces soft tofu, rinsed and drained
⅓ cup chopped scallions
⅔ cup water
1 tablespoon umeboshi vinegar
¼ teaspoon salt

In a blender or food processor, combine all of the ingredients and blend until smooth.

Serve immediately or refrigerate until ready to use. (This dressing can be stored, covered, in the refrigerator for 1–2 days.)

PEANUT-GINGER DRESSING

Preparation time 10 minutes.

Makes 2 cups.

What a tangy combination ginger and peanut butter make!

2 teaspoons ginger juice
  (one 2-inch length fresh gingerroot, peeled)
¾ cup unsalted unsweetened natural
  peanut butter
1 cup warm water
1½ tablespoons tamari

Prepare the ginger juice by grating and squeezing the gingerroot.

In a blender or food processor, combine the ginger juice and remaining ingredients and blend until smooth.

Serve immediately or refrigerate until ready to use. (This dressing can be stored, covered, in the refrigerator for 1–2 days.)

*The combination of
walnuts and white
miso makes this an
elegant dressing for
a Friday evening
soirée or Sunday
brunch.*

WALNUT-MISO DRESSING

1 cup whole walnuts
1½ tablespoons white miso
½ tablespoon tamari
½ tablespoon umeboshi vinegar
1 cup water

In a medium-sized skillet, dry roast the walnuts on medium heat for 5–7 minutes, stirring constantly, until the walnuts begin to brown. Remove and let cool for 5 minutes.

In a blender or food processor, combine the cooled walnuts, miso, tamari, and vinegar and blend until the walnuts are chopped. Add the water and blend for 30–60 seconds or until smooth.

Serve immediately or refrigerate until ready to use. (This dressing can be stored, covered, in the refrigerator for 1–2 days.)

PUMPKIN SEED DRESSING

Preparation time
10 minutes.

Cooling time
5 minutes.

Makes 2 cups.

1 cup dried pumpkin seeds
2 tablespoons brown rice vinegar
1 tablespoon umeboshi vinegar
1 teaspoon tamari
1 cup water

This hearty, health-ful dressing is especially suitable for brightening up chicory, endive, and other exotic greens.

In a medium-sized skillet, dry roast the seeds on medium heat for about 5 minutes, stirring constantly, until the seeds pop. Remove and let cool for 5 minutes.

In a blender or food processor, combine the cooled seeds, both vinegars, and tamari and blend until the seeds are chopped. Add the water and blend for 30–60 seconds or until smooth.

Serve immediately or refrigerate until ready to use. (This dressing can be stored, covered, in the refrigerator for 1–2 days.)

Here's an amazingly simple dressing with delightful umeboshi and scallion flavors.

UMEBOSHI
SCALLION DRESSING

1 ½ cups chopped scallions
¾ cup canola oil
2 tablespoons umeboshi vinegar
½ cup water

In a blender or food processor, combine all of the ingredients and blend until moderately smooth.

Serve immediately or refrigerate until ready to use. (This dressing can be stored, covered, in the refrigerator for 1 week.)

Greek Tamari Dressing

Preparation time
10 minutes.

Cooling time
5 minutes.

Makes 2 cups.

3 tablespoons white sesame seeds
¾ cup canola oil
3 tablespoons fresh lemon juice
2 tablespoons tamari
2 tablespoons tahini
2 tablespoons chopped fresh parsley
1 teaspoon ground mustard
½ teaspoon chopped garlic
½ teaspoon salt
⅛ teaspoon cayenne pepper
⅛ teaspoon black pepper
½ cup water

Something about the combination of tamari, tahini, fresh parsley, lemon juice, and canola oil makes this a robust topping for all types of salads. It is considered one of our prize dressings.

In a small skillet, dry roast the seeds on medium heat for about 5 minutes, stirring constantly, until the seeds begin to brown. Remove and let cool for 5 minutes.

In a blender or food processor, combine the cooled seeds and remaining ingredients and blend until smooth.

Serve immediately or refrigerate until ready to use. (This dressing can be stored, covered, in the refrigerator for 1 week.)

*Bright yellow-
orange in color and
tasting of sesame,
lemon, and tahini,
this is a perfect
dressing not only for
green salads, but
also for rice or pasta
salads.*

LEMON-SESAME DRESSING

3 tablespoons white sesame seeds
¾ cup canola oil
3 tablespoons fresh lemon juice
2 tablespoons finely chopped onions
1½ tablespoons tamari
1 teaspoon ground paprika
3 tablespoons tahini
½ teaspoon chopped garlic
½ teaspoon celery seeds
½ cup water
¼ teaspoon salt
⅛ teaspoon black pepper

In a small skillet, dry roast the seeds on medium heat for about 5 minutes, stirring constantly, until the seeds begin to brown. Remove and let cool for 5 minutes.

In a blender or food processor, combine the cooled seeds and remaining ingredients and blend until smooth.

Serve immediately or refrigerate until ready to use. (This dressing can be stored, covered, in the refrigerator for 1 week.)

PARSLEY-GARLIC DRESSING

**Preparation time
10 minutes.**

Makes 2 cups.

3 cups washed coarsely chopped fresh parsley
  (approximately 1 bunch parsley)
¼ cup tamari
½ cup fresh lemon juice
⅔ cup canola or sesame oil
1½ teaspoons chopped garlic

In a blender or food processor, combine all of the ingredients and blend until moderately smooth.

Serve immediately or refrigerate until ready to use. (This dressing can be stored, covered, in the refrigerator for 1 week.)

This dressing has zing! It combines a powerfully bright taste with a dose of vitamins A and C from the parsley.

*We often use this
versatile dressing on
holidays.*

Balsamic Vinaigrette

⅓ cup fresh orange juice
3 tablespoons balsamic vinegar
¼ cup olive oil
2 teaspoons Dijon-style mustard
1 teaspoon chopped garlic
1½ teaspoons salt
½ teaspoon black pepper

In a medium-sized bowl, combine all of the ingredients
and stir together with a fork or wooden spoon until well
blended.

Serve immediately or refrigerate until ready to use. (This
dressing can be stored, covered, in the refrigerator for 1
week.)

FRENCH DRESSING

½ cup olive oil
½ cup canola oil
¼ cup water
2 tablespoons cider vinegar
1½ tablespoons honey
1 tablespoon prepared brown mustard
1 teaspoon chopped garlic
½ teaspoon ground paprika
½ teaspoon salt
¼ teaspoon black pepper

In a blender or food processor, combine all of the ingredients and blend until smooth.

Serve immediately or refrigerate until ready to use. (This dressing can be stored, covered, in the refrigerator for 1 week.)

**Preparation time
5 minutes.**

Makes 2 cups.

This bright, sweet, and tangy dressing has been on the Kripalu menu for a long time. Enjoy!

**Preparation time
10 minutes.**

Makes 2 cups.

*The Cadillac of dairy
dressings and a cinch
to make,* Bleu
Cheese *turns a
simple salad into an
elegant statement of
good taste.*

Bleu Cheese Dressing

½ cup crumbled bleu cheese
½ cup sour cream
3 tablespoons mayonnaise
¼ cup plain yogurt
⅓ cup water
½ teaspoon black pepper

In a blender or food processor, combine ¼ cup of the cheese with the remaining ingredients and blend until smooth. Fold in the remaining cheese with a wooden spoon.

Serve immediately or refrigerate until ready to use. (This dressing can be stored, covered, in the refrigerator for 7–10 days.)

FETA-GARLIC DRESSING

Preparation time 10 minutes.

Makes 2 cups.

1 cup olive oil
²⁄₃ cup crumbled feta cheese
½ cup milk
1½ tablespoons white wine vinegar
½ teaspoon chopped garlic
½ teaspoon dried dill
½ teaspoon salt

In a blender or food processor, combine all of the ingredients and blend until creamy smooth. Or, reserve ⅓ cup cheese and add after blending to provide a contrasting texture.

Serve immediately or refrigerate until ready to use. (This dressing can be stored, covered, in the refrigerator for 7–10 days.)

Here's a recipe with spicy garlic and salty feta to dress up your favorite greens. Kuntal likes to combine it with Umeboshi Scallion Dressing *(see page 216) to make a doubly delicious topping for pasta salad.*

*Scallions and fresh
parsley, combined
with sour cream,
cottage cheese, and
buttermilk, make a
bright green, creamy
dressing — wonder-
ful for sprouts,
slaws, and greens.*

GREEN GODDESS DRESSING

½ cup sour cream
¼ cup cottage cheese
¼ cup buttermilk
½ cup canola or sunflower oil
2 tablespoons fresh lemon juice
3 tablespoons chopped scallions
2 tablespoons water
½ teaspoon salt
1 teaspoon chopped garlic
¼ teaspoon black pepper
¼ cup chopped fresh parsley
Pinch ground cardamom

In a blender or food processor, combine all of the ingredients and blend until creamy smooth.

Serve immediately or refrigerate until ready to use. (This dressing can be stored, covered, in the refrigerator for 7–10 days.)

CREAMY ITALIAN DRESSING

Preparation time 10 minutes.

Makes 2 cups.

½ cup buttermilk
½ cup sour cream
½ cup canola oil
⅓ cup cottage cheese
2 tablespoons water
½ tablespoon red wine vinegar
1 teaspoon salt
1 teaspoon chopped garlic
1 teaspoon dried onions
1 teaspoon dried oregano
¼ teaspoon black pepper
1 teaspoon dried basil
Pinch ground cardamom

In a blender or food processor, combine all of the ingredients and blend until creamy smooth.

Serve immediately or refrigerate until ready to use. (This dressing can be stored, covered, in the refrigerator for 7–10 days.)

One of our most versatile dressings, Creamy Italian *has some surprise ingredients, including buttermilk for richness and cardamom for sweetness, along with the Italian staples of oregano, basil, and garlic.*

Tamari-Ginger *is
more of a dipping
sauce than a dress-
ing. Use it for
dipping roasted
vegetables, tempura,
norimake, or your
favorite stir-fry.*

TAMARI-GINGER SAUCE

2 teaspoons ginger juice
  (one 2-inch length fresh gingerroot, peeled)
1½ cups water
¼ cup tamari
5 teaspoons brown rice vinegar
1 teaspoon fresh lemon juice
1 tablespoon finely grated daikon
  (Japanese white radish)
2 teaspoons finely chopped scallions

Prepare the ginger juice by grating and squeezing the gingerroot.

In a medium-sized bowl, stir together the ginger juice,
water, tamari, vinegar, and lemon juice. Add the daikon
and scallions so they float on top of the sauce.

Serve immediately or refrigerate until ready to use. (This
sauce can be stored, covered, in the refrigerator for 1–2
days.)

HOUSE SALSA

**Preparation time
15 minutes.**

Makes 5–6 cups.

1½ cups canned crushed tomatoes
2½ cups diced fresh tomatoes
¾ cup diced onions
¾ cup diced green bell pepper
2 tablespoons chopped fresh cilantro
¾ tablespoon olive oil
½ tablespoon balsamic vinegar
1 teaspoon diced jalapeño peppers or to taste
1 teaspoon diced garlic
1 teaspoon fresh lime juice
½ teaspoon salt
⅛ teaspoon black pepper
Pinch cayenne pepper or to taste
Dash Tabasco sauce or to taste

*Salsa is now the
best-selling condi-
ment in America.
Here's a tasty,
homemade recipe to
serve with Mexican
dishes, tortilla
chips, or any dish
desired.*

In a large bowl, combine all of the ingredients and mix
together well. Serve immediately or refrigerate until ready
to serve. (This salsa can be stored in an airtight container
in the refrigerator for 5–7 days.)

**Preparation time
15 minutes.**

Makes 2 cups.

*Chutney can provide
the perfect balance
to a spicy meal and
can brighten up a
simple meal. The
combination of
apples and cilantro
is sweet, piquant,
and flavorful.*

Apple-Cilantro Chutney

¼ cup raisins
½ cup water
1½ cups diced apples
¼ cup toasted shredded coconut
2 tablespoons chopped fresh cilantro
2 tablespoons whole almonds
½ tablespoon fresh lemon juice
½ tablespoon honey
½ teaspoon salt
½ teaspoon ground cumin
¼ teaspoon black mustard seeds
¼ teaspoon white sesame seeds
¼ teaspoon freshly grated black pepper
¼ teaspoon peeled grated fresh gingerroot
Pinch dried crushed red chili peppers
Pinch cayenne pepper

In a small bowl, cover the raisins with the water and soak
for 5–10 minutes. Drain.

In a medium-sized bowl, combine the remaining ingredients. Add the soaked raisins and mix together well.

Serve immediately or refrigerate until ready to use. (This
chutney can be stored, covered, in the refrigerator for 2–
3 days.)

*To toast shredded coconut: Preheat oven to 325 °F. Thinly
spread the shredded coconut on a baking sheet and
heat in the oven for about 10 minutes, stirring frequently.*

OLIVE RELISH

½ cup sliced carrots
½ cup chopped cauliflower
1 cup pitted whole green olives
¾ cup pitted whole black olives
¼ cup cider vinegar
½ cup olive oil
½ teaspoon salt
1 tablespoon chopped garlic
1 teaspoon dried oregano

In a blender or food processor, combine all of the ingredients in order and blend for 5–10 seconds. (Olives should be only slightly chopped, not mushy.)

Serve immediately or refrigerate until ready to use. (This relish can be stored, covered, in the refrigerator for 2–3 days.)

Preparation time 10 minutes.

Makes 2½ cups.

Olives, carrots, cauliflower, and herbs make this a deluxe condiment. Or, spread it on toasted, sliced pita bread for a quick and easy appetizer.

*Here's a nutty, salty
condiment, lower in
sodium than table
salt, to sprinkle on
soups, salads, or
stews. Since sesame
seeds are an excel-
lent source of
calcium and zinc,
consider making a
large batch of
gomasio to keep on
hand.*

GOMASIO

1 cup white sesame seeds
1 teaspoon freshly ground sea salt

In a small skillet, dry roast the seeds on medium heat for
about 5 minutes, stirring constantly, until begin to
brown.

Using a blender or mortar and pestle, blend or crush together the warm sesame seeds and salt.

Use immediately or refrigerate until ready to use. (This
condiment can be stored in an airtight container in the
refrigerator for several weeks.)

GOMA-WAKAME

1 cup white sesame seeds
1½ ounces wakame

In a small skillet, dry roast the seeds on medium heat for about 5 minutes, stirring constantly, until begin to brown.

Preheat oven to 400°F. On a baking sheet, place the wakame and bake for 10 minutes. (Check to prevent burning.) In a blender or food processor, combine the warm seeds and wakame and blend until well combined.

Use immediately or refrigerate until ready to use. (This condiment can be stored in an airtight container in the refrigerator for several weeks.)

**Preparation time
5 minutes.**

**Baking time
10 minutes.**

Makes 1 cup.

A variation of gomasio, Goma-Wakame *has the salty sea flavor and additional nutrients of dry roasted wakame.*

**Preparation time
5 minutes.**

**Baking time
3–5 minutes.**

**Cooling time
variable.**

Makes 1 cup.

*Here's another
savory condiment
with hints of the sea
and the flavor and
nutrients of pump-
kin seeds, which are
an excellent source
of zinc. Use it as a
topping for steamed
vegetables, brown
rice, or rice salads.*

PUMPKIN SEED-DULSE CONDIMENT

1 cup dried pumpkin seeds
1 tablespoon dried dulse flakes

In a small skillet, dry roast the seeds on medium heat, stirring constantly, until the seeds pop. Remove and let cool.

Preheat oven to 400°F. On a baking sheet, place the dulse and bake for 3–5 minutes. (Check to prevent burning.) Using a blender or a mortar and pestle, blend or crush together the cooled seeds and dulse.

Use immediately or refrigerate until ready to use. (This condiment can be stored in an airtight container in the refrigerator for several weeks.)

BEST OF BREADS AND BAKING

Chapter 10

 GOOD BREAD IS a Kripalu tradition. For years, we've perfected our whole-wheat yeasted breads, at the same time developing diverse recipes for quick breads, sourdough breads, biscuits, and baguettes. Express from our bakery, here are the best of our oven's offerings, along with some handy tips for foolproof bread preparation.

PUTTING BREADS TOGETHER

Generally, breads fall into three categories: yeasted breads, sourdough breads, and quick breads leavened with baking soda or baking powder. Since the majority of the breads in this chapter are yeasted breads, general instructions for them are offered first. Instructions for sourdough breads are briefly explained with their recipes. Quick breads have simpler instructions, because their fermentation, rising, and baking processes happen simultaneously in the oven.

The main ingredients that we use for baking include whole-wheat flour, unbleached white flour, active dry yeast, and other leavening agents, such as baking soda and baking powder. Feel free to try different varieties of flour, but unbleached flours are better, because they don't have the unpleasant by-products of bleaching. Where unbleached white flour is indicated, try Golden White Flour with Germ, a brand sold commercially by Arrowhead Mills, which is available at natural foods stores and specialty markets. Or, use the unbleached white flours marketed by the major, national brands.

For sweeteners, we use carob powder, molasses, rice syrup, and barley malt, each of which adds a distinctive flavor and color to the bread. Our quick bread recipes use a variety of interesting flours, sweeteners, and other ingredients, such as raisins, walnuts, herbs, cheeses, and even jalapeño peppers! We highly recommend using organic products as much as possible to avoid unwanted pesticides or contaminants in ingredients.

Most of the recipes are for two loaves of bread, except for a few of the quick bread recipes, which make only one loaf. Use standard 9 x 5 x 3-inch loaf pans, unless otherwise indicated.

INSTRUCTIONS FOR YEASTED BREADS

1. Mix active dry yeast with water that is very warm, about 100°–110°F.

2. Add the sweetening agent and mix well.

3. Let the mixture sit for 2–3 minutes; a foam head may appear.

4. Add the flour, oil, and salt that are called for in the recipe and mix until well combined. Let stand for 10 minutes, so the yeast mixture is fully absorbed.

5. On a lightly floured surface, knead the dough for 10 minutes: Push the dough together into a large mound and use the heels of your hands to push against its whole surface, rhythmically flattening the dough, then forming it back into a mound. Repeat this procedure to lengthen the fibers of gluten, so the dough will be able to rise.

6. As you knead the dough, it will probably become very sticky or tacky. The stickiness goes away or becomes less prominent as you continue to knead. If it hasn't changed after 5 minutes, then the dough is too wet, so add a little flour. The dough should, however, be fairly moist. If it gets too dry as you're kneading, add a little water. After some experience, you'll get better and better.

7. After the first 2–3 minutes of kneading, add any herbs or spices called for in the recipe. If there are raisins, seeds, or cheeses, add those close to the end of the kneading time, or after about 7 minutes. Total kneading time is about 10 minutes.

8. Place the dough in a large, lightly oiled bowl and cover with a clean cloth. Set in a warm, draft-free space (75°–80°F) and let rise for 40–60 minutes or until doubled in size. Use the finger test described below to check the amount of rise.

9. Return the dough to the lightly floured surface and punch down the dough, as you did for the first kneading. Shape the dough into a mound, cover again, and let rise for 20–30 minutes or half the time of the first rise. Use the finger test again to check the amount of rise.

10. Roll out the dough, divide into 2 loaves (if makes 2 loaves), and place in oiled loaf pan(s). Let rise in a warm, draft-free space until the dough has risen ¾–1 inch above the rim of the pan(s). This usually takes about 20 minutes.

11. Preheat the oven to 375°F. Bake the loaves for at least 45 minutes. The bread is done when the inside of the loaf is springy and not wet and when the bottoms sound hollow when tapped.

FINGER TEST

Lightly press your index finger into the dough.

1. If it springs up slightly, it can rise still more.

2. If nothing happens, it is time to punch down the dough and get ready for the next rise or for baking.

3. If the dough falls slightly around your indentation, it has risen too long. Be sure this doesn't happen on the second rise.

The rising time for yeasted breads, including all three rises, plus kneading time, is 2 hours. The preparation times listed in the individual recipes involve steps 1–4 in "Instructions for Yeasted Breads" above.

Preparation time
15 minutes.

Rising time
2 hours.

Baking time
45 minutes.

Cooling time
20–30 minutes.

Makes 2 loaves.

This classic whole-wheat bread has graced the Kripalu kitchen counter for years. We've toasted it for breakfast, served it with Chickpea of the Sea *or* Hummus Among Us *for lunch, and enjoyed it with* Golden Brown Tofu *at dinner (see pages 186–187, 201, and 90).*

YEASTED WHOLE-WHEAT BREAD

2½ cups very warm water
1 tablespoon active dry yeast
2½ tablespoons rice syrup
2 cups whole-wheat flour
1½ cups unbleached white flour
¼ cup canola oil
1 tablespoon salt

Prepare the dough according to the "Instructions for Yeasted Breads" (see page 235), using the ingredients listed above.

Remove the baked loaves from the pans and let cool for 20–30 minutes on a wire rack. Serve immediately or cool completely and wrap tightly in plastic wrap to store.

VARIATIONS ON YEASTED WHOLE-WHEAT BREAD

EARTH BREAD

⅓ cup uncooked millet
⅓ cup dried sunflower seeds
¼ cup white sesame seeds
1 recipe *Yeasted Whole-Wheat Bread* dough (see page 236)

In a small bowl, soak the millet in water to cover for 15 minutes. Drain and set aside.

In another small bowl, mix together the sunflower and sesame seeds and set aside.

Prepare the dough according to the "Instructions for Yeasted Breads" (see page 235), using the ingredients for *Yeasted Whole-Wheat Bread*. After the dough has stood for 10 minutes, knead for only 5 minutes.

Add the reserved soaked millet and reserved seed mixture and continue to follow the remaining instructions for *Yeasted Whole-Wheat Bread*.

Remove the baked loaves from the pans and cool for 20–30 minutes on a wire rack. Serve immediately or cool completely and wrap tightly in plastic wrap to store.

Preparation time 5 minutes. Rising time 2 hours. Baking time 45 minutes. Cooling time 20–30 minutes. Makes 2 loaves.

EVERYTHING BREAD

1 recipe *Yeasted Whole-Wheat Bread* dough (see page 236)
⅓ cup poppy seeds
⅓ cup white sesame seeds
½ tablespoon finely chopped garlic

Prepare the dough according to the "Instructions for Yeasted Breads" (see page 235), using the ingredients listed in *Yeasted Whole-Wheat Bread*.

Before placing the dough in the loaf

pans, mix together the poppy and sesame seeds and garlic in a large, shallow bowl. Roll the loaves in the seed mixture and place the loaves in the pans. Continue to follow the instructions for *Yeasted Whole-Wheat Bread*.

Remove the baked loaves from the pans and let cool for 20–30 minutes on a wire rack. Serve immediately or cool completely and wrap tightly in plastic wrap to store.

Preparation time 5 minutes. Rising time 2 hours. Baking time 45 minutes. Cooling time 20–30 minutes. Makes 2 loaves.

HONEY WHOLE-WHEAT BREAD

Topping:
1 teaspoon honey
1 tablespoon canola oil

Dough:
2½ cups very warm water
1 tablespoon active dry yeast

2 tablespoons rice syrup
⅓ cup unsulphured molasses
2 cups whole-wheat flour
4 cups unbleached white flour
¼ cup canola oil
2¼ teaspoons salt

To make the topping: In a small bowl, mix together the honey and oil and set aside.

Prepare the dough according to the "Instructions for Yeasted Breads" (see page 235), using the ingredients listed above, but bake the loaves for only 15 minutes. Remove the loaves from the oven and brush the reserved topping over the loaves with a pastry brush. Return the loaves to the oven and bake for 30 minutes more.

Remove the baked loaves from the pans and let cool for 20–30 minutes on a wire rack. Serve immediately or cool completely and wrap tightly in plastic wrap to store.

Preparation time 5 minutes. Rising time 2 hours. Baking time 45 minutes. Cooling time 20–30 minutes. Makes 2 loaves.

BAVARIAN BREAD

2½ cups very warm water
2 teaspoons active dry yeast
¼ cup unsulphured molasses
3 cups whole-wheat flour
2 cups unbleached white flour
¾ cup rye flour
⅔ cup rye flakes
⅓ cup rolled oats
2 tablespoons carob powder
2¼ teaspoons salt
¼ cup corn oil

In a medium-sized bowl, stir together the water, yeast, and molasses. In a large bowl, mix together all of the dry ingredients. Add the wet mixture to dry mixture and fold in the oil. Let stand for 10 minutes.

Continue to follow the "Instructions for Yeasted Breads" (see page 235).

Remove the baked loaves from the pans and let cool for 20–30 minutes on a wire rack. Serve immediately or cool completely and wrap tightly in plastic wrap to store.

Preparation time
20 minutes.

Rising time
2 hours.

Baking time
45 minutes.

Cooling time
20–30 minutes.

Makes 2 loaves.

This loaf has the flavor and texture of a European bread. Rolled oats, rye flour, and rye flakes impart the almost tart, very substantial taste of a durable peasant bread. Carob powder and molasses give this bread a dark color and sweetness.

Preparation time
15 minutes.

Rising time
2 hours.

Baking time
45 minutes.

Cooling time
20–30 minutes.

Makes 2 loaves.

The combination of cornmeal and wheat flours makes this a very special bread with a rich, sweet flavor. Toast for breakfast or serve with jam and butter for tea time. The origin of the name is unknown, though there's an improbable story about a Yankee hunter, who cursed at his wife Anna the first time she accidentally added cornmeal to the flour.

ANADAMA BREAD

2 cups very warm water
1¼ tablespoons active dry yeast
½ cup unsulphured molasses
2½ cups unbleached white flour
2½ cups whole-wheat flour
1 cup cornmeal
¼ cup corn oil
½ tablespoon salt

Prepare the dough according to the "Instructions for Yeasted Breads" (see page 235), using the ingredients listed above.

Remove the baked loaves from the pans and let cool for 20–30 minutes on a wire rack. Serve immediately or cool completely and wrap tightly in plastic wrap to store.

RAISIN BREAD

1¼ cups raisins
2 cups water
2⅔ cups very warm water
1 tablespoon active dry yeast
1 tablespoon unsulphured molasses
1 tablespoon barley malt
2⅔ cups whole-wheat flour
3 cups unbleached white flour
¼ cup canola oil
1 tablespoon salt
1 tablespoon ground cinnamon
1 tablespoon carob powder

In a small bowl, soak the raisins in the 2 cups water for 15 minutes. Drain and set aside.

Prepare the dough according to the "Instructions for Yeasted Breads" (see page 235), using the ingredients listed above, but let the dough rise for 1 hour for the first rise and 30 minutes for the second rise.

Remove the baked loaves from the pans and let cool for 20–30 minutes on a wire rack. Serve immediately or cool completely and wrap tightly in plastic wrap to store.

Preparation time
30 minutes.

Rising time
2 hours.

Baking time
45 minutes.

Cooling time
20–30 minutes.

Makes 2 loaves.

This raisin loaf is one of our specialty breads, nursed by Jayendra through many recipe tests until it emerged in its robust, full-bodied form, dotted with raisins and laced with cinnamon, carob, molasses, and barley malt.

Preparation time
30 minutes.

Rising time
2 hours.

Baking time
45 minutes.

Cooling time
20–30 minutes.

Makes 2 loaves.

This is a savory, high-protein bread with a wonderful aroma fresh from the oven. Mozza- rella, cheddar, and Parmesan cheeses combine with oregano, basil, and other herbs for a rich, salty under- tone al italiano. It's perfect accompany- ing Cream of Tomato Soup *for lunch or with* Antipasto *anytime (see pages 52–53 and 199).*

HERBED CHEESE BREAD

2¾ cups very warm water
1 tablespoon active dry yeast
3 tablespoons rice syrup
2½ cups whole-wheat flour
¼ cup canola oil
1 tablespoon salt
1 teaspoon dried oregano
1 teaspoon dried basil
1 teaspoon dried thyme
1 teaspoon dried dill
1 teaspoon dried marjoram
½ cup grated mozzarella cheese
½ cup grated cheddar cheese
½ cup grated Parmesan cheese

Prepare the dough according to the "Instructions for Yeasted Bread" (see page 235), using the ingredients listed above.

Remove the baked loaves from the pans and let cool for 20–30 minutes on a wire rack. Serve immediately or cool completely and wrap tightly in plastic wrap to store.

OATMEAL BREAD

1 cup rolled oats
4½ cups very warm water
2 teaspoons active dry yeast
⅓ cup unsulphured molasses
2½ cups whole-wheat flour
3 cups unbleached white flour
½ tablespoon salt

In a small bowl, combine the oats and 1½ cups of the water. Let stand for 15 minutes.

In a large bowl, mix together the remaining water, the yeast, and molasses and let stand for 5 minutes. Mix both flours and the salt into the yeast mixture. Add the oat mixture.

Continue to follow the "Instructions for Yeasted Breads" (see page 235, but let the dough rise 1–2 hours for the first rise and 30–60 minutes for the second rise.

Remove the baked loaves from the pans and let cool for 20–30 minutes on a wire rack. Serve immediately or cool completely and wrap tightly in plastic wrap to store.

Preparation time
25 minutes.

Rising time
1 hour 30 minutes – 3 hours.

Baking time
45 minutes.

Cooling time
20–30 minutes.

Makes 3 loaves.

Good old-fashioned oatmeal, commended for its many heart-healthy virtues, adds a sweet flavor and crusty texture, as well as durability and shelf life. Serve this bread with Guacamole (see page 200) or fill with salads and spreads for your child's lunch box.

**Preparation time
20–30 minutes.**

**Rising time
2 hours 20–25
minutes.**

**Baking time
45 minutes.**

**Cooling time
15–20 minutes.**

Makes 2 loaves.

*Seamus, our expert
baker, took great
pains to create this
excellent loaf,
which combines
caraway, sesame,
and poppy seeds,
rye, wheat, and
oats in an earthy
blend of flavors.*

Eight-Grain Bread

2¼ cups very warm water
2¼ teaspoons active dry yeast
2½ tablespoons rice syrup
2½ tablespoons unsulphured molasses
¼ cup canola oil
2 cups whole-wheat flour
2 cups unbleached white flour
1 tablespoon salt
½ cup rolled oats
⅓ cup caraway seeds
⅓ cup white sesame seeds
⅓ cup cooked rice (brown or white)
⅓ cup rye flakes
⅓ cup wheat bran
⅓ cup poppy seeds

In a medium-sized bowl, stir together all of the wet ingredients. In a large bowl, mix together all of the dry ingredients, except the poppy seeds. Let each mixture stand
for 5 minutes. Spread the poppy seeds on a large, rimmed
baking sheet and set aside.

Add the wet mixture to the dry mixture and mix together
until just combined. Let stand for 10 minutes more.

Knead the dough according to "Instructions for Yeasted
Breads" (see page 235), but let rise for 1 hour 30 minutes for the first rise and for 30 minutes for the second
rise.

Divide the dough into two equal mounds. With the palms of both hands, roll each mound into a 10-inch "rope." Curl each rope into a spiral and gently turn each loaf upside down onto a wet cloth to moisten the top of the loaf, then dip the top of each loaf into the reserved poppy seeds.

Place the loaves on a lightly oiled baking sheet and let rise for 20–25 minutes more. Continue to follow the "Instructions for Yeasted Breads."

Let the baked loaves cool for 15–20 minutes on a wire rack. Serve immediately or cool completely and wrap tightly in plastic wrap to store.

Preparation time
5 minutes.

Rising time
1 hour 45 minutes –
2 hours 15 minutes.

Baking time
45 minutes.

Cooling time
20–30 minutes.

Makes 2 loaves.

Caraway seeds and rye flour help make this a full-bodied, tart, and tasty bread. It's great for our Tofu Reuben (see pages 118– 119) or for grilled cheese and tomato sandwiches.

Swedish Rye Bread

3 cups very warm water
1 tablespoon active dry yeast
4 tablespoons unsulphured molasses
2½ cups whole-wheat flour
2 cups unbleached white flour
2 cups rye flour
2 tablespoons canola oil
1 tablespoon salt
2 tablespoons caraway seeds

Prepare the dough according to "Instructions for Yeasted Breads" (see page 235), using the ingredients listed above, but let the dough rise 1–1 hour 30 minutes for the first rise and about 45 minutes for the second rise.

Remove the baked loaves from the pans and let cool for 20–30 minutes on a wire rack. Serve immediately or cool completely and wrap tightly in plastic wrap to store.

FOCÀCCIA BREAD

2½ cups very warm water
2¼ teaspoons active dry yeast
¼ cup rice syrup
7 cups unbleached white flour
⅓ cup olive oil
1 tablespoon salt
½ cup chopped fresh rosemary
½ cup chopped fresh sage

Prepare the dough according to the "Instructions for Yeasted Breads" (see page 235), using the ingredients listed above, but preheat oven to 400°F and bake for 30 minutes.

Remove the baked loaves from the pans and let cool for 15–20 minutes on a wire rack. Serve immediately or cool completely and wrap tightly in plastic wrap to store.

Preparation time
30 minutes.

Rising time
2 hours.

Baking time
30 minutes.

Cooling time
15–20 minutes.

Makes 2 loaves.

Focàccia is a flat bread, adorned with olive oil and savory herbs, but we've turned it into a leavened bread that can be prepared with relatively little effort. Serve with Pasta Primavera Salad *or* Udons and Tempeh in Oriental Barbecue *(see pages 194–195 and 359–360).*

Preparation time
20 minutes.

Rising time
2 hours.

Baking timing
45 minutes.

Cooling time
20–30 minutes.

Makes 2 loaves.

Here's my favorite bread to serve with spaghetti or linguine. The long rolls are flatter than traditional French bread, but they have the same aroma and springy texture, plus the added healthy advantage of the combination of whole-wheat flour and unbleached white flour.

PEASANT FRENCH BREAD

2½ cups very warm water
2¼ teaspoons active dry yeast
3 tablespoons rice syrup
3 cups whole-wheat flour
2½ cups unbleached white flour
¼ cup canola oil
1 tablespoon salt

Prepare the dough according to the "Instructions for Yeasted Breads" (see page 235), using the ingredients listed above, but when ready to roll out the dough, divide the dough into two equal mounds.

Shape one mound into a long rectangle and pat it down somewhat firmly. Using your fingers and starting on the lower left-hand side of the rectangle, curl the dough as if you were rolling up a jelly roll. Move from the left side to the right, curling the dough for three or four rolls until it makes a long, round shape. With the palms of both hands, roll the dough on the surface two or three times so that the loaf firms up a bit.

Repeat this procedure with the remaining dough. Place the loaves on a baking sheet, cover, and let rise for 30 minutes or until doubled in size. Continue to follow the "Instructions for Yeasted Breads."

Let the baked loaves cool for 20–30 minutes on a wire rack. Serve immediately or cool completely and wrap tightly in plastic wrap to store.

FRENCH BAGUETTES

2½ cups water
1 tablespoon active dry yeast
2½ tablespoons rice syrup
3 cups white whole-wheat flour*
3 cups unbleached white flour
¼ cup canola oil
1 tablespoon salt

Prepare the dough according to the "Instructions for Yeasted Breads" (see page 235), using the ingredients listed above, but use the rolling technique described for *Peasant French Bread,* rolling the loaves, though, slightly longer and thinner. (These loaves are the length of traditional baguettes, but about twice the width.)

Preheat oven to 425°F. Place the loaves on baking sheets. Lightly spray the loaves with water and lightly coat with flour. (Also to keep the loaves moist while baking, lightly spray the oven with water before baking or set a pan of water in the oven.) Bake for 20 minutes.

Let the baked loaves cool for 20–30 minutes on a wire rack. Serve immediately or cool completely and wrap tightly in plastic wrap to store.

White whole-wheat flour (King Arthur brand) is available at natural foods stores and specialty markets.

Preparation time
20 minutes.

Rising time
2 hours.

Baking time
20 minutes.

Cooling time
20–30 minutes.

Makes 2 loaves.

Similar to Peasant French Bread *(see page 248), these baguettes have a crisp, hearty flavor due to using a naturally occurring white whole-wheat flour. If white whole-wheat flour is not available, use unbleached white flour. Serve with* French Onion Soup *(see page 49) or with hors d'oeuvres.*

SOURDOUGH BREADS

Sourdough breads are made from a starter mixture of wheat flour and water that, when left to sit, draws wild yeasts from the atmosphere into the dough in proportions that reflect naturally occurring processes; the yeasts are balanced by bacteria and other microorganisms that share in the fermenting/rising process. Richard Bourdon of Berkshire Mountain Bakery in Housatonic, Massachusetts, who helped train many of Kripalu's bakery staff in the art of sourdough bread baking, says that the acidity in sourdough is not something whimsically selected by bakers to enhance the flavor of their breads. Rather, it helps make the bread rise and breaks down certain chemicals in the bread so that the nutrients are more accessible. (See Sources.)

Once you've mixed together the required flour and water in a large glass, crockery, or plastic bowl, at a ratio of 1¼ cups flour to 1 cup warm water, and covered it with a *damp* cloth, you've alerted yeasts and microorganisms that, in Bourdon's words, "Food is here; come party." A 24-hour sit will create a spongy mixture (the starter), which can then be refrigerated and used to start new batches of sourdough. (Keep the starter in a 1–2-quart, covered container of glass, crockery, or plastic.)

Once you've made the starter, it's important to "feed" or freshen the spongy mixture the day before baking by adding more flour and water (1¼ cups flour and 1 cup warm water to ½ cup starter). When you begin bread baking, remember to remove and refrigerate a portion of the starter to use for future batches.

WHOLE-WHEAT SOURDOUGH BREAD

3 cups water
3 cups whole-wheat flour
3 cups unbleached white flour
1 teaspoon salt
8 ounces sourdough starter

Feed your starter the day before baking.

In a large bowl, mix together the water, both flours, and salt until well combined. Let stand for 10 minutes until the water is fully absorbed. Add the starter.

On a lightly floured surface, knead the dough for 10 minutes. Let the dough rise for a minimum of 1 hour, preferably 3–4 hours. (The dough will not rise as much as yeasted dough, but will rise some more while baking.)

Roll out the dough and divide the dough into two loaves. Let sit for 30 minutes.

Preheat oven to 425°F. Oil two 9 x 5-inch loaf pans. Roll out again and place the loaves in the pans. Let rise until the dough has risen about 1 inch above the rim of the pans. Bake for 30 minutes. Reduce heat to 375° and bake for 30 minutes more, or until the bottoms sound hollow when tapped.

Remove the baked loaves from the pans and let cool for 20–30 minutes on a wire rack. Serve immediately or cool completely and wrap tightly in plastic wrap to store.

Preparation time
25 minutes.

Rising time
2 hours.

Baking time
1 hour.

Cooling time
20–30 minutes.

Makes 2 loaves.

This bread has a mildly sour taste and a crisp, golden brown crust. It is excellent for sandwiches, French toast, and homemade croutons.

Preparation time
1 hour.

Rising time
20 minutes.

Baking time
1 hour.

Cooling time
20–30 minutes.

Makes 2 loaves.

A pleasant variation on wheat sour-dough, this rye bread is more dense and slightly more sour. It has a crispy crust, excellent for toast or peanut butter sandwiches.

RYE SOURDOUGH BREAD

3½ cups water
8 cups rye flour
1 teaspoon salt
8 ounces sourdough starter

In a large bowl, mix together the water, flour, and salt with a spatula until well combined. Add the starter and mix by hand for about 10 minutes. Mix dough by hand for 5–10 minutes every 30 minutes for the next hour, for a total of 3 times.

Preheat oven to 425°F. Oil two 9 x 5-inch loaf pans. Divide the dough into two loaves and place in the pans. Let the dough rise until it is even with the rim of the pans. Bake for 30 minutes. Reduce heat to 375° and bake for 30 minutes more, or until the bottoms sound hollow when tapped.

Remove the baked loaves from the pans and let cool for 20–30 minutes on a wire rack. Serve immediately or cool completely and wrap tightly in plastic wrap to store.

PAN CORN BREAD

Olive oil
2½ cups cornmeal
1½ cups whole-wheat pastry flour
1⅓ cups unbleached white flour
3 tablespoons baking powder
1 teaspoon salt
1¼ cups water
1⅓ cups soymilk
⅔ cup canola oil
½ cup pure maple syrup
½ teaspoon pure vanilla extract

Preheat oven to 400°F. Oil a 9 x 12-inch baking pan with the olive oil.

In a large bowl, mix together all of the dry ingredients. In a separate bowl, stir together all of the wet ingredients. Add the wet mixture to the dry mixture and mix together until just blended.

Pour the batter into the pan and bake for 20–25 minutes, or until a tester inserted in the center comes out clean. (The corners of the corn bread may start to turn brown; if so, reduce heat to 375° for remaining baking time.)

Let cool for 30 minutes on a wire rack. Cut into squares and serve.

**Preparation time
30 minutes.**

**Baking time
20–25 minutes.**

**Cooling time
30 minutes.**

Serves 6–8.

We are indebted to the late Frank Arcuri, who helped perfect many of our recipes, especially our Cajun and New Orleans-style dishes, and helped us turn out the best corn bread north of the Mason-Dixon line.

Preparation time
30 minutes.

Baking time
30–40 minutes.

Cooling time
30 minutes.

Serves 6–8.

*Here's part two of
the great corn bread
tradition! Add some
jalapeño peppers,
onions, red bell
peppers, and ched-
dar cheese for a
treat that's almost a
meal.*

JALAPEÑO CHEESE CORN BREAD

1⅔ cups cornmeal
2½ cups whole-wheat flour
2 teaspoons baking powder
1 teaspoon salt
½ teaspoon black pepper
¼ cup diced red bell peppers
⅓ cup diced jalapeño peppers
¾ cup diced Spanish onions
⅓ cup unsalted butter, melted
2 cups buttermilk
1½ tablespoons honey
1⅔ cups grated mild cheddar cheese

Preheat oven to 400°F. Oil a 9 x 12-inch baking pan.

In a large bowl, mix together all of the dry ingredients. In a separate bowl, combine both peppers, the onions, melted butter, buttermilk, and honey. Add the cheese and mix together until well combined. Add the wet mixture to the dry mixture with a spatula and mix together until well combined. (The texture will be thick and wet.)

Pour the batter into the pan and bake for 30–40 minutes, or until a tester inserted in the center comes out clean. (The corn bread will brown slightly and set up.)

Let cool for 30 minutes on a wire rack. Cut into squares and serve.

HERB BISCUITS

2 cups whole-wheat pastry flour
2½ cups unbleached white flour
2 teaspoons salt
3¾ teaspoons baking powder
1 teaspoon dried basil
1 teaspoon dried thyme
1 teaspoon dried oregano
1 teaspoon dried marjoram
2 teaspoons dried garlic granules
¾ cup canola oil
2 cups apple cider

Preheat oven to 350°F. Oil two baking sheets.

In a large bowl, mix together all of the dry ingredients. In a small bowl, combine the oil and cider. Add the oil mixture to the dry mixture with a spatula and mix together until well combined.

Drop the dough by tablespoonsful onto the baking sheets and bake for 12–15 minutes, or until the bottoms are brown.

Let cool for 10 minutes on a wire rack or serve warm.

Preparation time 15 minutes.

Baking time 12–15 minutes.

Cooling time 10 minutes.

Makes 18–20 biscuits.

One part biscuit and two parts heaven — these little breads are uncommonly soft and chewy, with a lovely herbal bouquet of basil, thyme, oregano, and garlic.

Preparation time
20 minutes.

Baking time
45–50 minutes.

Cooling time
20–30 minutes.

Makes 1 loaf.

*Among our quick
and sweet bread
offerings, this bread
is a favorite, and
it's easy to prepare.
It has the firm
texture and deep,
dark molasses flavor
of brown breads,
enhanced by the
addition of crushed
walnuts and two
kinds of raisins.*

BOSTON
BROWN BREAD

¾ cup unbleached white flour
1 cup whole-wheat flour
¾ cup whole-wheat pastry flour
¼ cup cornmeal
½ teaspoon salt
1 teaspoon baking soda
1 cup buttermilk
½ cup unsulphured molasses
⅓ cup roasted crushed walnuts
  (see page 132, substitute walnuts for almonds)
⅓ cup raisins
⅓ cup golden raisins

Preheat oven to 350°F. Oil an 8½ x 4½-inch loaf pan.

In a medium-sized bowl, mix together all of the dry ingredients, except the walnuts and raisins. In a large bowl,
stir together the buttermilk and molasses. Add the dry
mixture to the buttermilk mixture and mix together until
just blended. Stir in the walnuts and both raisins with a
wooden spoon and mix together until well combined.

Pour the batter into the pan and bake for 45–50 minutes,
or until a tester inserted in the center comes out clean.

Let cool for 20–30 minutes on a wire rack. Serve.

BANANA BREAD

2¾ cups sliced bananas
⅓ cup canola oil
½ cup rice syrup
1 cup whole-wheat pastry flour
1 cup unbleached white flour
½ teaspoon salt
1 teaspoon baking powder
1 teaspoon baking soda
½ teaspoon ground allspice
Pinch ground cardamom
⅔ cup roasted walnuts
    (see page 132, substitute walnuts for almonds)

Preheat oven to 375°F. Oil a 9 x 5-inch loaf pan.

In a blender or food processor, blend together the bananas and oil until just combined. Place the banana mixture in a large bowl. Stir in the syrup with a spatula. In a medium-sized bowl, mix together all of the dry ingredients, except the walnuts. Add the dry mixture to the banana mixture and mix together until well blended. Mix in the walnuts.

Pour the batter into the pan and bake for 40–50 minutes, or until a tester inserted in the center comes out clean.

Let cool for 20 minutes on a wire rack. Serve.

Preparation time
20 minutes.

Baking time
40–50 minutes.

Cooling time
20 minutes.

Makes 1 loaf.

Warm banana bread often greets us first thing in the morning at Kripalu. Ours is a perfect blend of flours, laced with walnuts and spiced with cardamom and allspice. This bread is a crowd pleaser, so serve on any holiday morning or any time you're feeling festive.

Preparation time
1 hour.

Baking time
1–1 hour 15 min-
utes.

Cooling time
30 minutes.

Makes 1 loaf.

*Cinnamon, cloves,
and figs combine
with lemon zest to
make a sweet and
tart loaf that is very
delicious. Use high-
quality dried figs,
such as Turkish or
Black Mission.*

FIG BREAD

8 ounces dried black figs
1¼ cups apple cider
⅓ cup canola oil
½ cup rice syrup
1 cup whole-wheat pastry flour
¾ cup unbleached white flour
¼ teaspoon salt
1½ teaspoons baking soda
1½ teaspoons baking powder
1 teaspoon ground cinnamon
½ teaspoon ground cloves
½ cup crushed walnuts
1½ tablespoons fresh lemon juice
1 teaspoon lemon zest

In a small saucepan, combine the figs and ¾ cup of the
cider and cook on medium-low heat for 10–15 minutes,
or until the figs are soft. In a blender or food processor,
blend the fig mixture to a paste.

Preheat oven to 350°F. Oil a 9 x 5-inch loaf pan. In a
medium-sized bowl, mix together the oil and syrup with
a wooden spoon. In a separate bowl, sift together all of
the dry ingredients, except the walnuts. Add the fig paste,
remaining cider, lemon juice and zest to the oil mixture
and stir together well. Add the dry mixture to the fig
mixture and mix together until well blended. Mix in the
walnuts.

Pour the batter into the pan and bake for 1–1 hour 15
minutes, or until a tester inserted in the center comes out
clean. Let cool for 30 minutes on a wire rack. Serve.

PRUNE BREAD

1 cup apple cider
1/3 cup canola oil
3/4 cup rice syrup
8 ounces prunes
1 cup whole-wheat pastry flour
1/4 teaspoon salt
1/2 tablespoon baking soda
1 teaspoon ground cinnamon
Juice of 1/2 lemon
1 teaspoon lemon zest
1/3 cup roasted walnuts
  (see page 132, substitute walnuts for almonds)

Preheat oven to 350°F. Oil a 9 x 5-inch loaf pan.

In a small bowl, stir together the cider, oil, and syrup. In a small saucepan, combine the prunes and half of the cider mixture and cook on medium-low heat for 5–10 minutes. Remove from heat, cover, and set aside for 30 minutes.

In a large bowl, mix together all of the dry ingredients. In a blender or food processor, blend the reserved prune mixture to a paste. Add the paste to the dry mixture and mix together well. Stir in the remaining half of the cider mixture and the lemon juice and zest. Mix in the walnuts.

Pour the batter into the pan and bake for 50–60 minutes, or until a tester inserted in the center comes out clean.

Let cool for 30 minutes on a wire rack. Serve.

**Preparation time
40 minutes.**

**Baking time
50–60 minutes.**

**Cooling time
30 minutes.**

Makes 1 loaf.

Another delectable loaf, this prune bread is sweet and fruity, with a slight hint of lemon. It makes a lovely breakfast bread or a treat for afternoon tea.

Preparation time
20 minutes.

Baking time
1 hour.

Cooling time
30 minutes.

Makes 1 loaf.

*Touches of carda-
mom, vanilla, and
apple cider make
this a hybrid,
halfway between a
bread and a sweet
baked dessert.*

POPPY SEED BREAD

1 cup whole-wheat pastry flour
1¼ cups unbleached white flour
½ teaspoon salt
½ teaspoon baking powder
½ tablespoon baking soda
1 teaspoon ground cardamom
½ cup poppy seeds
Juice and zest of ½ lemon
1 cup rice syrup
¼ cup canola oil
1 teaspoon pure vanilla extract
¾ cup apple cider

Preheat oven to 350°F. Oil a 9 x 5-inch loaf pan.

In a medium-sized bowl, mix together all of the dry ingredients, except the seeds and lemon zest. In a large
bowl, whisk together all of the wet ingredients, except the
lemon juice. Add the dry mixture to the wet mixture and
mix together until well blended. Stir in the seeds and
lemon juice and zest.

Pour the batter into the pan and bake for 1 hour, or until a tester inserted in the center comes out clean.

Let cool for 30 minutes on a wire rack. Serve.

DESSERTS AND OTHER DELIGHTS

Chapter 11

 MANY YEARS AGO, when Kripalu Center was still located in Pennsylvania, the Kripalu residents stopped eating sugar and sweet products in the hopes of attaining a more pristine, healthful diet. One of my favorite stories is about Dayaram, a young man who often sneaked away in his car, like many of us, to snack on forbidden treats.

One afternoon, telling no one about his clandestine purpose, he went out and bought an ice-cream cone. As he sat in his car, taking furtive licks from the cone, he spotted a police officer looking at him from across the street. In a frenzied reflex action, he shoved the ice-cream cone down under the seat. Equally startled by the gooey mess, he realized that his guilt about eating the "wrong thing" had surfaced so quickly that, imagining himself caught in the act, he had rushed to destroy the evidence!

Although we've come a long way since that time, we at Kripalu occasionally have bouts of panic or judgment about what we eat and about what's appropriate for a natural foods diet. But we've broadened our spectrum of choices considerably, as well as our attitudes about eating. In any form, dessert still comes under the category of "nice, but not necessary," as far as nutrition is concerned. So, whenever we entertain the idea of a postprandial treat, our philosophy, above all, is to enjoy ourselves fully.

Occasionally, we enjoy a voluptuous *Black Forest Cake* with real chocolate, cherries, and whipped cream, allowing for no substitutions. At the same time, our soy puddings will surprise you with their rich mouth feel, without using eggs, milk, cream, or sugar in their preparation. And try topping *Apple-Walnut Pie* or *Berry Cobbler* with *Soy Cream,* a nondairy topping, to discover how an elegant concoction can have simple ingredients.

While our assortment of end-of-the-meal treats runs the gamut from simple and healthy to devilishly decadent, you'll see that we rarely abandon nourishing food options. We like to choose from a variety of cakes, puddings, pies, and cookies to suit different occasions and times of the year, accommodating sweet and fat tooth cravings while still providing good nutrition. For that reason, you won't see granulated white sugar or cornstarch in our recipes, since those products are so refined that they're empty of anything but calories.

Sweeteners

In general, for sweetening purposes we use maple syrup, honey, granulated cane juice (Sucanat), rice syrup, and barley malt. Maple syrup and honey also have certain nutrients, because little if any refinement has occurred in producing them. Their sweetness is very pronounced, and each has a characteristic flavor, which may or may not be desirable, depending on the type of recipe that you're making.

Granulated cane juice is less refined than its counterpart, granulated white sugar, but it is still a very strong sweetener. We use it in cakes and pies where we want to approximate the texture and flavor of white sugar, without adding additional liquid. Barley malt and rice syrup are grain sweeteners that have distinctive flavors and less intense sweetness, so they work best when combined with other, stronger sweeteners, such as honey or maple syrup, that extend their sweetening ability, or they are used in desserts where natural, uncloying sweetness is an important feature. Although we suggest using chocolate chips sweetened with barley malt instead of white sugar, we use both. The barley malt chips are usually slightly less sweet.

We also use amasake as a liquid sweetener; it's a fermented rice drink that has a light, agreeable taste that blends well with cinnamon, almond, and fruit flavors. When preparing fruit pies or puddings, we often sweeten with fruits or fruit juice concentrates.

Thickeners

Agar-agar, a sea vegetable derivative, is our thickener of choice. It thickens to a gel-like consistency by itself, and when combined with other thickeners, agar-agar gives those sweeteners more body and firmness. Use agar-agar in powder or flake form (the flakes sometimes activate better if they're soaked before using); the proportion of powder to flakes is 1:2.

Agar-agar is variable in its thickening ability, since it comes from seaweeds, which have different strengths and go through different processing. If your agar-agar produces a very stiff, aspiclike consistency in a pudding that should be less congealed, you can make it over again! Simply return the mixture to the stove, reheat, and add more liquid ingredients. It will set up again in a looser fashion.

We also use arrowroot, which doesn't need boiling to thicken, and kuzu, which thickens to a pudding or stewlike consistency and therefore works better with a thickener like agar-agar. Kuzu is also a digestive aid and can be prepared as a comforting tea for stomachaches.

We use eggs in a few of our recipes, particularly in cake recipes that need the light, springy, and binding quality that eggs provide. We balance our dairy offerings with many soy and nondairy desserts. Any of our soy recipes can be converted to dairy, although I recommend that you give soymilk a chance — it's a very hearty, healthful drink that nearly equals dairy milk in protein, but has far fewer calories and no cholesterol. Soymilk, amasake, agar-agar, and kuzu are available at natural foods stores and specialty markets.

Basic Pie Crust (Butter)

Preparation time
10–15 minutes.

Chilling time
30 minutes.

Makes one
9–10-inch pie crust.

This fine, flaky crust can be prepared very quickly.

½ cup whole-wheat pastry flour
½ cup unbleached white flour
Pinch salt
⅓ cup cold butter, cut into large cubes
¼ cup ice water
1 teaspoon pure maple syrup

In a medium-sized bowl, mix together both flours and the salt. Using a pastry blender or two knives, cut the butter into the flour mixture until the mixture resembles cornmeal.

In a small bowl, mix together the water and syrup and add to the flour mixture, stirring with a fork. (The dough should form a ball and not be too sticky.) If too wet, add a sprinkling of flour. If too dry, sprinkle in a few more drops of water. (Do not overmix or the dough becomes tough.) Cover the dough and chill for 30 minutes or until firm.

On a lightly floured surface, roll out the chilled dough to ⅛-inch thickness or less. Use immediately or place in a pie pan and freeze. (This pie crust can be frozen for 4–5 weeks.)

*This nondairy crust
can be prepared as
easily as the butter
crust, but has the
advantage of no
cholesterol and little
saturated fat.*

BASIC PIE CRUST (NONDAIRY)

¾ cup whole-wheat pastry flour
¾ cup unbleached white flour
Pinch salt
¼ cup corn oil
⅓ cup ice water

In a medium-sized bowl, mix together both flours and
the salt. In a small bowl, whisk together the oil and water until the oil forms small globules throughout the water. Immediately add the oil mixture to the flour mixture,
stirring with a fork just until the dough forms a ball. If
the dough is too sticky, add a little flour.

On a lightly floured surface, roll out the dough to ⅛-inch
thickness or less. Use immediately or cover and chill until
ready to roll. (This pie dough can also be placed in a pie
pan and frozen for use later.)

STRAWBERRY-RHUBARB PIE

1 *Basic Pie Crust* (*butter*) or (*nondairy*)
  (see pages 265 or 266)
4 cups chopped fresh rhubarb (4–5 stalks)
½ cup plus 1 tablespoon water
½ cup apple juice
1 tablespoon arrowroot
1½ tablespoons agar-agar powder, or
  3 tablespoons agar-agar flakes
⅔ cup pure maple syrup
⅓ cup rice syrup
Dash salt
2 cups rinsed sliced fresh strawberries

Prepare the pie crust. Place the prepared pie crust in a lightly oiled, 9-inch pie pan and freeze for at least 1 hour.

In a large pot, combine the rhubarb and water and bring to a boil. Cook for 5–10 minutes, or until the rhubarb is soft. Drain and reserve the liquid.

In a large bowl, stir together the juice, arrowroot, and agar-agar and mix until well dissolved. Whisk in both syrups, the salt, strawberries, cooked rhubarb, and ½ cup of the reserved rhubarb liquid.

Preheat oven to 375°F. Pour the mixture into the frozen pie crust and bake for 35–40 minutes. Let cool on a wire rack for 10 minutes. Chill for 1–2 hours. Serve.

Preparation and cooking time 45 minutes.

Baking time 35–40 minutes.

Freezing time at least 1 hour.

Cooling time 10 minutes.

Chilling time 1–2 hours.

Serves 6.

This pie evokes thoughts of warm, lazy summer days. Serve topped with cold whipped cream or vanilla ice cream for a refreshing, summer treat.

Preparation and
cooking time
1 hour 10–15
minutes.

Baking time
50 minutes.

Cooling time
variable.

Serves 6.

*I don't know how
my good friend
Chitra managed to
come up with this
outstanding apple
pie, but every year I
beg her to repeat her
masterpiece for the
holidays or for any
commonplace
weekend that needs
dressing up.*

APPLE-WALNUT PIE

Crust:
1 recipe *Basic Pie Crust (butter)* (see page 265)

Filling:
8–10 cups peeled thinly sliced apples (10–12
   medium apples)
1 cup sour cream
$\frac{1}{2}$ cup sweetener*
$\frac{1}{3}$ cup unbleached white flour
$\frac{1}{2}$ tablespoon pure vanilla extract
$\frac{1}{2}$ teaspoon salt
$1\frac{1}{2}$ tablespoons arrowroot
$\frac{1}{2}$ tablespoon ground cinnamon

Topping:
$\frac{3}{4}$ cup coarsely chopped walnuts
$\frac{1}{4}$ cup unbleached white flour
$\frac{1}{2}$ teaspoon ground cinnamon
$\frac{1}{4}$ teaspoon salt
$1\frac{1}{2}$ cups rolled oats
$\frac{2}{3}$ cup butter
$\frac{1}{2}$ cup sweetener*
1 teaspoon pure vanilla extract

*Use $\frac{1}{2}$ cup pure maple syrup or Sucanat granulated cane juice,
$\frac{3}{4}$ cup barley malt, or $\frac{1}{3}$ cup honey.*

To make the crust: Prepare the crust. Place the prepared
crust in a lightly oiled, 9-inch pie pan and flute the edges.
Set aside.

To make the filling: In a large pot, steam the apples for 5 minutes or until barely softened. In a large bowl, combine the apples and the remaining ingredients and stir together until the apples are well coated. Place the filling in the reserved pie crust. (The crust should be nearly brimming over with apples.)

To make the topping: In a medium-sized bowl, mix together the walnuts, flour, cinnamon, salt, and oats. In a small saucepan, melt the butter and sweetener together. Remove from heat and stir in the vanilla. Add the butter mixture to the flour mixture and mix together well.

Preheat oven to 425°F. Crumble the topping over the apples until covered. Bake for 10 minutes. Reduce heat to 350° and bake for 40 minutes more, or until the apples are soft and the topping is brown. Let cool on a wire rack. Serve.

Preparation and
cooking time
45 minutes.

Baking time
10–15 minutes.

Chilling time at
least 1 hour.

Serves 6.

*This delightful,
easy-to-make pie
can perk up a
summer afternoon
with its combina-
tion of cool peach,
apple, and lemon
flavors.*

PEACH PIE

Crust:
1 cup rolled oats
1¼ cups whole-wheat pastry flour
¼ teaspoon salt
½ teaspoon ground cinnamon
¼ cup canola oil
¼ cup pure maple syrup
½ tablespoon ice water

Filling:
½ tablespoon agar-agar powder
1 cup cold apple cider
1 teaspoon pure vanilla extract
2 tablespoons kuzu dissolved in ⅓ cup cold
  apple cider
6 cups coarsely chopped fresh peaches
¼ cup pure maple syrup
1 teaspoon fresh lemon juice
½ tablespoon lemon zest
Pinch salt

To make the crust: In a food processor, process the oats for 30 seconds. Add the flour, salt, and cinnamon and process until just blended. In a small bowl, whisk together the oil and syrup. Add the oil mixture to the flour mixture in the processor and process until the dough forms wet clumps.

Preheat oven to 350°F. While the processor is running, add only enough ice water so the dough looks wet yet still holds together. (Do not make dough too sticky.) Pat the dough into a well-oiled, 9-inch pie pan, covering the bottom and sides. Bake for 10–15 minutes or until golden. Remove and let cool.

To make the filling: In a large, heavy-bottomed saucepan, stir together the agar-agar and the 1 cup cider and bring to a boil, stirring constantly until the agar-agar is fully dissolved.

In a small bowl, mix together the vanilla and the dissolved kuzu and set aside. When the cider mixture is boiling, add the peaches, syrup, lemon juice and zest, and salt. Reduce heat to medium and cook, stirring frequently until the mixture begins to boil. Stir the reserved kuzu mixture and add to the saucepan, stirring constantly. (The white of the kuzu should quickly turn transparent.) Continue cooking on medium heat, stirring constantly.

To check if mixture is done, remove 1 teaspoon of the mixture and set it on top of an ice cube. If the mixture gels, it's ready. Otherwise, cook for 2–3 minutes more.

Pour the hot peach mixture into the cooled crust and chill for at least 1 hour, preferably 2–3 hours. Serve.

Preparation and
cooking time
45–60 minutes.

Baking time
1 hour.

Cooling time
variable.

Serves 6–8.

*Both pumpkin and
chocolate have
unique flavors, yet
neither is overshad-
owed by the other in
this recipe. A pump-
kin layer rests on
top of a chocolate
cheesecake layer,
and together they
make an exotic,
rich-tasting pie.*

PUMPKIN-CHOCOLATE PIE

Crust:
4 ounces honey graham crackers
⅓ cup Sucanat (granulated cane juice)
⅓ cup butter

Chocolate Layer:
2 ounces unsweetened baker's chocolate
6 ounces cream cheese, at room temperature
1½ tablespoons arrowroot
¾ cup pure maple syrup

Pumpkin Layer:
2 eggs, well beaten
2 cups cooked or canned pumpkin
¾ cup Sucanat (granulated cane juice)
1 teaspoon ground cinnamon
½ teaspoon ground ginger
½ teaspoon ground cloves
1 teaspoon salt
1 cup milk

To make the crust: In a food processor, finely grind the
graham crackers. Add the Sucanat and process briefly. In
a small saucepan, melt the butter. With the processor
running, add the melted butter to the graham cracker
mixture and blend until the mixture is damp and holds
together.

Preheat oven to 425°F. Press the mixture into a lightly
oiled, 10-inch pie pan, covering the bottom and sides.
Bake for 3–5 minutes. Remove and let cool.

To make the chocolate layer: In a double boiler, melt the chocolate on medium heat. Remove from heat and let cool.

Meanwhile, in a food processor or with an electric mixer, blend the cream cheese at medium speed until fluffy. Add the arrowroot and blend until smooth. Add the melted (just barely warm) chocolate and blend at medium speed until smooth and thick. With the processor running, add the syrup in a steady stream until blended well.

Pour the mixture into the cooled crust and smooth to fill the bottom of the crust. Set aside.

To make the pumpkin layer: Preheat oven to 425°F. In a large bowl, combine the eggs, pumpkin, Sucanat, spices, and salt and mix together until well blended. Add the milk and mix with an electric mixer at low speed until well combined.

Pour the mixture over the chocolate layer. (The pie will be very full.) Bake for 15 minutes. Reduce heat to 350° and bake for 40–45 minutes more, or until a knife inserted 1 inch from the edge comes out clean. Let cool on a wire rack. Serve alone or topped with whipped cream.

Preparation and
cooking time
45–1 hour 15
minutes.

Baking time
45 minutes.

Cooling time
variable.

Chilling time
variable.

Serves 6.

*In this pie, we use
kuzu to bind and
thicken instead of
eggs, and the
double crust keeps
all of the flavors
locked inside.*

PECAN PIE

2 recipes *Basic Pie Crust* (*butter*) or (*nondairy*)
  (see pages 265 or 266)
6 cups roasted pecans
  (see page 132, substitute pecans for almonds)
2 cups barley malt
1 tablespoon kuzu dissolved in ¼ cup
  cold water
2 teaspoons pure vanilla extract
1 tablespoon barley malt
2 tablespoons water

Prepare the pie crusts. Place one recipe of the prepared
crust in a well-oiled, 9-inch pie pan.

In a spice grinder or with a mortar and pestle, grind the
cooled pecans to a coarse meal. In a medium-sized, heavy
saucepan, heat the 2 cups barley malt until warm. Remove from heat. Stir in the dissolved kuzu, pecan meal,
and vanilla. Heat the mixture for 5–10 minutes.

Preheat oven to 350°F. Pour the warm mixture into the
prepared pie crust and wet the edges surrounding the
rim. Place the remaining prepared crust over the top and
flute the top and bottom crusts together. Make 3 or 4
small slits in the top crust and bake for 35 minutes or
until golden.

Meanwhile, in a small bowl, mix together the 1 tablespoon barley malt and the water. Remove the baked pie
and brush the mixture over the top. Bake for 10 minutes
more. Let cool on a wire rack. Chill before serving. Serve.

BERRY COBBLER

Filling:
6 cups fresh or thawed frozen berries
  (blueberries, blackberries, or raspberries)
1 cup rice syrup
2 tablespoons fresh lemon juice
3 tablespoons arrowroot

Batter:
1½ cups whole-wheat pastry flour
1½ cups unbleached white flour
½ tablespoon baking soda
½ cup canola oil
½ cup rice syrup
1 teaspoon pure vanilla extract
2 cups buttermilk or soymilk

To make the filling: In a large bowl, combine the berries, syrup, lemon juice, and arrowroot and gently mix together until the berries are well coated. Set aside.

To make the batter: Preheat oven to 350°F. In a medium-sized bowl, mix together both flours and the baking soda. In a separate bowl, beat together the oil, syrup, vanilla, and buttermilk. Add the flour mixture to the oil mixture and mix together well. (The batter may be lumpy.)

Pour the batter into a well-oiled, 9 x 12-inch baking pan and spread the reserved berry mixture over the batter. Bake for 1 hour 15 minutes, or until a tester inserted in the center comes out clean. Let cool on a wire rack. Serve.

Preparation time
20 minutes.

Baking time
1 hour 15 minutes.

Cooling time
variable.

Serves 6–8.

This cobbler really doesn't need a sauce or topping, but try it with Vanilla Custard Sauce *(see page 298) or vanilla ice cream for a special treat. If it's not berry season, this recipe works well with frozen berries, too.*

Preparation time
30 minutes.

Baking time
30–35 minutes.

Cooling time
variable.

Serves 8–10 per
cake. (Makes two
2-layer 9-inch
cakes.)

*Here is a light and
versatile cake for
many occasions,
including birth-
days, graduations,
engagement par-
ties, or holiday
events. Top with
Cream Cheese
Frosting or Soy
Cream (see pages
297 and 299).*

MOCHA WALNUT CAKE

$1\frac{1}{2}$ cups roasted walnuts
  (see page 132, substitute walnuts for almonds)
1 cup whole-wheat pastry flour
$2\frac{1}{2}$ cups unbleached white flour
$\frac{1}{2}$ teaspoon salt
$\frac{1}{3}$ cup instant coffee powder
$1\frac{1}{2}$ tablespoons baking powder
$\frac{1}{2}$ cup canola oil
$\frac{1}{2}$ cup pure maple syrup
$\frac{1}{2}$ cup rice syrup
$\frac{1}{2}$ cup soymilk
$1\frac{1}{2}$ cups apple cider
1 teaspoon pure vanilla extract

Preheat oven to 350°F. Coarsely chop the cooled walnuts. In a large bowl, mix together the walnuts and the
remaining dry ingredients. In a separate bowl, whisk together the oil and both syrups until well combined. Add
the soymilk, cider, and vanilla to the oil mixture and
whisk until well blended. Add the wet mixture to the dry
mixture and mix together until smooth.

Divide the batter into four well-oiled and lightly floured,
9-inch cake pans and bake for 30–35 minutes, or until a
tester inserted in the center comes out clean.

Let cool in the pans for 10 minutes. Remove from the
pans and let cool completely on wire racks. Frost and
serve.

BLACK FOREST CAKE

Cake:
¾ cup unsweetened cocoa powder
1½ teaspoons baking soda
1½ teaspoons baking powder
2½ cups unbleached white flour
1 teaspoon salt
1⅓ cups Sucanat (granulated cane juice)
2 eggs
1 cup milk
1 cup rice syrup
½ cup canola oil
2 teaspoons pure vanilla extract
1 cup boiling water

Frosting:
One 14-ounce can pitted cherries, or one
  12-ounce package frozen dark sweet cherries
2 cups cold heavy whipping cream
⅓–½ cup honey
½ tablespoon pure vanilla extract
Shaved or grated chocolate (optional)

To make the cake: Preheat oven to 350°F. In a medium-sized bowl, sift together the cocoa, baking soda, baking powder, flour, and salt. Stir in the Sucanat and mix together well.

In a large bowl, combine the eggs, milk, syrup, oil, and vanilla with an electric mixer at low speed until well blended. Add the dry mixture to the wet mixture and beat at low speed until combined, then beat at medium

Preparation time
1 hour 10 minutes.

Baking time
35–45 minutes.

Cooling time
variable.

Chilling time
10–15 minutes.

Serves 8–10.
(Makes one 2-layer
9-inch cake or one
9 x 12-inch cake.)

This scrumptious, spectacular-looking cake will reward you with its blend of chocolate frosting, whipped cream, cherries, and two layers of deep dark chocolate cake. I was very fortunate to be greeted on my 50th birthday with this gem created by Sona, one of the best dessert chefs I know.

speed for 2 minutes. Turn off mixer, add the boiling water, and mix together well at low speed. (The batter will be thin.)

Divide the batter into two oiled and lightly floured, 9-inch cake pans or pour into one 9 x 12-inch baking pan and bake for 35–45 minutes, or until a tester inserted in the center comes out clean. Let cool in the pans for 20 minutes. Remove from the pans and cool completely on wire racks.

To make the frosting: Drain the cherries and place in a small bowl. Reserve the liquid separately.

In a medium-sized bowl, whip the cream with an electric mixer at highest speed, beating until begins to thicken. Turn off mixer, add the ⅓ cup honey and the vanilla, and beat again at highest speed until thicker. Adjust for sweetness and add the remaining honey, if desired. Continue beating at highest speed until the whipped cream forms stiff but soft-looking peaks. (At this point, be careful not to overbeat.) Set aside.

To assemble the cake: Check the cooled cake layers for evenness and, if necessary, trim until the tops are level. Place the first layer top down on a cake plate. Brush the layer with the reserved cherry liquid and spread with enough whipped cream to cover well. Reserve a few of the best-looking cherries for the top, then place the remaining cherries over the whipped cream layer. Place the second layer top up on the cherries and line up the layers.

Frost the top and sides of the cake with a very thin layer of whipped cream, so thin it can hardly be seen. Chill for 10–15 minutes. Frost the chilled cake's top and sides. If desired, use a pastry bag to decorate the top with rosettes, as well as with the reserved cherries.

Decorate the sides of the cake after frosting with the shaved or grated chocolate, if desired. Take a handful of the shaved chocolate and press lightly against the sides of the cake. Serve.

Variation: To make a 12-inch *Black Forest Cake:* Double the cake recipe. Yield will be one 12 x 3-inch high cake layer or two 12 x 1½-inch high cake layers. Baking time increases to 55–60 minutes for the 3-inch high cake and 45–55 minutes for the 1½-inch high cakes. If preparing the 3-inch high cake, when the cake has completely cooled, level the top and slice in half. Double the quantities for the *Black Forest Cake* frosting ingredients and follow the directions as given.

CARROT CAKE

**Preparation time
1 hour.**

**Baking time
55–60 minutes.**

**Cooling time
variable.**

**Serves 8–10. (Makes
one 2-layer 9-inch
cake.)**

*With a crunch and
sweetness that comes
from a blend of
pineapple, carrots,
coconut, and wal-
nuts, this cake is a
Kripalu favorite.
Top with* Maple
Glaze *or* Cream
Cheese Frosting
*(see pages 300 and
297) or use the
glaze between the
cake layers with the
frosting on top.*

2½ cups whole-wheat pastry flour
½ tablespoon baking soda
2 teaspoons ground cinnamon
½ teaspoon salt
3 eggs
½ cup canola oil
1 cup buttermilk
½ cup pure maple syrup
2 teaspoons pure vanilla extract
¾ cup well-drained canned crushed pineapple
2 cups grated carrots
¾ cup toasted shredded coconut (see page 228)
1 cup coarsely chopped roasted walnuts
  (see page 132, substitute walnuts for almonds)

Preheat oven to 350°F. In a medium-sized bowl, sift together the flour, baking soda, cinnamon, and salt. In a
large bowl, beat the eggs with an electric mixer at medium speed. Add the oil, buttermilk, syrup, and vanilla
and beat together at medium speed. Add the flour mixture to the oil mixture, beating at low speed until well
combined. Add the pineapple, carrots, coconut, and walnuts and beat at low speed until just combined.

Divide the batter into two well-oiled and lightly floured,
9-inch cake pans. Bake for 55–60 minutes, or until a
tester inserted in the center comes out clean. Let cool in
the pans for 10 minutes. Remove from the pans and cool
completely on wire racks. Frost and serve.

WHEATFREE GINGERBREAD CAKE

**Preparation time
20 minutes.**

**Baking time
45 minutes.**

**Cooling time
variable.**

**Serves 6–8. (Makes
one 9 x 12-inch
cake.)**

1¼ cups rye flour

¾ cup arrowroot

2 teaspoons baking soda

1 teaspoon ground cinnamon

¼ teaspoon ground cloves

¼ teaspoon ground ginger

½ cup rice syrup

1 cup unsulphured molasses

½ cup canola oil

2 tablespoons apple cider

½ cup boiling water

Preheat oven to 325°F. In a large bowl, sift together the flour, arrowroot, baking soda, cinnamon, cloves, and ginger. In a small bowl, whisk together the syrup, molasses, oil, and cider. Add the syrup mixture to the flour mixture and stir together with a wooden spoon until well combined. Add the water and gently mix together until blended.

Pour into a heavily oiled, 9 x 12-inch baking pan and bake for 45 minutes, or until the gingerbread pulls away from the sides of the pan. Let cool on a wire rack or serve warm.

Rye flour, seasoned with cinnamon, ginger, cloves, and molasses, makes this wheatfree gingerbread cake a unique delicacy — moist and gingery to the taste and pleasantly sticky to the fingers. Serve warm with whipped cream or Vanilla Custard Sauce (see page 298). Great for kids or adults with wheat allergies.

Preparation and
cooking time
30 minutes.

Baking time
15–20 minutes.

Freezing time
1 hour.

Chilling time
1–2 hours.

Cooling time
variable.

Serves 6–8.

*Imagine having a
cheesecake with
approximately half
the fat and calories!
This delicious
cheesecake delights
family and friends
with its thick, sweet
texture and fruity
topping. Garnish
with your choice of
orange slices,
strawberries, or
kiwifruit.*

AMASAKE CHEESECAKE WITH FRUIT GLAZE

Crust:
1 recipe *Basic Pie Crust* (*nondairy*) (see page 266)

Filling:
4 cups cold amasake
1 teaspoon pure vanilla extract
1 teaspoon pure almond extract
1/8 teaspoon salt
5 tablespoons pure maple syrup
1/4 teaspoon ground cardamom
4 tablespoons agar-agar powder, or
  6 tablespoons agar-agar flakes
3½ tablespoons kuzu dissolved in 1/4 cup
  cold water

Glaze:
1 teaspoon agar-agar powder dissolved in 3/4 cup
  cold fruit juice (any type)
1 teaspoon kuzu dissolved in 1/4 cup cold fruit
  juice (any type)

To make the crust: Prepare the pie crust. Place the prepared crust in a lightly oiled, 9-inch pie pan and freeze
for 1 hour.

Preheat oven to 350°F. Weight the bottom of the crust
with pie weights and bake for 15–20 minutes or until

lightly browned. Remove and let cool.

To make the filling: In a large saucepan, whisk together all of the ingredients, except the dissolved kuzu, and bring to a low boil, stirring constantly. Add the dissolved kuzu to the boiling mixture and boil for 1–2 minutes, or until the mixture thickens.

Pour the filling into the baked pie crust and chill for 1 hour before pouring the glaze on top.

To make the glaze: In a small saucepan, bring the dissolved agar-agar to a boil, stirring constantly. Add the dissolved kuzu and return to a boil. Cook on high heat for 1–2 minutes, or until the mixture turns clear and thickens.

Pour the glaze on top of the chilled filling, garnish with fresh fruit, and chill for 30–60 minutes. Serve.

Preparation time
30 minutes.

Baking time
30–35 minutes.

Cooling time
variable.

Serves 8. (Makes
one 9 x 12-inch
pan.)

*Something about
the ribbon of cream
cheese running
through these
delectable, dark
chocolate brownies
makes them a
winning dessert
year-round.*

CHOCOLATE CREAM CHEESE MARBLE BROWNIES

Chocolate Batter:
1 cup butter, at room temperature
½ cup Sucanat (granulated cane juice)
½ cup rice syrup
½ cup unsulphured molasses
2 eggs
½ tablespoon pure vanilla extract
¾ cup unsweetened cocoa powder
1 cup whole-wheat pastry flour
2 teaspoons baking powder
¼ teaspoon salt

Cream Cheese Batter:
¼ cup butter, at room temperature
½ cup cream cheese, at room temperature
⅓ cup honey
1 egg
1 teaspoon pure vanilla extract
¾ cup whole-wheat pastry flour

To make the chocolate batter: In a large bowl, cream the butter and Sucanat with an electric mixer at medium speed until fluffy. Add the syrup and molasses and cream together well. Add the eggs to the butter mixture, one at a time, beating well after each addition. Add the vanilla and beat until fluffy.

In a small bowl, sift the cocoa, then stir in the flour, baking powder, and salt. Add the flour mixture to the butter mixture and mix together well at low speed. Spread the chocolate batter in an oiled, 9 x 5-inch baking pan, covering the pan completely.

To make the cream cheese batter: Preheat oven to 350°F. In a large bowl, cream the butter and cream cheese with an electric mixer at medium speed until fluffy. Scrape the sides and beat until very smooth. Add the honey and beat until smooth. Add the egg and vanilla and beat until well combined. Add the flour and mix thoroughly.

Spread the cream cheese batter over the chocolate batter. With a knife, swirl the cream cheese and chocolate mixtures. Bake for 30–35 minutes, or until the cake pulls away from the sides of the pan and is lightly browned on top. Let cool on a wire rack. Cut into squares and serve.

Preparation time
30 minutes.

Baking time
35–40 minutes.

Cooling time
variable.

Serves 8. (Makes
one 9 x 12-inch
pan.)

*Perfect as a quick
dessert or afternoon
treat, these bars are
easy to make and
have a nondairy
filling that looks
and tastes like a
hearty granola
spread.*

Jelly-Coconut Bars

2 cups whole-wheat pastry flour
$\frac{1}{4}$ teaspoon salt
2 tablespoons lemon zest
$\frac{1}{4}$ cup corn oil
$\frac{1}{4}$ cup canola oil
1 cup rice syrup
$\frac{1}{4}$ cup apple cider
1 teaspoon pure vanilla extract
3 tablespoons almond butter
3 tablespoons soymilk
$1\frac{1}{2}$ cups shredded coconut
$1-1\frac{1}{2}$ cups all-fruit jam or jelly

Preheat oven to 350°F. In a small bowl, mix together the
flour, salt, and lemon zest. In a large bowl, combine both
oils, $\frac{1}{2}$ cup of the syrup, the cider, and vanilla with an
electric mixer, starting at low speed and increasing to
medium. Add the flour mixture and beat until smooth.
(The batter will be soft in texture.) Spread the batter into
a well-oiled, 9 x 12-inch baking pan until flat and
smooth. Bake for 15 minutes.

Meanwhile, in a blender or food processor, blend together the remaining syrup, the almond butter, and
soymilk until smooth to make the topping. Add the coconut and blend together well. Remove the crust from the
oven and spread the jam evenly over the crust. Sprinkle
the topping over the jam. Bake for 20–25 minutes. Let
cool on a wire rack. Cut into squares and serve.

RAIN FOREST BARS

1 cup roasted almonds (see page 132)
¾ cup softened butter
½ cup Sucanat (granulated cane juice)
¾ cup unbleached white flour
¾ cup whole-wheat pastry flour
½ cup nonfat dry milk powder
1 cup rice syrup
⅓ cup water
¾ cup shredded coconut
1 cup coarsely chopped dried dates
1 cup chocolate chips

Preheat oven to 375°F. Coarsely chop the almonds and set aside. In a large bowl, cream the butter and Sucanat with an electric mixer at medium speed until fluffy. In a small bowl, mix together both flours. Add the flour mixture to the butter mixture and beat well at low speed.

Pat the mixture into a well-oiled 9 x 12-inch baking pan, covering the pan completely. Bake for 10 minutes. Let cool for 10 minutes.

In a small bowl, combine the milk powder and syrup with an electric mixer at low speed until smooth. Slowly add the water, and mix at low speed until thick and syrupy.

On the cooled crust, spread the coconut to cover, then the reserved almonds, then the dates, and finally the chips. Gently pat down the filling and drizzle the topping over all. Bake for 25–35 minutes, or until the edges are golden brown and the center is lightly brown and looks solid. Let cool on a wire rack. Cut into squares and serve.

Preparation time 30–45 minutes.

Baking time 25–35 minutes.

Cooling time variable.

Serves 8. (Makes one 9 x 12-inch pan.)

Long a favorite of Kripalu Center guests and residents, who tend to load plates and pockets with them, these crisp bars are filled with chocolate, almonds, dates, and coconut, and topped with a sweet frosting.

Preparation time
20 minutes.

Baking time
10 minutes.

Cooling time
variable.

Makes 30 cookies.

This is a light, easy
chocolate chip
cookie recipe. As
with the richer
recipe that follows,
you can use barley
malt chips or choco-
late chips, depend-
ing on how sweet
you like your cook-
ies. (If you use
barley malt chips,
do not overbake,
because the chips
tend to caramelize
quickly and become
hard.)

CHOCOLATE CHIP
FAVORITES

¾ cup butter, at room temperature
1 cup rice syrup
1 teaspoon pure vanilla extract
1 egg
2½ cups unbleached white flour
1 teaspoon baking soda
1 teaspoon salt
2 cups barley malt chips or chocolate chips
1 cup coarsely chopped walnuts

Preheat oven to 375°F. In a large bowl, cream the butter
with an electric mixer at medium speed until fluffy. Add
the syrup and vanilla and cream at medium speed until
fluffy. Add the egg and beat until fluffy.

In a small bowl, combine the flour, baking soda, and salt.
Add the flour mixture to the butter mixture and beat at
low speed until smooth. Add the chips and walnuts and
mix at low speed until well combined.

Drop the dough by rounded teaspoonsful on a well-oiled
baking sheet. Bake for 10 minutes or until golden brown
on the bottom. Let cool on wire racks or serve warm.

CHOCOLATE CHIP SUPREMES

2¾ cups unbleached white flour
1 teaspoon baking powder
1 teaspoon baking soda
½ teaspoon salt
1 cup butter, at room temperature
1 cup Sucanat (granulated cane juice)
1 cup rice syrup
2 eggs, at room temperature
1 teaspoon pure vanilla extract
1 cup rolled oats
1 cup cornflakes
1 cup chocolate or barley malt chips
½ cup coarsely chopped roasted pecans
  (see page 132, substitute pecans for almonds)
½ cup shredded coconut

Preheat oven to 350°F. In a medium-sized bowl, sift together the flour, baking powder, baking soda, and salt. In
a large bowl, cream the butter and Sucanat with an electric mixer at medium speed until fluffy. Add the syrup
and beat at medium speed until fluffy. Add the eggs, one
at a time, beating after each addition until well combined
and creamy. Add the vanilla and beat well.

Add the flour mixture to the butter mixture and beat at
low speed until blended. Add the oats, cornflakes, chips,
pecans, and coconut and mix at low speed until just folded in. Drop the dough in 1½-inch balls on a well-oiled
baking sheet. Bake for 10–12 minutes or until golden brown
on the bottom. Let cool on wire racks or serve warm.

**Preparation time
30 minutes.**

**Baking time
10–12 minutes.**

**Cooling time
variable.**

Makes 40 cookies.

*These quintessential
chocolate chip
cookies have all
kinds of interesting
additions, including
cornflakes, pecans,
coconut, and, of
course, chocolate
chips.*

Preparation time
20–25 minutes.

Baking time
25–30 minutes.

Cooling time
variable.

Makes 20 cookies.

*Sometimes we hold
triathlons at
Kripalu, and we
always serve these
cookies afterward.
They're a great
pick-me-up after
exercise, and they
travel well on hikes
and outings.*

MAPLE
OATMEAL-RAISIN
COOKIES

½ cup roasted almonds (see page 132)
½ cup corn oil
⅓ cup pure maple syrup
⅓ cup rice syrup
3 tablespoons water
1 tablespoon almond butter
1¼ teaspoons pure vanilla extract
¾ cup whole-wheat pastry flour
¾ cup unbleached white flour
1 teaspoon ground cinnamon
½ teaspoon salt
1½ cups old-fashioned rolled oats
½ cup raisins

Preheat oven to 375°F. Coarsely chop the cooled almonds and set aside.

In a large bowl, combine the oil, both syrups, the water,
almond butter, and vanilla with an electric mixer at medium speed until well blended. In a small bowl, combine
both flours, the cinnamon, and salt. Add the flour mixture to the oil mixture and mix until just combined. Add
the oats, raisins, and reserved almonds and mix together
until well combined.

Drop the dough in 1-inch balls on a well-oiled baking
sheet and flatten the dough with a wet palm. Bake for
25–30 minutes. Let cool on wire racks or serve warm.

PECAN SANDIES

1½ cups whole pecans
1 cup butter, at room temperature
½ cup pure maple syrup
1½ teaspoons pure vanilla extract
2 cups whole-wheat pastry flour
¼ cup pecan halves (optional)
Jelly (optional)

Preheat oven to 350°F. In a blender or food processor, finely grind the pecans and set aside.

In a large bowl, cream the butter with an electric mixer at medium speed until fluffy. Add the syrup and vanilla and beat until creamy. In a small bowl, combine the flour and reserved pecan meal. Add the flour mixture to the butter mixture and mix until just combined. (The mixture will be soft.)

Drop the dough in 1-inch balls on a well-oiled baking sheet and flatten the dough with a wet palm. Garnish with the pecan halves or using a wet finger, make a small indentation in the middle of each flattened cookie and fill with jelly, if desired. Bake for 15 minutes, or until the edges and the bottoms are golden brown. Let cool on wire racks or serve warm.

**Preparation time
25 minutes.**

**Baking time
15 minutes.**

**Cooling time
variable.**

Makes 20 cookies.

These light, sweet cookies, laced with rich pecan meal, can be topped with pecan halves or made into thumb-print cookies with jelly. Since they tend to be very fragile, you should add ½ cup more flour if you want to take them on picnics or to gatherings.

Preparation time
25 minutes.

Baking time
10 minutes.

Chilling time at
least 1 hour.

Cooling time
variable.

Makes 40 cookies.

*Easy, elegant, and
graced with ginger
and cloves, these
cookies brighten up
any holiday menu.*

SWEDISH GINGER COOKIES

1 cup butter
1 cup unsulphured molasses
1 egg
1 teaspoon pure vanilla extract
3¼ cups unbleached white flour
3 teaspoons ground cinnamon
2 teaspoons ground ginger
1 teaspoon ground cloves
2 teaspoons baking soda

In a small saucepan, melt the butter. Stir in the molasses and bring to a boil. Remove from heat and place the mixture in a large bowl. Let cool to room temperature.

Beat the egg and vanilla into the cooled butter mixture with an electric mixer at low speed until well combined. In a medium-sized bowl, sift together the flour, cinnamon, ginger, cloves, and baking soda. Add the flour mixture to the egg mixture and mix at low speed until smooth. Cover and chill for at least 1 hour.

Preheat oven to 350°F. Roll out the dough and cut with cookie cutters or form the dough into a roll and cut ¼-inch slices with a sharp knife and place on an oiled baking sheet. Bake for 10 minutes (do not overbake). Let cool on wire racks or serve warm.

CINNAMON SOYMILK PUDDING

3½ cups soymilk or milk
1 tablespoon agar-agar powder, or
  2 tablespoons agar-agar flakes
½ teaspoon ground cinnamon
¼ teaspoon ground cardamom
Pinch ground nutmeg
Pinch salt
⅔ cup pure maple syrup
1 tablespoon kuzu dissolved in ½ cup cold
  soymilk or milk
1 teaspoon pure vanilla extract
Roasted almonds (see page 132)

In a blender, combine the milk, agar-agar, cinnamon, cardamom, nutmeg, salt, and syrup and blend on medium speed until well combined. In a medium-sized saucepan, combine the dissolved kuzu mixture and the milk mixture and cook on medium-high heat, stirring constantly, for 10–15 minutes, or until the mixture comes to a gentle boil.

Reduce heat to low and cook, stirring constantly, for 5 minutes more, or until the pudding thickens and turns slightly darker in color. Remove from heat. Stir in the vanilla and mix thoroughly with a wooden spoon. Let stand for 5 minutes.

Pour the pudding into dessert or parfait dishes and sprinkle with the almonds. Chill for 1 hour. Serve.

Preparation and cooking time 30 minutes.

Chilling time at least 1 hour.

Serves 4.

Here is a tasty pudding with one variation, Chocolate-Date Pudding *(see page 294). The key to perfection in both recipes is blending the thickening agents with the milk before heating.*

Preparation and
cooking time
30 minutes.

Chilling time at
least 1 hour.

Serves 4.

CHOCOLATE-DATE PUDDING

3½ cups milk or soymilk
1 tablespoon agar-agar powder, or
  2 tablespoons agar-agar flakes
¼ teaspoon ground cinnamon
¼ teaspoon ground cardamom
⅓ cup unsweetened cocoa powder
1 cup pure maple syrup
Dash salt
1 tablespoon unsulphured molasses
⅓ cup prepared coffee
1 tablespoon kuzu dissolved in ½ cup cold milk
  or soymilk
4–5 dried dates, chopped
¼ cup toasted shredded coconut (see page 228)

In a blender, combine the milk, agar-agar, cinnamon, cardamom, cocoa, syrup, salt, molasses, and coffee and blend together well.

In a large saucepan, combine the dissolved kuzu mixture and the milk mixture and cook on medium-high heat, stirring constantly, for 12–15 minutes, or until the mixture comes to a gentle boil and begins to thicken. Add the dates and remove from heat.

Pour the pudding into four dessert or parfait dishes and garnish with the coconut. Chill for at least 1 hour. Serve.

STRAWBERRY MOUSSE

2 cups fresh strawberries
  (approximately 1 pint strawberries)
Dash salt
1 tablespoon agar-agar powder, or
  2 tablespoons agar-agar flakes dissolved in
  1 cup apple juice
½ tablespoon kuzu dissolved in ½ cup
  cold water
1 cup apple juice
½ cup rice syrup
2 tablespoons pure maple syrup
4 teaspoons tahini
Fresh mint leaves
Kiwifruit slices

Rinse the strawberries in a sieve and remove the stems. Sprinkle with the salt (helps berries retain color) and set aside.

In a large saucepan, bring the dissolved agar-agar mixture to a boil and cook for 5 minutes. Reduce heat to simmer and stir in the dissolved kuzu mixture. Remove from heat as soon as the kuzu turns from milky white to clear.

In a blender, combine the reserved strawberries and the apple juice and blend until liquified. Add both syrups and blend thoroughly. Add the strawberry mixture to the agar/kuzu mixture and bring to a boil, then reduce heat.

Pour the mousse into four dessert or parfait dishes, fill-

Preparation and cooking time 20 minutes.

Chilling time 1–2 hours or overnight.

Serves 4.

Here is a simple two-layer dessert that requires little preparation, yet pleases the palate with contrasting flavors of straw-berry, tahini, and maple syrup.

ing halfway. Set aside ¼–⅓ of the mousse for the topping. Chill all of the dishes and reserved mousse for at least 1 hour.

In a blender, combine the chilled reserved mousse and the tahini. Remove the chilled dessert dishes and pour the tahini mixture on top of each. Chill for 1 hour more. Garnish with the mint leaves or the kiwifruit slices. Serve.

Variation: An alternative to serving in separate dessert dishes is to pour the two layers into one large baking pan or casserole dish and continue following the recipe directions.

CREAM CHEESE FROSTING

**Preparation time
20–30 minutes.**

**Makes frosting for
one 2-layer 9-inch
cake or one 9 x 12-
inch cake.**

*Use this rich and
delicious frosting to
top our* Carrot
Cake *(see page
280) or your favor-
ite cake creation.*

½ cup butter, at room temperature
1 pound cream cheese, at room temperature
¾ cup honey
1½ teaspoons pure vanilla extract
1 pint heavy whipping cream
2 tablespoons honey

In a medium-sized bowl, cream the butter and cream cheese with an electric mixer at medium speed until smooth and fluffy. Scrape the beaters and bowl with a spatula and beat again for 1–2 minutes. Add ½ cup of the honey and 1 teaspoon of the vanilla and beat until smooth, again scraping the sides. Adjust for sweetness and add the remaining ¼ cup honey, if needed.

In a separate bowl, beat the whipping cream at high speed until begins to thicken. Add the 2 tablespoons honey and the remaining vanilla and beat until the cream forms stiff peaks. (Do not overbeat.)

Fold the whipped cream, in three batches, into the cream cheese mixture. (The frosting should be soft but spreadable.) Spread on cooled cake layers or on cooled sheet cake.

*Here's a velvety,
vanilla topping that
lends itself to a
variety of uses. Pour
it over* Berry Cob-
bler, *on top of*
Mocha Walnut
Cake *or* Apple-
Walnut Pie *(see
pages 275, 276,
and 268–269), or
on your favorite
pastry.*

VANILLA
CUSTARD SAUCE

12 egg yolks, at room temperature
¾ cup pure maple syrup
4 cups milk
1 tablespoon pure vanilla extract

In a medium-sized bowl, whisk together the egg yolks and
syrup. In a large, heavy-bottomed saucepan, heat the milk
on medium heat until bubbles appear around the sides of
the saucepan. Pour a small amount of the heated milk
into the egg yolk mixture, so the yolks gradually reach the
same temperature as the milk.

Add the egg yolk mixture to the hot milk and mix together well, stirring around the sides of the saucepan,
until the sauce reaches 185°F, or until the sauce thickly
coats the back of a wooden spoon. (If the sauce curdles
or separates due to overcooking, whisk well and it should
restabilize.)

Immediately pour the sauce in a large bowl and add the
vanilla. Let cool. Use as a topping.

SOY CREAM

½ cup chilled soymilk
1 cup chilled canola oil
2 tablespoons pure maple syrup
1 tablespoon Sucanat (granulated cane juice)
1 teaspoon pure vanilla extract
1 teaspoon Cafix instant beverage powder*
Dash salt
Dash ground cardamom

In a blender, combine the chilled soymilk and ½ cup of the chilled oil and blend together at medium speed for 15 seconds.

With the blender running, slowly pour in the remaining oil and blend for 15–30 seconds, or until the mixture thickens, forming soft peaks. Add the remaining ingredients and blend for 5–10 seconds more. Use immediately as a topping.

*Cafix is available at natural foods stores and many large supermarkets.

Adapted from *Naturally Delicious Desserts* by Cherie Baker. © 1985 by Cherie Baker. Reprinted by permission of Ballantine Books, a division of Random House, Inc. (See Bibliography.)

**Preparation time
5–10 minutes.**

Serves 4.

This nondairy topping, adapted from Cherie Baker's Creamy Soy Whip recipe, has become a Kripalu favorite. It whips up quickly and easily, and it has the delicate sweetness and rich mouth feel of a dairy frosting, without the cholesterol and saturated fat.

*This sweet but
simple glaze goes
well with many of
our dessert recipes,
either as a top
frosting or as an
icing between cake
layers.*

MAPLE GLAZE

⅓ cup pure maple syrup
¼ cup rice syrup
¼ cup butter
¼ cup buttermilk
¾ teaspoon baking soda
¼ teaspoon pure vanilla extract

In a medium-sized saucepan, combine all of the ingredients, except the vanilla. On medium heat, bring the mixture to a boil. Cook for 5 minutes, stirring frequently.

Remove from heat and stir in the vanilla. Immediately pour the glaze over cakes just removed from the oven. (The glaze will sink into the cake surfaces, making them very moist and sweet.)

INDIAN COOKERY

Chapter 12

 IN INDIA, thousands of years of practice in blending the world's best spices with vegetables, grains, and fruits have produced a gold mine of flavors, colors, and food combinations. At Kripalu, we've been inspired by Urmila Desai, the coauthor of *The Ayurvedic Cookbook* (see Bibliography), which not only has excellent Indian recipes, but also explains the dietary principles of Indian cooking. With her help and the supervision of Chandrakant, our head chef, we've been adapting Indian recipes to American palettes for years.

Most traditional Indian meals contain several of the following:
- dahl (a thick, spiced soup).
- grain (usually white rice).
- one or two well-spiced vegetable side dishes.
- chutney (a relish).
- baked or fried bread (chapati or puri).
- raita (a yogurt-based condiment that serves as a cooling agent to balance the meal's hotter ingredients).
- a sweet or dessert (often eaten with the main meal).

Although eating Indian-style is a treasured pastime of ours, we have adapted our recipes to reflect our inclination toward a healthier, less spicy, less oily diet, while retaining the spicy potpourri of flavors that is the trademark of Indian food. The recipes in this chapter offer some latitude, so you can adapt them to your taste.

In general, we use less oil than is traditional in Indian cooking; we use fewer spicy and hot ingredients; and we use black pepper more frequently than cayenne pepper. We also use Sucanat granulated cane juice as a substitute for granulated white sugar, although purists will argue that to replicate the original recipes one must use white sugar. In certain recipes we do use white sugar, but we encourage you to try experimenting with Sucanat or milder sweeteners.

In our rice recipes, we follow the Indian tradition of not adding salt while the rice is cooking. Since most of the rice dishes are designed to be eaten with dahl or vegetables, less salt is needed, because dahl is quite salty. Feel free, however, to add salt in rice dishes where it's indicated as optional.

THE USE OF A VAGAR

A vagar is a type of sauté in which spices are cooked in oil or butter. This technique helps release the flavor of the spices before other ingredients are added.

To make vagar, seeds are added to hot cooking oil. Most often mustard seeds are used; occasionally fenugreek seeds or ajwan, a wild celery seed, are also used. As soon as the seeds pop, their flavors are released into the oil, and it's time to add the next ingredients, which usually include garlic and ground ginger or fresh gingerroot, followed by turmeric, asafetida (a subtle Asian seasoning, not unlike garlic and also called hing), and paprika. The garlic and gingerroot slightly cool the temperature of the cooling oil; nevertheless, when the powdered ingredients are added, care should be taken to stir them in quickly so they do not burn.

The vagar can be added to steamed vegetables, or the steamed vegetables can be added to the vagar. In either case, the idea is to coat the vegetables well with the oil, so the spices can adhere to them. If more oil is needed, add during this stage, before the vegetables are baked or stir-fried. Also, adjust the mixture for sweetness and saltiness and balance those flavors before proceeding to the final stage of cooking.

THE CRADLE OF SEASONINGS

It helps to study the diagram below, created by Chandrakant, to get an idea of how flavors balance one another in vagar-style cooking. Then you can taste test and adjust which flavor(s) needs balancing as you cook.

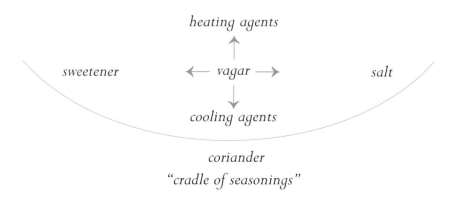

heating agents

sweetener ← *vagar* → *salt*

cooling agents

coriander
"cradle of seasonings"

At the heart of the preparation is the vagar, which sets all the flavors in motion and imparts a distinctive, pungent flavor. To add heat, add chili powder, curry powder, or garam masala, a mixture of hot spices (see recipe on page 324). To cool down, add yogurt, sour cream, milk, or tofu. If too salty, add sweetener; if too sweet, add salt.

Supporting the interplay of all of these flavors is coriander, which is called "the cradle of seasonings." It balances and enhances the flavors of the spices and provides a background of richness.

I heartily recommend a trip to an Indian food shop or specialty market, where you can buy a great assortment of spices, including asafetida, ajwan, cardamom, cinnamon sticks, and a much less expensive saffron. It can be a great adventure in food shopping.

MENUS

For your ease in combining different dishes to make a balanced meal, this chapter contains two basic, full-course meals that include a dahl or vegetable main dish, rice, chutney, raita, and a sweet.

Madrasi Red Lentil Dahl

Gujarati Mixed Vegetables

Cilantro Chutney

Punjabi Cucumber Raita

Golden Basmati Rice

Shiro

*Here is an out-
standing dahl, or
thick soup, made
with red lentils,
eggplant, and
potatoes. It is
prepared using the
vagar technique (see
page 303). The
whole meal revolves
around the quality
of the dahl, which
in India is used like
a thick, spicy sauce
for coating rice and
vegetables and
dipping chapati.*

MADRASI RED LENTIL DAHL

1 $\frac{1}{4}$ cups dried lentils

8 cups water

$\frac{1}{4}$ cup canola oil

1 teaspoon black mustard seeds

$\frac{1}{2}$ teaspoon fenugreek seeds

1 $\frac{1}{2}$ tablespoons finely chopped garlic

1 $\frac{1}{2}$ tablespoons ground ginger

$\frac{3}{4}$ teaspoon ground turmeric

$\frac{3}{4}$ teaspoon ground paprika

2 pinches ground asafetida (hing)

$\frac{3}{4}$ cup diced onions

$\frac{3}{4}$ cup diced tomatoes

$\frac{1}{2}$ cup diced bell peppers

$\frac{1}{2}$ cup diced red potatoes

$\frac{1}{2}$ cup diced eggplant

$\frac{1}{4}$ cup shredded coconut

1 tablespoon fresh lemon juice

1 tablespoon ground coriander

1 $\frac{1}{2}$ teaspoons Sucanat (granulated cane juice)

1 $\frac{3}{4}$ teaspoons salt

$\frac{1}{2}$ teaspoon garam masala (see page 324)

Wash the lentils. In a large saucepan, combine the lentils and 6 cups of the water and bring to a boil. Reduce heat to simmer, cover, and cook for 30 minutes, or until the lentils are soft.

In a small skillet, heat the oil and sauté the mustard and fenugreek seeds until the seeds pop. Add the garlic and ginger and sauté for 1–2 minutes. Stir in the turmeric, paprika, and asafetida and sauté for 1 minute.

In a large, deep skillet, place all of the diced vegetables, pour the vagar over the vegetables, and sauté for 2–3 minutes. Add the sautéed vegetable mixture to the cooked lentils (dahl). Also add the remaining water, if needed for thinning. Add the remaining ingredients and bring to a boil. Reduce heat to low and cook for 20 minutes.

Adjust the lemon juice and salt and serve immediately.

This is a spicy mixture of eggplant, potatoes, lima beans, peas, and sweet potatoes. It is prepared using a vagar (see page 303) to coat vegetables that have been steamed.

GUJARATI MIXED VEGETABLES

2 cups cubed potatoes
2 cups cubed sweet potatoes or yams
3 cups cubed eggplant
  (approximately 1 small eggplant)
¾ cup cubed green bell peppers
¾ cup frozen lima beans
¼ cup canola oil
1½ teaspoons black mustard seeds
¾ teaspoon ajwan seeds
1 tablespoon chopped garlic
1 tablespoon finely chopped fresh gingerroot
1 teaspoon ground turmeric
¾ teaspoon ground paprika
2 pinches ground asafetida (hing)
¾ cup frozen peas
3 tablespoons ground coriander
¾ teaspoon garam masala (see page 324)
1½ teaspoons salt
½ teaspoon black pepper
1½ teaspoons Sucanat (granulated cane juice)
⅓ cup shredded coconut
1 cup water

In a large, covered saucepan with a steamer basket, steam the potatoes and sweet potatoes in water for 15 minutes. Remove and set aside. Steam the eggplant for 5 minutes. Remove and set aside. Steam the bell peppers and lima beans for 5 minutes. Remove and set aside.

In a small skillet, heat the oil and sauté the mustard and

ajwan seeds until the seeds pop. Add the garlic and gingerroot and sauté for 2–3 minutes. Stir in the turmeric, paprika, and asafetida and sauté for 1–2 minutes.

In a large saucepan or cast-iron pot, place all of the reserved steamed vegetables and pour the vagar over the vegetables. Add the remaining ingredients and stir carefully to create even color and flavor throughout. Cook on low heat for 8–10 minutes.

Adjust the water and salt and serve immediately.

This is a hot, spicy blend of hot peppers, garlic, sweet coconut, and sesame seeds — a perfect complement to Gujarati Mixed Vegetables *(see pages 308–309).*

CILANTRO CHUTNEY

1 tablespoon chopped jalapeño peppers
1¼ cups coarsely chopped fresh cilantro
1½ tablespoons water
2 teaspoons ground cumin
2 teaspoons fresh lemon juice
1 teaspoon Sucanat (granulated cane juice)
1 teaspoon salt
½ teaspoon ground ginger
½ teaspoon finely chopped garlic
1½ tablespoons shredded coconut
½ teaspoon white sesame seeds
¼ teaspoon black pepper

In a blender or food processor, blend together half of the peppers, the cilantro, and 1 tablespoon of the water for 15 seconds or until thoroughly chopped.

Adjust for hotness. If desired, add the remaining half of the peppers and blend again. If needed, add the remaining water to make the mixture easier to blend.

In a small bowl, combine the pepper mixture and the remaining ingredients and mix together well. Serve.

PUNJABI CUCUMBER RAITA

Preparation time 10 minutes.

Serves 4–6. (Makes 2 cups.)

In this piquant side dish, cucumbers come alive combined with yogurt, sweet raisins, and the contrasting flavors of fresh cilantro, ground cumin, and mustard seeds.

¼ teaspoon black mustard seeds
1 cup peeled diced cucumbers
¾ cup plain yogurt
3 tablespoons sour cream
3 tablespoons raisins
1 tablespoon chopped fresh cilantro
1 teaspoon ground cumin
¼ teaspoon salt
⅛ teaspoon black pepper

With a mortar and pestle or a spice grinder, crack the mustard seeds. In a medium-sized bowl, combine the cracked seeds and the remaining ingredients and mix together well.

If the yogurt is very sour, increase the sour cream, reducing the yogurt proportionately. Serve.

*This dish gets its
bright golden color
from the addition of
ground turmeric
and cumin seeds,
which also impart a
robust, spicy flavor.*

GOLDEN BASMATI RICE

2 cups uncooked white basmati rice
4 cups water
$\frac{1}{3}$ cup diced onions
1 teaspoon ghee (see page 325)
5 whole cloves
$\frac{1}{2}$ teaspoon ground turmeric
$\frac{1}{2}$ teaspoon cumin seeds
$\frac{1}{2}$ teaspoon salt (optional)

Wash and drain the rice. In a large saucepan, combine
the rice and the remaining ingredients, except the salt,
and bring to a boil. Reduce heat to simmer, cover, and
cook for 15 minutes.

When the water is no longer visible on top of the rice, use
a long fork to fluff the rice, turning the bottom rice to the
top and the top rice to the bottom. Add the salt, if desired. Cook for 5 minutes more, or until the water is absorbed.

Fluff the rice with a fork and serve immediately.

SHIRO

1 cup unsalted butter
1½ cups uncooked farina
3½ cups milk
⅓ cup whole almonds
⅔ cup golden raisins
1 tablespoon ground cardamom
1½ cups granulated sugar

In a medium-sized saucepan, melt the butter and slowly add the farina, coating well with the butter. In a separate saucepan, heat the milk on very low heat.

Add the almonds, raisins, and cardamom to the farina mixture and cook, stirring constantly, on medium-high heat for 15 minutes, or until the raisins begin to plump, and the farina turns slightly golden brown.

Stir in the warmed milk and cook for 5–10 minutes more on medium heat, or until the mixture becomes thick, and the raisins and almonds begin to separate or fall out of the grain. Add the sugar (the mixture will again turn to a liquid consistency) and stir over medium heat. Adjust the sugar and cardamom. Set aside and let cool for 5–10 minutes.

Fluff the farina with a fork. Serve immediately by scooping into serving bowls, but do not pack down. In Chandrakant's words, it should be "an exploded grain dish," ready to eat with or at the close of your Indian feast.

Preparation and cooking time 40 minutes.

Cooling time 5–10 minutes.

Serves 4–6.

Shiro is a sweet dessert made from farina, milk, cardamom, almonds, and raisins that, because of its unusual cooking process, becomes a very light, fluffy dish, rather than a thick porridge or cereal.

The secret to preparing Shiro lies in roasting the farina, with the almonds, raisins, and spices, in butter until the farina turns golden brown. This technique plumps the raisins and prepares the farina grains to cook individually, so they do not stick together.

MATAR PANEER

INDIAN HOME FRIES

GINGER-RAISIN CHUTNEY

KACHUMBAR

SPICED BASMATI RICE

KHIR

MATAR PANEER

1 pound firm tofu, rinsed and drained
2 tablespoons canola oil
2½ teaspoons chopped garlic
1 tablespoon chopped fresh gingerroot
One 28-ounce can crushed tomatoes
¾ cup water
3½ teaspoons curry powder
½ teaspoon ground paprika
5 teaspoons ground coriander
5 teaspoons ground cumin
1 teaspoon garam masala (see page 324)
½ teaspoon ground turmeric
2 cups frozen peas
2½ teaspoons salt
½ teaspoon black pepper
1 tablespoon fresh lemon juice
2½ teaspoons Sucanat (granulated cane juice)

Wrap the tofu in a clean towel and place a weight on top. Press for 15 minutes, unwrap, and cut the tofu into ¾-inch cubes. Set aside.

In a large skillet, heat the oil and sauté the garlic and gingerroot for 2–3 minutes. Whisk in the tomatoes and water. Add the curry powder, paprika, 3 teaspoons of the coriander, 3 teaspoons of the cumin, the garam masala, and turmeric and cook on medium heat until the spices are absorbed into the sauce. Add the peas and reserved tofu and cook for 5 minutes more. Stir in the salt, black pepper, lemon juice, and Sucanat. Adjust for saltiness, sweetness, and hotness. Mix in the remaining coriander and cumin and serve immediately.

Preparation and cooking time 40 minutes.
Serves 4–6.

A tomato-based, spicy curry dish, Matar Paneer contains peas, tofu, and seasonings, cooked in a thick stew and served with rice and other vegetables.

Preparation and
cooking time
30 minutes.

Baking time
15 minutes.

Serves 4–6.

*A spicier version of
American home
fries, these potatoes
are coated with
turmeric, paprika,
garlic, coriander,
and black pepper.
They go well with
the dishes on Dinner
Menu One (see page
305), or they can be
served to perk up
Southern Fried
Tofu or Tempeh
Barbecue (see pages
91 and 99).*

INDIAN HOME FRIES

10 cups cubed potatoes (7–8 medium potatoes)
⅓ cup canola oil
1½ teaspoons black mustard seeds
1 tablespoon finely chopped garlic
3 tablespoons ground coriander
¾ teaspoon ground turmeric
¾ teaspoon ground paprika
1 teaspoon black pepper
3 teaspoons salt
2 pinches ground asafetida (hing)
2¼ teaspoons Sucanat (granulated cane juice)
1–2 tablespoons canola oil

In a large, covered pot with a large steamer basket, steam the potatoes in water for 15 minutes or until thoroughly cooked yet still firm. Place the potatoes in a 9 x 12-inch baking pan and set aside.

In a small skillet, heat the ⅓ cup oil and sauté the mustard seeds until the seeds pop. Add the garlic and sauté for 2–3 minutes more.

Preheat oven to 375°F. Add the remaining ingredients, except the 1–2 tablespoons canola oil, and stir-sauté for 30 seconds, or until all of the spices are coated with oil. Pour the vagar over the reserved potatoes, covering well. Add the 1–2 tablespoons oil, if needed. Bake for 15 minutes. Turn the potatoes and bake for 10 minutes more.

Adjust for saltiness, sweetness, and hotness. Serve.

GINGER-RAISIN CHUTNEY

Preparation time 25 minutes.

Serves 6. (Makes 2 cups.)

This distinct chutney has a sweet raisin flavor, perked up by gingerroot and lemon and punctuated by jalapeño peppers. Increase or decrease the hot ingredients to suit your taste. This recipe will probably serve more than six, since most people take only a small serving as a condiment to accompany their rice, vegetables, and dahl.

1¾ cups golden raisins
1 cup hot water
5 teaspoons finely chopped fresh gingerroot
4 teaspoons finely chopped jalapeño peppers
1 tablespoon red wine vinegar
6 tablespoons shredded coconut
½ teaspoon salt
1 tablespoon fresh lemon juice

In a medium-sized bowl, soak the raisins in the hot water for 15–20 minutes. Drain.

Add the gingerroot, peppers, vinegar, and coconut to the drained raisins and mix together well with a wooden spoon. Add the salt and lemon juice. Adjust for hotness and serve.

**Preparation time
15 minutes.**

Serves 4.

*Kachumbar is a raw
vegetable dish made
from vegetables
finely chopped and
seasoned with
cumin, salt, black
pepper, and lemon
juice. It's the Indian
equivalent of a salad
accompanying the
main meal. This*
kachumbar *is
composed of cucum-
bers, green bell
peppers, and toma-
toes, with peanuts
giving contrast and
crunch.*

KACHUMBAR

1½ cups finely chopped cucumbers
1½ cups finely chopped green bell peppers
1½ cups finely chopped fresh tomatoes
¾ cup blanched peanuts
½ tablespoon ground cumin
½ teaspoon black pepper
1 teaspoon salt
5 teaspoons fresh lemon juice
1 tablespoon chopped fresh cilantro

In a large bowl, mix together all of the vegetables, the peanuts, cumin, black pepper, salt, and 3 teaspoons of the lemon juice. Adjust for hotness, sourness, and saltiness.

If more sourness is desired, add the remaining lemon juice. Add a pinch of salt or black pepper to intensify the flavors, if needed. Sprinkle with the cilantro and serve.

SPICED BASMATI RICE

This rice dish has interesting scents of clove and cumin that are sure to brighten a meal.

2 cups uncooked white basmati rice
4 cups water
1 teaspoon ghee (see page 325)
¼ teaspoon black pepper
½ teaspoon cumin seeds
7 whole cloves
½ teaspoon salt (optional)

Wash and drain the rice. In a large saucepan, combine the rice and the remaining ingredients, except the salt, and bring to a boil. Reduce to simmer, cover, and cook for 15 minutes.

When the water is no longer visible on top of the rice, use a long fork to fluff the rice, turning the bottom rice to the top and the top rice to the bottom. Add the salt, if desired. Cook for 5 minutes more, or until the water is absorbed.

Fluff the rice with a fork and serve immediately.

Preparation and
cooking time
35 minutes.

Cooling time
15–20 minutes.

Serves 4–6.

*Khir is a liquid
dessert made from
milk, slivered
almonds, and white
basmati rice, with a
delicious contrast of
cardamom, ghee,
saffron, and almond
flavors. In this
recipe, we use
granulated sugar to
achieve the texture
and sweetness of the
traditional Indian
version. Khir can be
served with the meal
or as a dessert,
though it will
appear thin by
comparison with
standard rice creams
or puddings.*

KHIR

1 teaspoon cardamom seeds, or
  ½ teaspoon ground cardamom
1 tablespoon ghee (see page 325) or melted
  unsalted butter, at room temperature
3 tablespoons uncooked white basmati rice
1 quart milk
1½ tablespoons slivered almonds
1 strand saffron, or ⅛ teaspoon ground saffron
½ cup granulated sugar

With a mortar and pestle or a spice grinder, crack the
cardamom seeds. Set aside. Rub the ghee into the rice.

In a large saucepan, combine the rice mixture and milk
and cook on medium heat, stirring frequently, for 5–10
minutes. Stir in the almonds and reserved cardamom and
cook for about 20 minutes, stirring occasionally.

Turn off heat and let cool for 15–20 minutes. Mix in the
saffron and sugar. Serve immediately.

More Indian Recipes

Here are a few more delectable Indian dishes that you can experiment with and enjoy with friends and family.

Khadi

1½ cups steamed chopped cauliflower
1 cup water
1½ tablespoons ghee (see page 325) or melted unsalted butter
1½ teaspoons cumin seeds
½ teaspoon yellow mustard seeds
7 whole cloves
½ cinnamon stick, broken into small pieces
¼ teaspoon ground turmeric
Pinch ground asafetida (hing)
½ teaspoon finely chopped garlic
2 cups plain yogurt
2 cups water
1 tablespoon fresh lemon juice
2 teaspoons salt
¼ teaspoon black pepper
2½ teaspoons Sucanat (granulated cane juice)
1 tablespoon chopped fresh cilantro

In a food processor, blend together the cauliflower and the 1 cup water for 2–3 minutes, or until the cauliflower is pureed. Set aside.

In a medium-sized saucepan, melt the ghee and sauté the cumin and mustard seeds until the seeds pop. Add the cloves, cinnamon, turmeric, and asafetida and sauté for

Preparation and cooking time 30 minutes.

Serves 4.

A thin, yogurt-based soup, khadi has a slight lemon-butter flavor that combines very well with Khichari *(see page 323) and other fragrant rice dishes.*

3–5 minutes, stirring frequently.

Add the reserved cauliflower mixture to the vagar and mix together well. Add the garlic, yogurt, water, lemon juice, salt, black pepper, and Sucanat and cook on medium heat for 10–15 minutes, stirring constantly with a whisk.

Add the cilantro just before adjusting flavors. Adjust for saltiness and sweetness and serve hot.

KHICHARI

½ cup dried mung beans
1¼ cups water
2 cups uncooked white basmati rice
4 cups water
1½ teaspoons salt
1 tablespoon ghee (see page 325)
1 teaspoon ground cumin
1 teaspoon ground coriander
½ teaspoon ground turmeric
Pinch ground asafetida (hing)
Pinch ground cardamom
⅛ teaspoon black pepper

In a large pot, combine the beans and the 1¼ cups water and cook on medium-high heat for 15–20 minutes, or until the beans are soft and the water is evaporated.

Wash and drain the rice. Add the rice and the 4 cups water to the beans and bring to a boil. Add the salt.

In a small skillet, melt the ghee and sauté the remaining ingredients until well coated with the ghee. Stir the ghee mixture into the boiling bean mixture. Reduce heat to simmer and cook, covered, for 15–20 minutes, or until the rice is soft and the water is absorbed.

Turn off heat and let stand, covered, for 5 minutes. Serve immediately.

Preparation and cooking time 50 minutes.

Serves 4–6.

Khichari is a seasoned rice and mung bean dish that is well loved among Kripalu residents. Make it festive by adding onions, peas, carrots, or green bell peppers or serve with Khadi (see pages 321–322) or one of the dahl recipes in this chapter.

*Chandrakant would
not willingly give up
the secret recipe that
has earned him
accolades for years
at Kripalu. It's a
recipe for Indian
tea, or* chai, *a
milky, sweet brew of
strong black tea and
the spice mixture
known as garam
masala. To make
this in true Indian
fashion, you'll need
an Indian tea called
CTC, which can be
found in Indian
shops or specialty
markets.*

CHANDRAKANT'S SECRET CHAI RECIPE

2 heaping teaspoons CTC tea or
  orange pekoe/pekoe-cut black tea
1⅓ cups milk
⅔ cup water
½ teaspoon garam masala (see recipe below)
¼ teaspoon ground cardamom
3–4 teaspoons granulated sugar to taste
½ teaspoon grated fresh gingerroot (optional)

In a small saucepan, combine all of the ingredients and
bring to a boil. Reduce heat and simmer for 1–2 minutes.

Tea should be a golden tan color when brewed. Adjust for
sweetness and serve immediately.

GARAM MASALA

2 tablespoons ground ginger
1 tablespoon black pepper
½ tablespoon ground cinnamon
¾ teaspoon ground cloves

In a small bowl, mix together all of the ingredients.
(Garam masala can be stored in a glass jar with a tight-
fitting lid in a cool, dark place.)

Makes about ¼ cup.

Ghee is butter that has been clarified and simmered until the milk solids settle out and a clear, golden oil is left behind. With the removal of the milk solids, ghee is considered superior to butter for cooking. It is more stable, with a very high smoking point of 375°F. An additional benefit is that environmental pollutants that may have been concentrated in the animal fat will be destroyed in the boiling process. In the Ayurvedic tradition, ghee is not only used as a condiment and a cooking oil, but also is considered to have healing properties. It is often used as the basis for medicinal preparations.

GHEE

4 pounds unsalted butter

In a large, heavy saucepan, melt the butter on low heat (do not burn). Bring to a boil until the butter foams. Stir gently and reduce heat to simmer. Simmer for 5–10 minutes, or until the solids settle to the bottom and brown slightly. Remove the foam that continues to form on the top and simmer for 10–15 minutes more.

Line a strainer with several layers of cheesecloth. Ladle the ghee through the strainer into a medium-sized bowl, being careful not to disturb any solids on the bottom of the saucepan. Scoop out the solids and discard or store with the foam in a small jar for use in cooking and baking.

When the ghee has completely cooled, pour into a glass jar with a tight-fitting lid. (Ghee can be stored for two months in a cool place, four months in the refrigerator, and even longer in the freezer.)

Preparation and cooking time 40 minutes.

Makes 6½–7 cups.

Since 1 pound of butter yields 1¾ cups of ghee, it is helpful to cook several pounds of butter at a time and store the ghee in a covered glass jar. Always use unsalted butter for making ghee.

The Light Line:

Low-Fat Meals

Chapter 13

THE HEALTH FOR LIFE PROGRAM began in 1986 at the request of many Kripalu guests. They had come to Kripalu for brief periods, and each time they had left feeling renewed, but they wanted a longer time in which to revitalize themselves and learn new life skills. Consequently, we created Health for Life, a three-week program that offered a panorama of healthy lifestyle activities, including daily walks, exercise classes, yoga classes, relaxation and stress management workshops, and low-fat cooking lessons.

The program resulted in dramatic, therapeutic changes for many of the participants. Just as important was the increase in energy, self-esteem, and joy that our Health for Lifers took home with them.

Many of the recipes in this chapter are adaptations of the Health for Life menu, but we've added many more; other low-fat recipes can be found throughout this book, especially in Chapters 6, 7, 8, and 9.

Most meals at Kripalu are already significantly lower in fat than the standard American diet due to our minimal use of animal products and our frequent use of fresh vegetables, whole grains, legumes, and other whole foods. In addition, there are a few special factors that need to be considered to create successful, low-fat meals:

Satiation. Satiation refers to our degree of satisfaction, both while we're eating, which is "mouth feel" and after eating, which is "stomach feel." Two important food characteristics that contribute to satiation are thickness and smoothness. In low-fat cooking, thickness can be achieved through the judicious use of thickening agents, such as arrowroot, agar-agar, and kuzu (see Chapter 11 for a discussion of thickeners and their uses). Also, the addition of a small quantity of rich-tasting foods, such as tahini, ghee, cashew butter, and other nut butters can contribute greatly to thickness and smoothness.

Flavor balance. Another important factor is the balancing of the five major flavors — salty, sour, sweet, pungent, and bitter. Enjoyable foods tend to combine or contrast elements of these five flavors. For example, a little salt and lemon juice help bring out a carrot's natural sweetness, while an astringent green vegetable like asparagus may call for a sweet sauce with a touch of ghee or almond butter.

Cooking method. Modifying the way we cook makes a big difference in lightening meals. For example, using a cast-iron skillet, which imparts an earthy flavor to foods, greatly reduces the need for added fats and oils. Tofu and tempeh, for example, can be simply pan-sautéed without any additional fat; just set the pan on medium heat and turn the tofu or tempeh frequently to keep it from sticking, then serve with a light sauce.

Baking and roasting are very effective low-fat cooking methods, not only for the old standby, potatoes, but also for beets, squash, carrots, zucchini, eggplant, bell peppers, onions, garlic, and sweet potatoes. And, when sautéing, you can replace some of the oil with water.

Trusting our taste buds. When we've simplified our diet by eating more whole grains, more fresh fruits and vegetables, and fewer commercially prepared or processed foods, we begin to finely tune our taste buds to the natural qualities of food. As we eat less added sweetener, for example, we start to taste the natural sweetness in foods; the less fat and oil we add to achieve satiation, the more we appreciate food in its pure state.

Preparation and
cooking time
1 hour.

Cooling time
variable.

Chilling time
1 hour.

Serves 4–6.

Visualize a beautiful, chilled terrine in layers of white, orange, and green. With this recipe, you can create a work of art as well as a luscious, highly nutritious, low-fat meal. Two hints: Dissolve the agar-agar completely and chill the terrine until firm.

TRICOLOR TERRINE

Carrot Layer:
2 cups chopped carrots
1 tablespoon pure maple syrup
1 teaspoon fresh lemon juice
½ teaspoon dried dill
1 tablespoon agar-agar powder
Salt to taste

Cauliflower Layer:
2 cups chopped cauliflower
2 pounds soft tofu, rinsed and drained
1 tablespoon agar-agar powder
1½ teaspoons white miso
1 teaspoon fresh lemon juice
Salt to taste

Asparagus Layer:
2 cups chopped asparagus
½ cup chopped celery
1 tablespoon umeboshi vinegar
1 tablespoon agar-agar powder
2 teaspoons tahini
⅓ pound soft tofu, rinsed and drained

Several sprigs fresh parsley or dill

For each of the layers, the procedure is approximately the same. Steam the vegetables of each layer in separate, covered saucepans with steamer baskets in water until tender. Save the water in which each layer of vegetables was steamed and let cool.

In separate, small saucepans, using ½ cup of each quantity of vegetable water, bring the water to a boil and add the amount of agar-agar required for each vegetable, stirring constantly until well dissolved, about 5 minutes for each. (With the cauliflower layer, after the agar-agar is well dissolved, dissolve the miso in the agar mixture.)

In a food processor, blend *separately* each set of steamed vegetables, agar mixture, remaining required ingredients, and remaining cooled soak water.

Layer the mixtures in a baking dish in any order desired. Chill for at least 1 hour before serving. Garnish with the parsley and serve with your favorite pasta or fresh greens salad.

Preparation and
cooking time
1 hour 20 minutes.

Baking time
20–30 minutes.

Serves 4–6.

*Here's a variation
on traditional
Shepherd's Pie,
which is made with
ground meat,
potatoes, and peas.
This dish has three
layers that are
prepared in stages,
simultaneously.
Serve with a salad
for a complete
meal.*

SHEPHERD'S PIE

Potato Layer:
2½ cups unpeeled coarsely chopped
  red potatoes
¼ cup soymilk
1 teaspoon ghee (see page 325)
½ teaspoon salt
Dash black pepper

Bulgur Layer:
½ cup uncooked bulgur
1 cup water
1 teaspoon olive oil
2–3 teaspoons water
1 cup chopped onions
½ cup sliced fresh mushrooms
½ cup chopped celery
1 tablespoon dried tarragon
1 teaspoon dried thyme
1 tablespoon tamari
½ teaspoon salt
Dash black pepper

Asparagus Layer:
3 cups chopped fresh asparagus
  (approximately 1 pound asparagus)
1 teaspoon cashew butter*
1 tablespoon umeboshi vinegar
¼ teaspoon salt

To make the potato layer: In a medium-sized saucepan,
boil the potatoes in water to cover for 15–20 minutes.
Drain, cover, and set aside.

To make the bulgar layer: Place the bulgar in a small bowl. In a small saucepan, boil the 1 cup water and pour over the bulgur. Let stand for 15–20 minutes, or until the water is absorbed. Set aside.

Meanwhile, in a medium-sized skillet, heat the oil and 2–3 teaspoons water and sauté the onions for 3–5 minutes or until translucent. Add the mushrooms, celery, tarragon, thyme, tamari, salt, and black pepper and sauté on low heat for 10 minutes more. Set aside.

To make the asparagus layer: In a large, covered saucepan with a steamer basket, steam the asparagus in water for 10–15 minutes. Drain and place the asparagus in a food processor. Add the cashew butter, vinegar, and salt and puree the mixture. Remove the mixture and set aside.

Preheat oven to 350°F. Add the reserved bulgar and reserved mushroom mixture to the processor and blend together well. Spread the bulgar mixture 1 inch thick on the bottom of an ovenproof casserole dish.

Add the reserved potatoes, the soymilk, ghee, salt, and black pepper to the processor and blend together until very smooth, but not watery. Spread the potato mixture 1 inch thick on top of the bulgur layer. Spread the reserved asparagus puree on top and bake for 20–30 minutes. Serve immediately.

Cashew butter is available at natural foods stores and specialty markets.

Here's an haute
cuisine *dish with a
light touch. Even
without cream or
cheese, it's as rich
as its namesake
because of the
blended vegetables,
tofu, and cashews.*

ZUCCHINI
ALFREDO LIGHT

1 cup sliced carrots
2 cups sliced zucchini
2 cups sliced yellow squash
1 teaspoon olive oil
2 cups chopped fresh mushrooms
½ cup chopped fresh basil
1–2 tablespoons dried seasoned bread crumbs

Sauce:
1 teaspoon olive oil
1 teaspoon water
1 cup diced onions
2 teaspoons chopped garlic
1 cup chopped cauliflower
½ pound firm tofu, rinsed and drained
½ cup whole cashews
1 tablespoon white wine vinegar
1 teaspoon brown rice vinegar
2 teaspoons umeboshi paste
1 teaspoon Dijon-style mustard
Dash ground nutmeg
½ cup vegetable stock

In a large, covered saucepan with a steamer basket, steam
the carrots, zucchini, and squash in water for 4–6 minutes. Drain and set aside. In a medium-sized skillet, heat
the oil and sauté the mushrooms for 5–8 minutes, turning frequently. Set aside.

To make the sauce: In a separate skillet, heat the oil and

water and sauté the onions and garlic for 3–5 minutes, or until the onions are translucent. Set aside.

Preheat oven to 275°F. In separate, covered saucepans with steamer baskets, steam the cauliflower and tofu in water for 3–6 minutes, or until the cauliflower is tender. Drain and set aside.

Place the cashews in a shallow pan and dry roast in the oven for 10–15 minutes or until lightly browned. In a food processor, grind the cashews into cashew meal. Add, one at a time, the onion mixture and the reserved cauliflower and tofu and process with the cashew meal until smooth.

In a small bowl, stir together both vinegars, umeboshi paste, mustard, and nutmeg. Add the vinegar mixture to the cashew mixture and process until well blended, adding the stock, as needed, for a pourable, creamy texture.

Preheat oven to 375°F. In an oiled, ovenproof 1-quart casserole dish, combine the reserved carrot mixture, reserved mushrooms, cashew sauce, and basil.

Top with the bread crumbs, cover, and bake for 25 minutes. Serve immediately. (If desired, place the casserole under the broiler for 3–4 minutes at the end of baking and lightly brown the top.)

Preparation and
cooking time
1 hour 15 minutes.

Baking time
20 minutes.

Serves 4.

Here's a Thanksgiv-
ing-style dish:
squash stuffed with
rice, zucchini puree,
and savory season-
ings. Be creative and
add your favorite
vegetables or spices
to the stuffing.

SQUASH BOATS
WITH SAVORY RICE

4 medium whole zucchini
1 cup washed drained brown basmati rice
1⅓ cups water
Sprig fresh rosemary
1 cup chopped onions
1 teaspoon canola or olive oil
1–2 teaspoons water
1 cup chopped fresh mushrooms
½ cup chopped celery
1 tablespoon tamari
⅛ teaspoon salt
⅛ teaspoon Spike seasoning*
1 teaspoon dried thyme
½ teaspoon dried sage
½ teaspoon dried marjoram
1 teaspoon nutritional yeast
Dash black pepper
2 tablespoons water
½ cup finely chopped carrots
½ cup finely chopped red bell peppers

In a large, deep skillet, cook the zucchini whole, in water
to cover two-thirds of the zucchini, for about 5 minutes
or until just tender. Drain, cover, and set aside.

In a large saucepan, combine the rice, the 1⅓ cups water,
rosemary, and onions and bring to a boil. Reduce heat to
low, cover, and cook for about 35 minutes, or until the
rice is soft and the water is absorbed. Set aside.

In a small skillet, heat the oil and the 1–2 teaspoons water and sauté ½ cup of the mushrooms, the celery, and the next eight ingredients for 5–7 minutes, or until the mushrooms and celery are tender-crisp. Set aside.

With a sharp knife, halve the reserved zucchini and trim a little off the bottom sides so they lie flat in a baking pan. Scoop out the zucchini meat, finely chop, and add to the reserved mushroom mixture. Cook for 3–5 minutes, or until the zucchini is tender.

In a blender or food processor, blend together the cooked zucchini mixture and half of the reserved rice mixture. Combine the zucchini-rice mixture with the remaining rice.

Preheat oven to 350°F. Fill the zucchini shells with the combined zucchini mixture and place in a shallow baking pan with a small amount of water.

In a small skillet, heat the 2 tablespoons water and sauté the remaining mushrooms, the carrots, and bell peppers for about 5 minutes or until limp. Sprinkle these vegetables over the stuffed zucchini shells and bake for 20 minutes. Serve immediately.

*Spike seasoning is available at natural foods stores and specialty markets.

With the bright colors of squash and the aroma of sage, this dish celebrates the arrival of au-tumn or makes a nutritious holiday entrée. The gravy is a lower fat version of Autumn Gravy (see page 80).

Spaghetti Squash with Tofu and Autumn Gravy

1 medium spaghetti squash, halved and seeded
8 ounces firm tofu, rinsed, drained, and cut into ½-inch cubes
2 tablespoons tamari
2 teaspoons nutritional yeast
Dash freshly ground black pepper
½ tablespoon olive oil
4 cups finely chopped onions
  (3–4 medium onions)
1½ cups water
1 cup chopped celery
½ teaspoon dried sage
½ teaspoon salt
1 tablespoon tamari
1 teaspoon fresh lime juice

Preheat oven to 375°F. Place the squash halves face down in a baking pan and add water to cover a ½ inch. Bake for 45 minutes. (Note the time that the squash be-gins baking because the tofu should begin baking 15 min-utes *later.*)

Place the tofu in a separate baking pan and add less than ¼ inch water. Sprinkle the tamari evenly over the tofu and top with the nutritional yeast and black pepper. Bake for 30 minutes.

To make the gravy: In a large skillet, heat the oil and sauté the onions for 2 minutes. As the oil is absorbed, add $\frac{1}{2}$ cup of the water and cook for 10 minutes. Add the celery and cook for 10 minutes more. Restore the water level by adding another $\frac{1}{2}$ cup of the water. Mix in the sage, salt, tamari, and lime juice and cook for 10 minutes.

In a blender or food processor, blend two-thirds of the celery mixture, adding the remaining water only if needs thinning. Combine the blended mixture with the remaining onion mixture and set the gravy aside.

Scoop out the baked squash, place in a large serving bowl, and gently fold in the tofu. Gently fold the reserved gravy into the squash mixture and serve immediately.

This entrée takes advantage of dry sautéing and baking to avoid the use of oil. It also includes a tasty kuzu marinade sauce.

BROCCOLI WITH TOFU AND MUNG BEAN SPROUTS

¼ cup tamari
⅛ cup rice vinegar
½ cup water
1 teaspoon ground ginger
1½ cups cubed firm tofu
   (approximately 8 ounces tofu)
Pinch salt
3 cups broccoli florets
   (approximately 2 stalks broccoli)
½ cup fresh mung bean sprouts
2 teaspoons kuzu dissolved in ¼ cup cold water

Preheat oven to 350°F. In a medium-sized bowl, combine the tamari, vinegar, water, and ginger to make a marinade. Place the tofu in the marinade and marinate for at least 10 minutes. Drain and reserve the marinade.

On an oiled baking sheet, place the tofu and bake for 15 minutes or until browned and lightly crisped. (Overbaking will make the cubes rubbery and hard.)

Meanwhile, heat a large skillet on high heat and add the salt and broccoli. Cook the broccoli without water for 6–10 minutes, stirring constantly, until bright green and tender-crisp. Stir in the baked tofu and bean sprouts.

In a small saucepan, mix together the dissolved kuzu and the reserved marinade and bring to a boil. Reduce heat to simmer and cook for 1–2 minutes, or until the sauce thickens. Pour the sauce over the broccoli mixture and stir together well. Serve immediately.

**Preparation time
30 minutes.**

**Baking time
30 minutes.**

Serves 4.

A hearty, whole-wheat, dairy-free version of Greek spanakopita, these turnovers are a surprisingly quick and complete meal.

TOFU-SPINACH TRIANGLES

Crust:
½ cup whole-wheat pastry flour
½ cup unbleached white flour
1 tablespoon ghee (see page 325)
3 egg whites
⅓ cup ice water

Filling:
1½ teaspoons olive oil
1 teaspoon finely chopped or pressed garlic
⅔ cup diced onions
20 ounces frozen spinach, thawed and
   well drained, or 8 ounces fresh spinach,
   well washed and trimmed
8 ounces firm tofu, rinsed, drained, and
   crumbled
½ teaspoon dried basil, or
   1 teaspoon chopped fresh basil
½ teaspoon dried oregano
Pinch ground nutmeg
Pinch black pepper
½ teaspoon fresh lemon juice
1 tablespoon umeboshi vinegar
1 tablespoon nutritional yeast
Salt to taste

Before preparing, chill all of the crust ingredients until ice-cold.

To make the filling: In a large skillet, heat the oil and

sauté the onions and garlic for 3–5 minutes, or until the onions are translucent. Add the spinach and sauté for 3 minutes more.

In a medium-sized bowl, combine the spinach mixture and the remaining filling ingredients. Set aside.

Preheat oven to 375°F. To make the crust: In a large bowl, combine both flours and mix in the ghee and egg whites to form a lumpy dough. Add the ice water, a little at a time, until the dough is smooth and pliable.

Divide the dough into four balls and roll out into 6-inch squares, $\frac{1}{8}$–$\frac{1}{4}$ inch thick. Place a heaping $\frac{1}{3}$ cup of the reserved filling in the center of each square and fold into triangles.

Using a fork or pastry crimper, crimp the seams where the edges meet and make holes in the top crusts with a fork. Place on a baking sheet and bake for 30 minutes or until golden brown. Serve immediately.

Preparation and
cooking time
50 minutes.

Marinating time
2 hours or over-
night.

Serves 4–6.

*This is a pleasant
dish that has the
crisp flavor and
bright colors of a
stir-fry, but with
less oil. The secret
lies in marinating
the tofu beforehand,
then baking it so it
holds its shape and
adds a crisp texture.*

LIGHT AND LIVELY STIR-FRY WITH TOFU

1 pound firm tofu, rinsed, drained, and
   cut into bite-sized cubes

Marinade:
1 teaspoon finely chopped garlic
1 teaspoon peeled finely chopped fresh
   gingerroot
3 tablespoons tamari
1/2–2/3 cup water

Stir-Fry:
1 cup chopped broccoli
1 cup chopped carrots
1 cup chopped zucchini
1/2 cup water
2 teaspoons sesame oil
1–2 tablespoons water
1 cup chopped onions
1 clove garlic, finely chopped
1 teaspoon peeled finely chopped fresh
   gingerroot
1/2 cup chopped celery
1 cup chopped fresh mushrooms
1/2 cup chopped red cabbage
1/4 cup chopped canned water chestnuts
Tamari to taste
1/4 cup chopped scallions
1/4–1/2 cup chopped fresh mung bean sprouts

Place the tofu in a large, shallow bowl. To make the marinade: In a small bowl, mix together all of the marinade ingredients and pour over the tofu. Marinate for at least 2 hours or overnight. Drain and reserve the marinade.

Preheat oven to 400°F. On an oiled baking sheet, place the drained tofu and bake for 20 minutes or until golden brown. Set aside.

To make the stir-fry: In a large, covered skillet or wok with a steamer basket, steam the broccoli, carrots, and zucchini in the ½ cup water for about 5 minutes, or until the vegetables are tender and the water is evaporated. Remove the broccoli mixture and set aside.

In the same skillet, heat the oil and the 1–2 tablespoons water and stir-fry the onions, garlic, and gingerroot for 1–2 minutes. Add the celery and mushrooms and stir-fry for 1–2 minutes. Add the cabbage and water chestnuts and stir-fry for 2 minutes.

Stir in the reserved broccoli mixture and reserved tofu and heat through. Mix in the tamari and sprinkle the scallions and bean sprouts on top. Serve immediately with the reserved marinade on the side.

Here's a colorful and delicious teriyaki that is light, yet makes a complete meal.

Seitan Teriyaki

1 pound dried rice noodles or soba noodles
1 tablespoon canola oil
1 tablespoon peeled chopped fresh gingerroot
2 cloves garlic, chopped
1 pound seitan, cut into strips
1 cup sliced halved carrots
1 cup sliced green bell peppers
1 cup sliced red bell peppers
3 cups chopped Chinese (napa) cabbage
  (8–10 ounces cabbage)
1⅓ cups vegetable stock or water
⅓ cup tamari
¼ cup rice syrup
1 tablespoon arrowroot dissolved in
  2 tablespoons water
¼ cup chopped scallions
2 tablespoons brown sesame seeds

In a large saucepan, cook the noodles in boiling water until tender but still firm. Drain and rinse. Set aside and keep warm.

In a large skillet, heat the oil and sauté the gingerroot and garlic for 4–6 minutes or until lightly brown, then move the ginger and garlic to the side of the skillet. (Repeat this procedure of adding an ingredient, sautéing, moving to the side, then adding the next ingredient.) Add the seitan and sauté for 1 minute, then the carrots for 1 minute, then all of the bell peppers for 2 minutes, then the cabbage for 1 minute.

Add the stock, tamari, and syrup and bring to a boil. Reduce heat to medium-low and stir in the dissolved arrowroot. Cook, stirring constantly, for about 5 minutes or until clear.

Place the reserved noodles in a serving dish and spoon the mixture over the noodles. Garnish with the scallions and seeds and serve immediately.

Preparation and
cooking time
1 hour.

Cooling time
variable.

Serves 8.

*The sauce for this
seitan dish has
much of the Stroga-
noff character,
without the heavy
doses of milk,
cream, and cheese
as in the traditional
recipe.*

SEITAN STROGANOFF LIGHT

3 cups whole fresh mushrooms
  (8–12 ounces mushrooms)
1 large red bell pepper
1 tablespoon olive oil
2 tablespoons water
2½ cups chopped onions
2 cloves garlic, peeled
1 teaspoon dried tarragon, or
  2 teaspoons chopped fresh tarragon
Pinch ground nutmeg
1 teaspoon black pepper
3 cups chopped seitan
  (approximately 1 pound seitan)
4 cups chopped cauliflower
  (approximately 1 large head cauliflower)
1 pound soft tofu, rinsed and drained
1 teaspoon salt
⅛ cup brown rice vinegar
⅔ cup mirin
1 cup frozen peas
1 pound dried egg noodles

Preheat oven to 400°F. In a large bowl, toss together the mushrooms, bell pepper, and oil. On a lightly oiled, rimmed baking sheet, place the mushrooms and bell pepper and roast in the oven, turning constantly, for 20 minutes or until well roasted. Remove and set aside.

In a large skillet, heat the water and sauté the onions and garlic for 3–5 minutes, or until the onions are translucent. Remove and set aside.

In the same skillet, combine the tarragon, nutmeg, black pepper, and seitan in the onion liquid and sauté until the seitan is browned. In a large, covered saucepan with a steamer basket, steam the cauliflower in water for 3–6 minutes. Drain and set aside to cool.

Meanwhile, in a food processor, puree the tofu, salt, vinegar, and mirin until smooth. Add the pureed tofu mixture to the browned seitan. In the processor, also puree the reserved cauliflower and reserved onion mixture and up to 1½ cups water, as needed, to lighten the texture of the vegetables. Add the pureed cauliflower mixture to the seitan mixture and heat through. Gently stir in the roasted mushrooms.

Seed and julienne the roasted bell pepper and add to the seitan mixture. Add the peas and cook on low heat for 15–20 minutes. Adjust the seasonings.

In a large saucepan, cook the noodles in boiling water until tender but still firm. Drain and rinse. Place in a serving bowl and spoon the hot seitan mixture over the noodles. Serve immediately.

**Preparation and cooking time
1 hour 5 minutes.**

**Soaking time
1 hour.**

**Baking time
40 minutes.**

**Cooling time
variable.**

Makes two 8-inch pies or one 9 x 12-inch pan.

Here is a hearty quiche, without the extra fat calories, that will satisfy everyone. Besides the tofu, carrots, and onions, this recipe uses hiziki, which gives the quiche a faint sea flavor and lots of calcium and trace minerals. You can prepare the crust and filling ahead of time, then pop the quiche in the oven

TOFU-HIZIKI QUICHE

Crust:
2 cups whole-wheat flour, or combination
  1 cup whole-wheat flour and 1 cup
  unbleached white flour
1 teaspoon salt
2–3 tablespoons canola oil
⅓–½ cup cold water

Filling:
1 ounce dried hiziki, well rinsed in cold water
  and drained
4 tablespoons water
3 cups sliced onions (2–3 medium onions)
3 cups julienned carrots
  (approximately 3 large carrots)
1½ tablespoons tamari
2¼ teaspoons brown rice vinegar
1 pound soft tofu, rinsed and drained
2 tablespoons umeboshi vinegar
2 tablespoons white miso
2 tablespoons tahini
1½ tablespoons kuzu

To make the crust: In a medium-sized bowl, combine all of the crust ingredients and roll out on sheets of wax paper to ⅛-inch thickness, either in two 8-inch rounds or one 9 x 12-inch rectangle. Place the dough in chosen pans and set aside.

To make the filling: In a small bowl, soak the drained hiziki in 2 tablespoons of the water for at least 1 hour.

In a large, deep skillet, heat the remaining water and sauté the onions for 3–5 minutes or until translucent. Drain the hiziki and layer on top of the onions, then layer the carrots on top of the hiziki. Add water to cover only the hiziki layer. Cover and simmer for 30 minutes, *without* stirring.

Preheat oven to 400°F. Stir the tamari and rice vinegar into the hiziki mixture and simmer for 15 minutes more. Let cool.

In a blender or food processor, blend together the tofu, umeboshi vinegar, miso, tahini, and kuzu until smooth. Add the tofu mixture to the hiziki mixture and mix together well. Place the mixture in the pie shell and bake for 40 minutes or until golden brown. Let cool for 5–10 minutes and serve.

Variation: Omit the pie crust and bake the filling in a lightly oiled baking pan for the same baking time and temperature.

shortly before serving. If desired, cook extra hiziki to use as a side dish for tomorrow's meal.

*If you are unfamiliar
with the use of millet
and tend to pass it
up in favor of rice or
noodles, try this
dish. It provides a
very tasty, nonfat
alternative to but-
tered mashed pota-
toes. Serve with the
gravy in* Kasha
Varnishkas with
Shiitake Mushroom
Gravy *(see pages
356–357) or try
any of the variations
below.*

MASHED MILLET WITH CAULIFLOWER

¼ cup water
1½ cups diced onions
6⅓ cups water
Pinch salt
2 cups uncooked millet
4–6 cups chopped cauliflower
   (approximately 1 large head cauliflower)

In a large pot, heat the ¼ cup water and sauté the onions for 3–5 minutes or until translucent. Add the 6⅓ cups water and the salt and bring to a boil. Stir in the millet and cauliflower and return to a boil. Reduce heat to simmer, cover, and cook for about 25 minutes, or until the water is absorbed. Turn off heat and let steam, covered, for 15 minutes.

In a blender or food processor, process the millet mixture until well mashed. Place in a serving bowl and serve warm after the mixture firms.

Variations:

With herbs: Add 1–2 tablespoons finely chopped fresh dill or basil; or add 1½ teaspoons prepared horseradish.

With onions: Add 1½ cups diced onions sautéed in 1 tablespoon canola oil and ¼ cup water.

With vegetables: Add 1½ cups cooked grated zucchini or carrots; or add 1½ cups cooked finely chopped fresh spinach.

With leftovers: Combine leftovers with sautéed onions and finely chopped cooked carrots. Shape the mixture into patties and coat with flour or bread crumbs. Bake at 400°F for 20 minutes or fry in 1 tablespoon canola oil.

Here's a pasta dish with the basil-scented flavors of Italy and the earthiness of root vegetables. If you allow the linguine to stand for a while in the sauce, it will be tinted a lovely magenta color, contributing to a colorful, pleasing dish.

LINGUINE IN RED VEGETABLE SAUCE

1½ cups vegetable stock
2 cups diced carrots
1½ cups scrubbed diced fresh beets
1 bay leaf
3–4 pieces kombu, broken into small pieces
¼ teaspoon salt
Dash freshly ground black pepper
½ tablespoon olive oil
1¼ cups chopped onions
½ tablespoon chopped garlic
1 teaspoon dried oregano
1 teaspoon dried thyme
1½ tablespoons chopped fresh basil
2 cups water
1 tablespoon umeboshi vinegar
1 pound dried linguine pasta
1 teaspoon umeboshi vinegar (optional)
1–2 fresh basil leaves, finely chopped

In a large saucepan, bring the stock to a boil. Add the carrots, beets, and bay leaf, and return to a boil. Add the kombu, salt, and black pepper, cover, and reduce heat to simmer.

In a medium-sized saucepan, heat the oil and sauté the onions and garlic for 3–5 minutes, or until the onions are translucent. Stir in the oregano, thyme, and basil and sauté for 5 minutes more. Add the water and simmer for

5 minutes. Add the 1 tablespoon vinegar and reduce heat to low.

Meanwhile, in a separate saucepan, cook the linguine in boiling water until tender but still firm. Drain and rinse. Set aside and keep warm.

Remove the bay leaf from the carrot mixture. In a blender or food processor, blend half of the carrot mixture. Return the blended mixture to the saucepan. Adjust the seasonings, adding the 1 teaspoon vinegar, if desired.

Stir in the onion mixture and pour the sauce over the reserved pasta. Garnish with the basil and serve immediately.

*This is a traditional
dish with a simple,
healthy mushroom
sauce — a great
dish to warm you up
in the winter.*

Kasha Varnishkas with Shiitake Mushroom Gravy

2 teaspoons canola oil
1 tablespoon water
1 cup chopped onions
$\frac{1}{2}$ teaspoon dried dill
$\frac{1}{2}$ teaspoon dried parsley, or
  2 teaspoons chopped fresh parsley
$1\frac{2}{3}$ cups water
1 cup roasted buckwheat
Pinch salt
8 ounces dried semolina noodles or bow tie
  noodles

Gravy:
2 cups water
One 2-inch strip kombu, broken into
  several pieces
2 tablespoons mirin
3 tablespoons tamari
1 tablespoon arrowroot dissolved in $\frac{1}{4}$ cup
  cold water
1 tablespoon kuzu dissolved in $\frac{1}{4}$ cup cold
  water
1 cup soaked, trimmed, and sliced dried
  shiitake mushrooms

1 cup sliced fresh button mushrooms
2 teaspoons pure maple syrup
Salt to taste

In a large skillet, heat the oil and sauté the onions for 3–5 minutes, adding the 1 tablespoon water while sautéing. After 4 minutes, add the dill and parsley and sauté for 5 minutes more. Add the 1⅔ cups water, buckwheat, and salt and bring to a boil. Reduce heat to low, cover, and cook for 15–20 minutes, or until the water is absorbed. Turn off heat and let steam, covered, for 10 minutes.

In a large saucepan, cook the noodles in boiling water until tender but still firm. Drain and rinse. Set aside and keep warm.

To make the gravy: In a large saucepan, combine the water and kombu and bring to a boil. Stir in the mirin, tamari, dissolved arrowroot, dissolved kuzu, shiitake mushrooms, and button mushrooms and return to a boil. Reduce heat to medium and add the syrup and salt, stirring constantly.

After 10–15 minutes, remove the mixture from the heat. Remove the kombu and stir in the reserved noodles. Serve warm over the steamed buckwheat.

*This light, aromatic
dish is a lovely cross
between soup and
pasta.*

Udons in Miso with Daikon and Watercress

1 pound dried udon noodles
Pinch salt
1 tablespoon ginger juice
   (one 2-inch length fresh gingerroot, peeled)
8 cups water
1½ cups julienned daikon
   (Japanese white radish)
1 medium carrot, julienned
½ cup tamari
2 tablespoons brown rice vinegar
1 tablespoon pure maple syrup
2 tablespoons white miso
4 scallions, finely chopped
½ cup washed chopped fresh watercress

In a large saucepan, cook the noodles in boiling water
with the salt until tender but still firm. Rinse and drain.
Set aside.

Prepare the ginger juice by grating and squeezing the gingerroot. In a large pot, bring the water to a boil and add
the ginger juice, daikon, carrot, tamari, vinegar, and
syrup. In a small bowl, dilute the miso in ½ cup of the
broth. After the broth has simmered for about 5 minutes,
add the reserved noodles, scallions, and watercress. Remove from heat. Stir in the diluted miso and let stand,
covered, for 5–10 minutes. Serve.

Udons and Tempeh in Oriental Barbecue

8 ounces tempeh, cut into ½ x 3-inch strips

Marinade:
3 tablespoons tamari
2 tablespoons rice vinegar
½ cup water
3 tablespoons rice syrup
1 clove garlic, finely chopped
1 teaspoon peeled finely chopped fresh
 gingerroot
2 tablespoons tomato puree or ketchup

1 pound dried udon noodles
2 teaspoons olive oil
½ cup chopped scallions
1 teaspoon peeled finely chopped fresh
 gingerroot
1 clove garlic, finely chopped
½ cup chopped celery
½ cup chopped green bell peppers
1 cup shredded green cabbage
2 cups chopped fresh mushrooms
½ cup frozen peas

Place the tempeh in a large, shallow bowl. To make the marinade: In a medium-sized bowl, mix together all of

**Preparation and
cooking time
40 minutes.**

**Marinating time
30 minutes.**

Serves 4–6.

*Here's a delightful
indoor barbecue
with little fuss and
lots of flavor.
Marinating the
tempeh gives it a
rich, smoky taste.*

the marinade ingredients. Pour 1 cup of the marinade over the tempeh and marinate for at least 30 minutes.

In a large saucepan, cook the noodles in boiling water until tender but still firm. Rinse and drain. Set aside and keep warm.

Meanwhile, in a large, deep skillet, heat the oil and sauté the scallions, gingerroot, garlic, and celery for 3 minutes. Gradually add the bell peppers, cabbage, mushrooms, and peas and sauté for 5–8 minutes more, or until the vegetables are tender-crisp.

On an oiled baking sheet, broil the marinated tempeh for 2–3 minutes per side. Add the broiled tempeh and reserved noodles to the vegetable mixture. Place the combined mixture in a serving bowl and ladle the remaining marinade on top or serve on the side. Serve immediately.

WHITE BEAN-
TORTILLA CASSEROLE

Filling:
3 cups well-cooked navy beans or canned
  navy beans with liquid
1 teaspoon salt
1½ teaspoons ground cumin
2 teaspoons fresh lime juice
2½ teaspoons dried cilantro, or
  2 tablespoons chopped fresh cilantro
½ teaspoon mirin
¼ teaspoon cayenne pepper
Pinch black pepper

Sauce:
1 cup scrubbed chopped fresh beets
1 cup chopped carrots
1¾ teaspoons olive oil
1 cup chopped onions
1 clove garlic, finely chopped
1½ teaspoons dried cilantro, or
  1 tablespoon chopped fresh cilantro
¼ teaspoon ground cumin
1 tablespoon umeboshi vinegar
¼ cup water

4 soft corn tortillas
1 tablespoon shredded low-fat cheese or
  soy cheese
1 teaspoon grated Parmesan cheese

To make the filling: In a blender or food processor, blend
together the cooked beans and all of the remaining filling

*This recipe is baked
in one dish, so it
makes for a simple
but tasty Mexican-
style meal.*

ingredients. Adjust the seasonings and set aside.

To make the sauce: In a medium-sized, covered saucepan with a steamer basket, steam the beets and carrots in water for 8–10 minutes, or until the beets are tender. In a medium-sized skillet, heat the oil and sauté the onions and garlic for 3–5 minutes, or until the onions are translucent. Reduce heat to low. Stir in the steamed beets and carrots, the cilantro, cumin, and vinegar and cook, stirring constantly, for 5–10 minutes.

In a blender or food processor, blend the beet mixture, adding water, if needed, until smooth and thick.

Preheat oven to 375°F. Place a corn tortilla on the bottom of a casserole dish and add layers of ingredients in the following order: half of the reserved filling, another tortilla, a small amount of the sauce, another tortilla, the remaining filling, a small amount of the low-fat cheese, another tortilla, and the remaining sauce. Sprinkle with the Parmesan cheese, cover, and bake for about 25 minutes. Serve immediately.

Variations:
Use *House Salsa* (see page 227) or other salsa on top of the casserole in place of the sauce.
For enchiladas, place ¼ cup of the filling in the center of a flour tortilla, add grated cheese, and fold. Place seam-side down in a baking pan and spread the sauce down the center. Bake at 350°F for about 25 minutes.

PARTY MEALS FOR

LARGE GROUPS

Chapter 14

 PREPARING MEALS FOR LARGE GROUPS is among the most challenging yet satisfying of cooking projects. My advice to prospective hosts and caterers is to keep it "elegantly simple." In other words, prepare a number of foods that, though simple in themselves, combine for an elegant presentation.

Some people enjoy getting their adrenaline pumping, approaching the meal as a victory over limited time. But I recommend taking it slowly, keeping it simple, and attending to details ahead of time as much as you can, so you're free to enjoy the company of your guests.

You can, however, include on your party menu some dishes that are complex and time consuming, if you plan them well in advance, and prepare or cook them ahead of time. This chapter has a few creatively complex recipes, as well as a number of dishes that can be prepared in minutes.

When planning your menu, create a time line for preparing not only dishes that can be made in advance, but also the dishes that can be prepared quickly. I find it helpful to proceed systematically and keep to-do lists of what needs to get done in what order. With many tasks and a tight calendar, no amount of organization is too much. (My mom, for example, sets her table three days before a big dinner!) So get out the coffeemaker and teapot, set out your serving dishes, ladles, and spoons, and let's begin!

The following are four special, very different dinner menus suitable for entertaining. There are also recipes for a few hors d'oeuvres and specialty items.

DINNER MENU ONE

EASY GAZPACHO

VEGETABLE PAELLA

Easy Gazpacho

3 cups V-8 Juice or tomato juice
5 cups chopped tomatoes
   (6–8 medium tomatoes)
1 tablespoon chopped garlic
2 cups chopped onions
3 cups peeled chopped cucumbers
   (approximately 2 medium cucumbers)
3 cups chopped red bell peppers
   (approximately 2 medium peppers)
2 cups chopped green bell peppers
3 tablespoons chopped fresh basil
¼ cup chopped fresh cilantro
¼ cup chopped fresh parsley
½ cup finely chopped scallions
Pinch cayenne pepper, or
   several drops Tabasco sauce
2 tablespoons olive oil
¼ cup umeboshi vinegar
½ teaspoon salt or to taste
½ teaspoon black pepper
Splash fresh lime juice (optional)

In a food processor, blend together all of the ingredients
in batches until well combined. Adjust the seasonings.
Chill before serving.

Variation: Blend together only two-thirds of the vegetables
and keep one-third in chopped form for a variety of textures.

VEGETABLE PAELLA

½ cup dulse (4–5 pieces, broken apart)
½ cup kelp (3–4 pieces, broken apart)
2 cups water
1 pound firm tofu, rinsed and drained

Marinade:
2 tablespoons olive oil
¼ cup tamari
¼ cup umeboshi vinegar
1 tablespoon balsamic vinegar
1 tablespoon rice vinegar
½ teaspoon finely chopped fresh gingerroot
½ teaspoon finely chopped garlic
1 teaspoon fresh lime juice

Rice:
2½ cups uncooked white basmati rice
3 cups water
2 vegetable bouillon cubes
½ teaspoon saffron strands (1–2 strands)
4 teaspoons olive oil
2 cups chopped Bermuda onions
2 cloves finely chopped garlic
2 cups chopped red bell peppers
4 cups chopped fresh mushrooms (12 ounces)
2 cups chopped zucchini
One 10-ounce package frozen peas
½ cup artichoke hearts
1 teaspoon ground paprika
1–2 teaspoons finely chopped jalapeño peppers
⅓ cup chopped fresh cilantro
Salt and black pepper to taste

Preparation and cooking time 1 hour 15 minutes.

Baking time 30 minutes.

Soaking time variable.

Serves 10–12.

This is a very exotic vegetarian offering, patterned after a Spanish seafood and rice dish, of tofu, mushrooms, artichoke hearts, peas, and saffron-dyed rice. Guests will hardly notice the lack of fish, yet will delight in the sea flavors of dulse and kelp, which alone provide lots of B vitamins, iodine, iron, calcium, potassium, magnesium, and vitamins A, C, and E.

In a small bowl, soak the dulse and kelp in the 2 cups water. Set aside.

Preheat oven to 375°F. To make the marinade: In a small bowl, mix together the oil, tamari, all three vinegars, gingerroot, garlic, and lime juice. Slice the tofu into three ¼-inch thick slices. Then cut each slice into triangular pieces. Pour the marinade in a baking pan and add the tofu, coating each piece well. Bake for 30 minutes.

Meanwhile, to make the rice: Drain the reserved dulse and kelp and reserve all soak water. Slice the dulse and kelp into small pieces and set aside.

Wash and drain the rice. In a large saucepan, combine the rice, 3 cups water, and 2 cups reserved soak water and bring to a boil. Gently stir in the bouillon cubes and saffron without disturbing the bottom layer of rice. Reduce heat to low and place the reserved dulse and kelp on top. Cover and cook for 20–25 minutes, or until the water is absorbed. Set aside, covered.

In a large skillet, heat 2 teaspoons of the oil and sauté the onions and garlic for 3–5 minutes, or until the onions are translucent. Add the bell peppers and sauté for 5 minutes more. Transfer the bell pepper mixture to a large stew pot or cast-iron pot. Heat the remaining 2 teaspoons oil in the skillet and sauté the mushrooms for 5 minutes.

Meanwhile, remove the baked tofu from the oven and reserve the marinade in a small bowl. Set aside the tofu.

Add the zucchini to the mushroom mixture and sauté for 5 minutes or until tender-crisp, using the reserved marinade as needed for sautéing. Add the peas, artichoke hearts, paprika, jalapeño peppers, cilantro, and additional marinade as needed and cook for 5 minutes, or until the peas are tender, and the seasonings are well blended. Add the mushroom mixture to the bell pepper mixture in the pot.

Blend the reserved dulse and kelp into the cooked rice, then add the rice mixture to the pot. Gently add the reserved tofu and mix together well the contents of the pot. Add the salt and pepper and any remaining marinade, if needed. Serve immediately.

DINNER MENU TWO

Seitan
Kabobs

Baked Stuffed
Potatoes

Green Beans
and Garlic

Seitan Kabobs

30 skewers, 8–10 inches long

30 or more small fresh mushrooms
(approximately 2 pounds mushrooms)

5 green, red, or yellow bell peppers,
deveined, seeded, and cut into 2-inch squares

30 or more cherry tomatoes
(approximately 2 pints)

30 or more very small onions
(approximately 3 pounds)

2 pounds seitan, rinsed, drained, and cut into
1½-inch cubes

Marinade:

1½ cups tamari

4½ cups water

½ cup olive oil

¼ cup fresh lemon juice, or your favorite
vinegar: balsamic, cider, raspberry

Prepare the mushrooms, bell peppers, and tomatoes. Set aside.

Wash the onions and remove the outermost layer, if unsightly. Otherwise, remove the skin after the grilling. In a large saucepan, boil or steam the onions for 5 minutes. Drain and set aside.

To make the marinade: In a large bowl, mix together all of the marinade ingredients. In a large, shallow bowl, place all of the reserved vegetables and the seitan and pour the marinade over the top, covering well. Marinate for at least 1 hour or refrigerate overnight, turning occasionally.

Preparation and cooking time 55 minutes.

Marinating time 1 hour or overnight.

Serves 14–16. (Makes 30 kabobs on 8–10-inch skewers.)

With savory chunks of seitan interspersed with mushrooms, cherry tomatoes, baby onions, and green bell peppers, these kabobs are the hit of the party.

Remove the vegetables and seitan from the marinade and place on the skewers in different combinations. Grill on an outdoor grill for 3–5 minutes per side or under the broiler for 5–7 minutes per side. Serve immediately.

Baked Stuffed Potatoes

16 large baking potatoes, scrubbed and
   wrapped in aluminum foil
¼ cup butter
¾ cup milk
2 teaspoons salt
1 teaspoon black pepper
1 cup finely grated cheddar cheese
2 tablespoons ground paprika
¼ cup chopped fresh chives

Preheat oven to 400°F. Bake the potatoes for 45 minutes
or until soft. Cool slightly, then slice in half and scoop the
contents into a large bowl. Reserve half of the potato
shells (16 shells) for restuffing.

Add the butter, milk, salt, and pepper to the potatoes and
mash with a potato masher or a large fork until well combined. (Use an electric mixer if desire a more whipped
texture.)

Restuff the reserved potato shells with the mashed potato
mixture. Sprinkle each stuffed shell with the cheese and
paprika. Place the stuffed shells on a baking sheet and
broil for 2–5 minutes. Sprinkle on the chives and serve
immediately.

**Preparation and
cooking time
45 minutes.**

**Baking time
45 minutes.**

**Serves 14–16.
(Makes 16 stuffed
potatoes.)**

*If you bake the
potatoes, prepare
the stuffing, and
restuff the shells a
day in advance, you
can broil these
potatoes the day of
your party and have
a rich, tasty dish
that comes out of
the oven in less than
5 minutes.*

Preparation and
cooking time
20 minutes.

Chilling time
variable.

Serves 14–16.

*This dish never fails
to win compliments,
yet it is very easy to
prepare. Slender
green beans are
tossed with garlic,
oil, and vinegar to
be served either as a
cold salad or as a
piping hot side dish.*

GREEN BEANS AND GARLIC

2 pounds fresh green beans, tipped, tailed,
  and washed
¼ cup olive oil
2 tablespoons finely chopped garlic
4 teaspoons umeboshi vinegar
4 teaspoons balsamic vinegar

In a large, covered pot with a steamer basket, steam the
beans in water for 8–10 minutes or until tender-crisp.

To serve as a cold salad: Let the beans cool completely. In
a small bowl, stir together all of the remaining ingredients
and blend well. In a large bowl, toss the beans with the
mixture. Serve immediately or chill before serving.

To serve as a hot side dish: In a large, deep skillet, heat
the oil and add the garlic and both vinegars. Stir-fry the
beans for 5 minutes, coating with the hot oil mixture.
Serve immediately.

DINNER MENU THREE

Hot Beet Borscht with Sour Cream

Stuffed Cabbage with Tomato-Raisin Sauce

Potato Latkes

*What a hot, sooth-
ing soup to begin a
meal. The ultimate
secret to making
excellent beet
borscht, as passed on
to us by my mom,
Sophie Levitt, is to
add a small amount
of sweet, salty, and
sour flavors, one at a
time, and keep
tasting. There is a
certain point when
all of the flavors
come together, and
you know that you
have reached the
perfect balance.*

Hot Beet Borscht with Sour Cream

5 cups peeled chopped fresh beets
   (approximately 5 medium beets)
10 cups water
Dash salt
2 whole medium onions, peeled
1½–2 tablespoons salt
2 tablespoons fresh lemon juice
½ cup pure maple syrup
½ cup apple cider or apple juice
½–1 cup sour cream or plain yogurt

In a large stew pot or cast-iron pot, combine the beets, water, dash salt, and onions and bring to a boil. Reduce heat to medium-low, cover, and cook for 30–40 minutes. In the last 15 minutes, stir in half of *each:* the salt, lemon juice, syrup, and cider. Cook for 5 minutes, then taste.

Depending on your taste preference, add the remaining half of the salt, lemon juice, syrup, and cider or a portion of that half until the taste is balanced. Pour into serving bowls and top with dollops of the sour cream. Serve hot.

Stuffed Cabbage in Tomato-Raisin Sauce

**Preparation and cooking time
2 hours 30 minutes.
Serves 8–10.**

This sumptuous cabbage dish features the hearty flavors of oregano, chives, and parsley blended in a tofu-rice stuffing and served in a tomato sauce, lightly sweetened by raisins and herbs. This dish will be even more tasty, having marinated for a while, if prepared and refrigerated for several days in advance.

Stuffing:
1 tablespoon olive oil
1 cup finely chopped onions
½ cup finely chopped celery
½ cup finely chopped red bell peppers
1 cup finely chopped fresh mushrooms
2 teaspoons olive oil
1 cup diced zucchini
1 tablespoon finely chopped fresh parsley
1 tablespoon finely chopped fresh chives
1 teaspoon dried oregano, or
  2 teaspoons chopped fresh oregano
8 ounces soft tofu, rinsed, drained, and
  crumbled
2 cups cooked white basmati rice
Dash fresh lemon juice
2 tablespoons red wine vinegar
1½ tablespoons pure maple syrup
4 tablespoons tamari
Salt and black pepper to taste

Sauce:
3 cups canned tomato sauce
1 cup water
½ cup golden raisins
1 tablespoon pure maple syrup
Salt or tamari to taste
2 large heads green cabbage, or
  2 heads Savoy cabbage, trimmed and cored

To make the stuffing: In a large Dutch oven or cast-iron pot, heat the 1 tablespoon oil and sauté the onions for 3–5 minutes or until translucent. Add the celery and bell peppers and sauté for 5 minutes. Add the mushrooms and sauté for 2–3 minutes more. Remove the sautéed vegetables and set aside. Add the 2 teaspoons oil to the pot and sauté the zucchini, herbs, and tofu for 3–5 minutes.

Meanwhile, in a separate pot, heat the cooked rice for 15 minutes. Stir in the lemon juice, vinegar, syrup, and tamari. Adjust for sweetness and saltiness. Fold in the reserved sautéed vegetable mixture and the zucchini mixture and add the salt and pepper. Set aside.

To make the sauce: In the large Dutch oven or cast-iron pot, combine the tomato sauce and water and cook on medium-low heat for 15 minutes. Stir in the raisins, syrup, and salt and continue to cook on low heat.

Meanwhile, half-fill a large saucepan with water and bring to a boil. Gently peel off the large leaves of the cabbage, one by one, taking care not to tear or break off any leaves. Drop the leaves in the boiling water, 3 or 4 at a time, and cook for 3–5 minutes, or until the leaves wilt but the stem is still sturdy. Remove the leaves and drain on a wire rack, repeating the procedure with 3 or 4 more leaves.

As you cook more leaves, stuff the leaves that have cooled. Take a leaf, spread it open, place 1–2 tablespoons of the reserved stuffing in the center, and fold the leaf like an envelope. Place the cabbage rolls, one at a time, in the sauce, folded side face down. When all of the cabbage rolls are in the pot, cook on very low heat for about 1 hour. Turn off heat and let stand for 15–20 minutes. Serve immediately.

Potato Latkes

1 cup chopped onions, divided
8 cups peeled chopped potatoes, divided
  (7–8 medium potatoes)
1½ cups water
½ cup matzoh meal
3 eggs
2 teaspoons salt
⅛ teaspoon black pepper
¼ cup butter
Sour cream (optional)
Applesauce (optional)

In two medium-sized bowls, combine each ½ cup onions with each 4 cups potatoes. Place the first onion-potato batch in a food processor with ½ cup of the water and process for 1–3 minutes, or until the potatoes are well pureed with no lumps.

Place the pureed mixture in a large bowl, then process the second onion-potato batch with ½ cup of the water. Add the second batch to the bowl and stir in the matzoh meal, eggs, salt, and black pepper until well combined. Mix in the remaining water to make the batter pourable.

In a small skillet, melt the butter and lightly butter two large, cast-iron skillets. Heat both skillets and preheat oven to 300°F. Spoon the batter into the well-heated skillets and thinly spread the batter to form 2½-inch circles. Cook for 3–4 minutes per side. Keep the cooked latkes hot by placing on a lightly oiled baking sheet in the oven. Serve hot with the sour cream and a touch of the applesauce, if desired.

Preparation and cooking time 50 minutes.

Serves 10–12. (Makes 34–36 medium latkes.)

Around holiday time, the smell and sizzle of potato latkes, thin pancakes of onions, potatoes, eggs, and matzoh meal, wake up any dormant appetite.

ROASTED
PORTABELLA
MUSHROOMS,
PEPPERS, AND
ZUCCHINI

ANGEL HAIR
PASTA WITH
PARMESAN

ROASTED PORTABELLA MUSHROOMS, PEPPERS, AND ZUCCHINI

Preparation and cooking time 25 minutes.

Marinating time at least 30 minutes.

Serves 14–16.

1½–2 pounds fresh portabella mushrooms, washed and trimmed (approximately 6 medium mushrooms)
4 large red bell peppers, deveined, seeded, and cut into 1 x 3-inch strips
4 large zucchini, cut into 1 x 3-inch strips

Marinade:
1½ cups olive oil
4 cups water
¼ cup balsamic vinegar
1½ tablespoons finely chopped garlic
2 teaspoons salt
2 teaspoons ground paprika
½ teaspoon cayenne pepper

Prepare all of the vegetables and place in one or two large, shallow bowls. Set aside.

To make the marinade: In a large bowl, mix together all of the marinade ingredients. Pour the marinade over the reserved vegetables and marinate for at least 30 minutes, preferably 1–2 hours.

Preheat oven to 375°F. Drain the vegetables and place on one or two large baking sheets. Roast in the oven for 10–

Here's a delightfully easy main dish for a party or gathering. The red bell peppers and zucchini contribute lots of color, and the portabella mushrooms have a meaty, almost tenderloin flavor after soaking in the marinade. Roast these vegetables in the oven or grill outdoors in the summer. Serve on a bed of Angel Hair Pasta with Parmesan *(see page 383) or with rice or couscous.*

15 minutes, turning once.

For faster results, place under the broiler and broil for 3 minutes per side. On an outdoor grill, grill for 3–5 minutes per side. Serve immediately.

Angel Hair Pasta with Parmesan

Preparation and cooking time 20–25 minutes.
Serves 14–16.

This pasta dish can be quickly prepared and when served with Roasted Portabella Mushrooms, Peppers, and Zucchini *(see pages 381–382) makes an elegant presentation. Add a fresh green salad for an even more satisfying meal.*

3 pounds dried angel hair pasta
1 cup olive oil
2 tablespoons chopped garlic
1 cup grated Parmesan cheese
3 tablespoons umeboshi vinegar
2 tablespoons chopped fresh parsley or basil

In a large, two-gallon pot, cook the pasta in boiling water until tender but still firm. Stir occasionally to prevent sticking. Rinse and drain.

Place the pasta in a large mixing bowl or two separate bowls and mix in the oil, garlic, cheese, vinegar, and parsley until well combined. Serve warm or at room temperature.

HORS D'OEUVRES AND PARTY ADDITIONS

Here is a selection of hors d'oeuvres, sandwiches, and side dishes to round out your party or special event.

Preparation and cooking time 1 hour 20–30 minutes.

Cooling time 45–60 minutes.

Serves 14–16. (Makes 48 squares.)

This delicious casserole provides all of the elements of norimake, that tasty, rolled rice and sea vegetable finger food, without the inconvenience of preparing and rolling individual servings.

NORIMAKE CASSEROLE

8 nori sheets
4 cups uncooked short-grain brown or
  white rice
7 cups water
½ teaspoon salt
1 tablespoon umeboshi paste diluted in
  3 tablespoons water
2 small avocados, peeled and cut into
  long, flat strips
2 cups grated cucumbers
1½ cups julienned scallions
⅓ cup roasted sesame seeds (see page 178)
3–4 teaspoons wasabi horseradish paste*

Place the nori sheets on a baking sheet and toast under the broiler for *only* 30 seconds. Set aside.

Wash and drain the rice. In a large saucepan, combine the rice and water and bring to a boil. Add the salt. Reduce heat to simmer and cook, covered, for 45 minutes. (For white rice, cook for 20 minutes.)

Turn off heat and let stand, covered, for 10 minutes. Place the rice in a large bowl and fluff with a fork. Let cool for 45–60 minutes.

In two 9 x 12-inch baking pans, layer a small amount of rice, enough to form a thin coating on the bottom of each pan. Place a sheet of the reserved nori on top of the rice and cover with another layer of rice. Add a thin layer of the diluted umeboshi paste. Then layer on half of the avocados, cucumbers, scallions, and sesame seeds in each pan. Add another layer of nori, then a layer of the remaining rice. Top with a final sheet of nori.

Use a very sharp knife to cut the norimake into 24 two-inch squares per pan. Serve immediately with the wasabi horseradish paste or chill before serving.

Wasabi horseradish paste is available in natural foods stores and Asian markets.

**Preparation and
cooking time
40 minutes.**

**Baking time
35 minutes.**

**Serves 10–12.
(Makes 32 mush-
rooms.)**

*This hors d'oeuvre
adds a gourmet
touch to your gath-
ering. Tempeh,
mixed with onions,
bell peppers, al-
monds, and tamari,
makes a wonderfully
rich, nutty filling
that complements
the earthy tones of
the mushrooms.*

STUFFED MUSHROOMS WITH TEMPEH PÂTÉ

32 large fresh mushrooms
2 tablespoons olive oil
2 cups diced onions
2 cups diced fresh mushrooms
8 ounces tempeh, cut into small cubes
3 tablespoons tamari
1 tablespoon brown rice vinegar
1 cup diced red bell peppers
½ cup roasted almonds (see page 132)

Wash the mushrooms and carefully pull out the stems, instead of trimming, so that a small indentation is left in each mushroom for stuffing. Set the mushrooms aside.

In a large skillet, heat the oil and sauté the onions for 10 minutes or until begin to caramelize. Add the diced mushrooms and sauté for 5 minutes. Stir in the tempeh, tamari, and vinegar and sauté for 10 minutes. Add the bell peppers and sauté for 5 minutes more. Turn off heat.

In a food processor, chop the cooled, roasted almonds into small pieces. Add the sautéed vegetable mixture to the processor and process for 30 seconds. (The mixture should be semichunky in texture.) Adjust for saltiness and other flavors.

Preheat oven to 400°F. Stuff each mushroom cap with 1½ tablespoons pâté. Place the stuffed mushrooms in a large baking pan with ½ cup water on the bottom. Cover with aluminum foil and bake for 30 minutes. Uncover and bake for 5 minutes more. Serve immediately.

Preparation and cooking time 30 minutes.

Marinating time overnight.

Serves 16. (Makes 16 sandwiches.)

These great submarine sandwiches are long French bread loaves, stuffed with cheddar, provolone, "tempeh bacon," Olive Relish, lettuce, and tomatoes. If you prepare the Olive Relish and the first stage of the tempeh bacon a day ahead, these sandwiches can be quickly assembled on the day of your special event.

NEW ORLEANS SUBS

Tempeh Bacon:
4 cups water
2 bay leaves
2 tablespoons sesame oil
2 tablespoons chopped garlic
¼ cup barley miso
¼ cup prepared brown mustard
1 teaspoon freshly ground white pepper
2 teaspoons ground cumin
2 pounds tempeh, thawed and cut into
    2 x 3½-inch pieces
2 tablespoons canola oil

Sandwiches:
4 medium thick French bread loaves,
    16–18 inches long
1–2 tablespoons olive oil
1–2 tablespoons cider vinegar or
    red wine vinegar
½ teaspoon dried oregano
Salt and black pepper to taste
16 fresh lettuce leaves (1 large head)
16 thin slices fresh tomato
    (approximately 3 medium tomatoes)
16 thin slices cheddar cheese
16 thin slices provolone cheese
5 cups *Olive Relish* (see page 229)

To make the tempeh bacon: In a large bowl, mix together the first eight ingredients to make a marinade. Place the tempeh pieces in a 9 x 12-inch baking pan. Pour the marinade over the tempeh, covering well, and marinate in the refrigerator overnight.

When ready to prepare the subs, in a large skillet, heat the canola oil and cook the drained tempeh pieces for 3–4 minutes per side or until brown on both sides. Drain on paper towels and set aside.

To make the sandwiches: Slice the loaves lengthwise and sprinkle the oil, vinegar, oregano, salt, and black pepper on each bottom length of bread. Layer on the lettuce, tomatoes, both cheeses, and reserved tempeh.

Spread the relish on top and cover with the top length of bread. Cut each loaf into 4 sandwiches and pierce each with a toothpick to hold it together. Serve.

Preparation and
cooking time
1 hour.

Cooling time
variable.

Soaking time
5 minutes.

Serves 10–12.
(Makes 30 dolmati.)

*These stuffed grape
leaves are not only
wonderful party
appetizers, but
they're also great
snacks to have on
hand or to serve as
part of a main
meal.*

DOLMATI

1½ cups uncooked white basmati rice
3 cups water
¾ cup diced onions
⅓ cup pine nuts
1 teaspoon salt
¼ cup raisins
2 tablespoons olive oil
½ teaspoon dried dill
¼ teaspoon black pepper
30 preserved medium grape leaves*
¼–½ cup fresh lemon juice

Wash and drain the rice. In a large saucepan, combine
the rice, water, onions, and pine nuts and bring to a boil.
Add the salt. Reduce heat to simmer and cook, covered,
for 20 minutes, or until the water is absorbed.

Meanwhile, in a small bowl, cover the raisins with water
and soak for 5 minutes. Drain and set aside.

When rice is cooked, stir in the soaked raisins, oil, dill,
and black pepper with a fork. Let the rice mixture cool
enough to handle. Spoon 1–1½ tablespoons of the rice
mixture onto each grape leaf and fold the leaf like an envelope. Sprinkle each leaf with a dash of lemon juice and
place the stuffed leaves on a serving tray. Serve immediately.

*Grape leaves can be purchased in 16- or 32-ounce jars; check
the label for number of leaves in jar.*

APRICOT KUGEL

12 ounces dried wide egg noodles
3 tablespoons butter, at room temperature
8 ounces cream cheese, at room temperature
½ cup finely chopped dried apricots
4 eggs, beaten
4¼ cups milk
Dash salt
¾ cup pure maple syrup
½ cup Sucanat (granulated cane juice)
2 teaspoons pure vanilla extract
1 teaspoon ground cinnamon
Dash ground cardamom
1 tablespoon agar-agar powder, or
  2 tablespoons agar-agar flakes
½ cup all-fruit apricot preserves
½ cup fresh orange juice
¼ cup pure maple syrup

In a large saucepan, cook the noodles in boiling water for 8–10 minutes or until soft. Drain. In a large bowl, combine the hot noodles, butter, and cream cheese and mix together well. Stir in the apricots and set aside.

Preheat oven to 300°F. In a separate, large bowl, whisk together the eggs, milk, salt, ¾ cup syrup, Sucanat, vanilla, cinnamon, cardamom, and agar-agar until smooth and well combined.

Place the reserved noodle mixture in a 9 x 12-inch baking pan and add the egg mixture, covering the noodles well. Bake, covered, for 1 hour. Remove and let cool for 5–10 minutes.

Preparation and cooking time 20 minutes.

Baking time 1 hour 10 minutes.

Cooling time 20 minutes.

Serves 10–12. (Makes 12–16 squares.)

Adapted from Sophie Levitt's kitchen, this kugel has all the richness of the traditional noodle pudding that's served on holidays and special occasions. It can be part of a meal, a sweet appetizer, or a satisfying dessert. Since kugel is very rich, a little goes a long way.

Meanwhile, in a small bowl, mix together well the preserves, orange juice, and ¼ cup syrup to make a glaze. Gently pour the glaze on top of the slightly cooled noodle mixture and smooth out with a spoon or spatula. Bake for 10 minutes more. Let cool for 10 minutes. Cut into small squares and serve.

COOKING FOR THE KIDS

Chapter 15

ANYBODY WHO READ the Mrs. Piggle Wiggle books while growing up will remember her magic tonics that tasted like vanilla ice cream and helped cure children of their bad habits, such as gossiping, bullying, and "crybabyitis."

Many of us still wish for secret ingredients to restore our balance and health. And now we're searching for the magical kinds of foods that not only delight our children, but also provide optimal nutrition and wholesomeness for them. Fortunately, many supermarkets now support that quest, providing organic vegetables, tofu hot dogs, honey-sweetened cereals with almonds and raisins, whole-grain breads, fresh sprouts, and many other healthful foods.

Incorporating elements of vegetarianism in kids' diets requires a creative approach to working with their nutritional needs, while dealing with their often hyped-up romance with burgers and fast foods. But there are many delicious and enjoyable whole foods that you can prepare to perk up their meals and to restore your confidence that they're getting what they need.

Luckily, cooking for kids is a simple rather than a complex affair. In general, children prefer fewer spices, lighter amounts of cooking oil, and ingredients that are easy to digest, yet captivating to the taste buds. Their nutritional needs can be met by a steady diet of complex and simple carbohydrates, with an emphasis on beans, grains, breads, pasta, and vegetables and good-quality protein, fats, and oils. In this chapter, we present some simple, but popular recipes for entrées, vegetable dishes, snacks, quick and easy breakfasts, and some winning lunch-box items to accompany kids to school.

For other favorites, see the "Pizza Magic" section in Chapter 5; children love our gourmet pizza and often take pride in helping put it together. Chapter 10 provides a wonderful selection of breads for the lunch-box sandwiches included in this chapter, and Chapter 11 has many dessert options that kids will happily devour without giving one thought to wholesomeness.

MUESLI IN THE MORNING

1 cup rolled oats
1½ cups milk, soymilk, or oat milk
1¼ cups raisins or dates

In a medium-sized bowl, cover the oats with the milk and add the raisins. Let stand for at least 15 minutes, preferably 1 hour, or soak overnight in the refrigerator.

Stir and serve immediately.

Variation: Add chopped apples or your favorite chopped nuts.

Preparation time 20 minutes.

Soaking time overnight (optional).

Serves 1–2.

This cereal can be prepared ahead of time, and it's unbelievably simple — no cooking or fuss. Try it without sweeteners first and see if your children are satisfied by the sweetness of just raisins or dates.

**Preparation time
10 minutes.**

**Baking time
5–7 minutes.**

**Serves 4–6. (Makes
8 waffles or 8–10
pancakes.)**

*This delightful
recipe for waffles or
pancakes uses
freshly ground oat
flour, which makes
a surprisingly light,
airy waffle or pan-
cake. (Make your
own oat flour by
using a coffee
grinder or food
processor to grind
rolled oats to a fine
powder.) If you have
a child who's intol-
erant of wheat or
dairy, this is an
excellent breakfast
or snack option.*

OAT WAFFLES

1–2 tablespoons canola oil for waffle iron or
   skillet
2 eggs, beaten
2 cups oat flour*
1⅔ cups milk, rice milk, or soymilk

Preheat a well-oiled waffle iron or a medium-sized skillet. In a medium-sized bowl, combine the eggs, flour, and
milk and mix together well with a whisk or wooden
spoon.

Ladle the batter into the waffle iron and bake for 5–7
minutes or until golden brown, or ladle into a skillet to
form 3-inch circles and cook until bubbles form. Turn
the pancakes and cook until golden brown. Serve immediately with your favorite topping.

*Oat flour is available in natural foods stores and specialty mar-
kets.*

BLUEBERRY-BANANA SMOOTHIE

Preparation time 5 minutes.

Serves 2–3.

This smoothie makes a tasty after-school snack and is also great on top of cereal or granola.

1 cup fresh or frozen blueberries
1 large banana
1½ cups cold milk, rice milk, or soymilk
1 tablespoon pure maple syrup (optional)

In a blender or food processor, combine all of the ingredients and blend on medium-high for 30 seconds or until smooth and frothy. Serve immediately.

Variation:
For an even cooler smoothie, use a frozen banana. Peel the banana, place in a sealable, freezer bag and freeze for several hours or overnight.

For a crunchy smoothie, add ¼ cup chopped walnuts and blend well.

*This is the closest
we get to chicken-
rice soup, and it
genuinely delights
children. Using a
light miso, such as
barley or mellow
white, gives a mild,
slightly sweet flavor.
If using cold leftover
rice, add the rice
when you add the
carrots, so it can
warm up suffi-
ciently.*

LIGHT MISO SOUP WITH RICE

5 cups water
½ cup julienned carrots
½ cup sliced celery
½ cup small broccoli florets
2 tablespoons white miso or barley miso
1 cup cooked brown or white rice
½ cup chopped scallions (optional)

In a large saucepan, bring the water to a boil. Add the
carrots and celery and cook for 6–8 minutes. Add the
broccoli after 6 minutes and cook for 4–6 minutes more,
or until all of the vegetables are well cooked.

Dilute the miso in 1 cup of the broth and return the diluted miso to the saucepan. Reduce heat to simmer. Stir
in the rice and scallions and cook for 10 minutes. Serve
immediately.

Variation: Use cooked dried noodles instead of the rice.

CARROT-BEET-POTATO TOSS

Preparation and cooking time 1 hour.

Serves 4.

1 cup diced carrots
1 cup diced fresh beets
1 cup diced potatoes
1¼ cups water
½ teaspoon salt
1½ tablespoons butter

In a medium-sized saucepan, combine the carrots, beets, potatoes, and water and bring to a boil. Reduce heat to medium-low. Add the salt. Cook for 45 minutes, or until the vegetables are very soft. (Check occasionally to prevent burning.)

Drain the vegetables and toss with the butter before serving. Serve immediately.

Variation: Melt light mozzarella cheese or Parmesan cheese on the top of the vegetables before serving.

Although some children shy away from vegetables, there are ways to make vegetables attractive and fun to eat. The trick in this recipe is to dice all of the vegetables into very small, same-sized pieces. When the vegetables cook together, they all take on one color, and the kids can play a guessing game of which vegetables are carrots, beets, or potatoes.

Preparation and cooking time 30 minutes.

Serves 4.

Easy and quick to prepare, this recipe has cheese as its winning ingredient. This vegetable mixture is great stuffed in pita bread or rolled up in a tortilla!

CAULIFLOWER, CARROT, AND CELERY SAUTÉ

1½ cups chopped cauliflower
1 cup julienned carrots
1 cup diced celery
½ tablespoon olive oil or canola oil
Pinch salt
½ cup shredded soy cheese or dairy cheese

In a large, covered saucepan with a steamer basket, steam all of the vegetables in water for 5–7 minutes or until tender-crisp. Remove and set aside.

In a large skillet, heat the oil on medium-high heat and sauté the reserved steamed vegetables for 5 minutes or until lightly browned.

Stir in the salt. Add the cheese after 4 minutes. Coat the vegetables with the cheese and cover for 5–10 minutes. Serve immediately.

Broccoli Bagel Melt

Here's an easy, tasty sandwich that gets kids to eat their broccoli.

1 cup broccoli florets
2 bagels, sliced
Mayonnaise or prepared mustard
4 slices fresh tomato (optional)
4 slices cheese (American, Muenster, or Swiss)

In a small, covered saucepan, steam the broccoli in water for 5–10 minutes or until tender-crisp. Remove and set aside.

Spread the bagel halves with the mayonnaise and place the reserved steamed broccoli on the bagels. Top with a slice of tomato and a slice of cheese.

Toast in a toaster oven or broil for 3–5 minutes. Serve immediately.

These are oven-baked fries, low in oil. They're quick to prepare and very tasty. Since adults love these as much as kids, one baking sheet may not be enough, so consider preparing more potatoes for a second round.

BAKED FRENCH FRIES

3 large potatoes
2 tablespoons olive or canola oil
1½ teaspoons salt

Preheat oven to 400°F. If the potatoes are badly marked or starting to sprout, peel them. Otherwise, wash and leave in their skins. Thinly slice the potatoes lengthwise, then slice again to make long, fairly flat fries.

Coat a baking sheet with the oil. Spread out the potatoes on the sheet and sprinkle with the salt. Bake for 20–25 minutes, turning once. (For crispier fries, place under the broiler for the last 3 minutes of cooking.) Serve immediately.

Rice Balls

½ cup uncooked brown rice
2 tablespoons dried lentils
¼ cup finely chopped yams or carrots
½ cup finely chopped fresh broccoli or
  green beans
1½ cups water

Wash the rice and lentils. In a medium-sized saucepan, combine all of the ingredients and bring to a boil. Reduce heat to simmer and cook, covered, for 30–40 minutes, or until the rice and lentils are soft. Let cool slightly.

Using a baby food grinder, grind the mixture, and place in a bowl. Roll the mixture into nickel-sized balls and place within your child's reach. Watch them vanish!

Variation: Use other vegetables to create different combinations.

Preparation and cooking time 1 hour.

Cooling time variable.

Makes 2–3 meals for infants or toddlers.

Here's a great way to feed toddlers nutritious grain, beans, and vegetables in a form that's compelling and easy to grab. These rice balls quickly disappear when the 7–11-months age group gets ahold of them.

LUNCH-BOX SPECIALS

Send your child to school with a variety of healthy, but popular sandwiches and snacks.

Preparation and cooking time 1 hour 30 minutes.

Soaking time overnight.

Serves 4.

The secret to getting kids to eat chickpeas is to cook them for a very long time. The chickpeas then taste almost sweet and are very easy to digest.

CHICKPEA DELIGHT SANDWICH

½ cup dried chickpeas, or
  1½ cups canned chickpeas, well rinsed
2 cups water
1 teaspoon salt
¼ cup finely chopped celery
¼ cup finely chopped scallions (optional)
⅓–½ cup finely chopped dill pickles
5 tablespoons mayonnaise
½ teaspoon ground paprika
Bread slices

Wash the chickpeas. Soak overnight or use the quick-soak method (see page 128).

In a large saucepan, combine the soaked chickpeas and water and bring to a boil. Reduce heat to simmer and cook, stirring occasionally, for 1 hour, or until the chickpeas are soft. Add the salt. Cook for at least 15 minutes more. Drain. In a large bowl, mash the chickpeas with a large fork or potato masher. Mix in the celery, scallions, pickles, mayonnaise, and paprika.

Spread the mixture on the bread. Serve or wrap tightly with plastic wrap for lunch box.

AVOCADO AND CHEESE SANDWICH

1 ripe avocado, peeled, sliced, and dipped in
  lemon juice
4 slices cheese (American, Muenster, or Swiss)
4–6 thin slices fresh tomato
1 cup fresh alfalfa sprouts or to taste
4 tablespoons mayonnaise
8 slices whole-wheat bread

Put all of the ingredients together into sandwiches. Serve
or wrap tightly in plastic wrap for lunch box.

PITA WABBITS

4–6 tablespoons mayonnaise
4 whole-wheat pita bread pockets, or
  8 slices bread
4 servings fresh salad ingredients:
  sliced lettuce, tomatoes, and cucumbers,
  sprouts, small broccoli florets, fresh spinach,
  grated carrots, grated beets

Place liberal amounts of the mayonnaise in the pita pockets or on the bread. Kids can stuff their own pockets or
put the salad inside bread slices. Serve or wrap tightly
with plastic wrap for lunch box. (If your child has a long
wait until lunch, you may want to wrap the salad ingredients separately, so the bread doesn't get soggy.)

**Preparation time
5–10 minutes.
Serves 4.**

*I was informed by two
young boys in the
Kripalu community
that the only sandwich
choice for their crowd is
avocado and cheese on
whole wheat (though
one boy holds out for
Wonder Bread).*

**Preparation time
5–10 minutes.
Serves 4.**

*Make this sandwich
look like a "wabbit" by
placing cucumber ears
and sprout whiskers in
the pita bread.*

*Let the kids roast
the sunflower seeds
and help combine
the ingredients.
Serve with tomatoes
and lettuce in pita
bread.*

SUNNY TOFU SPREAD

1 pound soft tofu, rinsed and drained
⅓ cup finely chopped carrots
1½ tablespoons tahini
1½ tablespoons umeboshi vinegar
1½ tablespoons tamari
¼ cup roasted sunflower seeds (see page 167)
2 teaspoons rice syrup
2 teaspoons prepared mustard

In a medium-sized bowl, combine all of the ingredients and mash with a fork until well combined.

Make sandwiches and serve or wrap tightly in plastic wrap for lunch box.

*Avocados are an
excellent source of
protein. Use this
spread also as a dip
with corn chips or
raw vegetables.*

AVOCADO SPREAD

1 large ripe avocado, peeled, or
  1½ medium avocados, peeled
⅓ cup diced fresh tomatoes
⅓ cup diced cucumbers
1 teaspoon umeboshi vinegar
¼ teaspoon salt
½ tablespoon fresh lemon juice
1 tablespoon mayonnaise

In a medium-sized bowl, mash the avocado with a fork. Add the remaining ingredients and mix together until well combined. Serve immediately or make sandwiches.

ALMOND-DATE ROLLS

2 cups slivered almonds
½ cup shredded coconut
1 cup chopped pitted dried dates
¾ cup raisins
¾ cup golden raisins
1 teaspoon ground cardamom

Roast the almonds in the oven (see instructions on page 132). Remove and set aside. Let cool. In a food processor, briefly chop the cooled almonds.

Toast the coconut in the oven (see instructions on page 228). Remove and set aside. Let cool.

In a food processor, combine half of the dates and half of both types of raisins. Pulse on and off until the mixture begins to blend. (If needed, add a small amount of water to help blending.) While blending, gradually add the remaining dates and raisins through the feed tube.

When the fruit is thoroughly blended and pastelike in consistency, add the cooled almonds and the cardamom. Process until the mixture congeals in a ball.

Place the cooled coconut in a shallow baking pan or on a baking sheet. Roll the date-almond mixture into one-inch balls, then roll and cover in the coconut. Serve or chill until ready to serve.

Preparation time
15 minutes.

Baking time
10–15 minutes.

Cooling time
variable.

Chilling time
variable.

Makes 25 balls.

Take some chopped dates and almonds, combine them with two kinds of raisins, roll them in coconut, and you've captured the tasty simplicity of Almond-Date Rolls.

*Here's the perfect
treat for kids for any
day you're wanting
crunchy snacks
without too much
effort.*

PEANUT CRISPY CLUSTERS

3½ ounces organic, sweetened milk chocolate
   or carob
½ cup crispy brown rice cereal
¼ cup roasted blanched peanuts
   (see page 132, substitute peanuts for almonds)
¼ cup toasted shredded coconut (see page 228)

In a double boiler, melt the chocolate on medium heat.
(Turn off heat as soon as the chocolate melts. Do not
overheat.)

Add the cereal, peanuts, and coconut and stir together
until well coated. Drop the mixture by teaspoonful onto
a very lightly oiled baking sheet and refrigerate until the
clusters are hard. Serve or continue to chill until ready to
serve.

DINNERTIME FOR KIDS

Here are four main-meal offerings that are child-friendly and easy to prepare.

KENTUCKY FRIED TOFU

2 pounds firm tofu, rinsed, drained, and cut
  into ¼-inch thick slices
½ cup tamari
1 cup nutritional yeast
½ cup cornmeal or unbleached white flour
2–3 tablespoons canola oil

In a medium-sized bowl, drench and coat the tofu slices well with the tamari. In a separate bowl, mix together the yeast and cornmeal and coat each tofu slice thoroughly with the yeast mixture.

In a well-heated cast-iron skillet, heat 2 tablespoons of the oil and brown the tofu slices on one side, then turn, and brown the other side. Sprinkle more of the yeast mixture on the top side and turn again, adding the remaining oil to the skillet. Brown only that side.

When the tofu is crunchy, serve immediately.

Preparation and cooking time 30 minutes.

Serves 4.

This dish uses a combination of nutritional yeast and cornmeal to provide a wonderfully crunchy crust for the tofu. The secret to this recipe is to brown the tofu on three sides!

Preparation and cooking time
1 hour 30 minutes.

Baking time
30–40 minutes.

Soaking time
1 hour.

Serves 4–6.

Here's an all-time favorite dish brought up-to-date by adding tofu frankfurters. These healthy franks are fast becoming very popular with kids. Cooked with navy beans, mustard, and maple syrup, this dish is a plentiful source of protein.

TOFU FRANKS AND BEANS

1½ cups dried navy beans
6 cups water
2 teaspoons salt
⅓ cup ketchup
¼ cup water
2½ tablespoons prepared mustard
1 tablespoon Sucanat (granulated cane juice)
1 tablespoon pure maple syrup
4 tofu frankfurters, cooked and cut into
  ½-inch lengths*

Wash the beans. In a large saucepan, combine the beans and 2 cups of the water and bring to a boil. Turn off heat, cover, and let soak for 1 hour. Drain and return the beans to the saucepan.

Add the remaining water to the beans and bring to a boil. Reduce heat to medium and cook for 1 hour. Add 1 teaspoon of the salt. Cook for 15–20 minutes more, or until the beans are very soft.

Preheat oven to 375°F. Stir in the remaining salt, the ketchup, ¼ cup water, mustard, Sucanat, syrup, and franks and mix together well. Place the mixture in a baking dish, cover, and bake for 30–40 minutes. Serve immediately.

Tofu frankfurters are available in natural foods stores, specialty markets, and many supermarkets.

CHEESE-SEITAN STROGANOFF

Preparation and cooking time 35 minutes.

Serves 4.

This is a great introduction to seitan, a tasty wheat-gluten product that tastes like meat. Prepared in this dish with lots of noodles, peas, and cheese (soy or dairy), it's a sure-fire hit.

8 ounces dried ribbon egg noodles
¼ cup butter
1½ cups sliced onions
2 cups cubed seitan
1 cup diced carrots
½ tablespoon dried tarragon
2½ cups milk or soymilk
⅓ cup unbleached white flour
½ cup grated soy cheese or dairy cheese
1 cup cooked peas
½ tablespoon salt
¼ teaspoon ground nutmeg

In a large saucepan, cook the noodles in boiling water until tender but still firm. Drain, rinse, and set aside.

In a large, deep skillet, melt the butter and sauté the onions for 3–5 minutes or until translucent. Add the seitan and carrots and sauté for 10 minutes. Stir in the tarragon and remove from heat.

In a medium-sized saucepan, heat the milk and whisk in the flour, stirring constantly, until smooth. Add the cheese and stir until well blended.

In the skillet, combine the reserved noodles, seitan mixture, milk mixture, peas, salt, and nutmeg. Heat through until hot and well combined. Serve immediately.

**Preparation and
cooking time
40 minutes.**

Serves 4.

*Many seasoned
cooks find that their
children pass up
gourmet offerings
for simpler fare.
This easy, one-pot
meal may not win
any fancy awards,
but it may become
your kids' favorite.*

BASMATI, TOFU, AND BROCCOLI

1 cup uncooked white basmati rice
½ cup rinsed, drained, and diced firm tofu
1¾ cups water
1 cup chopped broccoli
½ teaspoon salt
2 tablespoons unsalted butter or ghee
  (see page 325)

Wash and drain the rice. In a medium-sized saucepan, combine the rice, tofu, and water and bring to a boil. Reduce heat to medium-low and add the broccoli and salt.

Cover and cook for 15 minutes. Add the butter and cook, covered, for 5–7 minutes more. Remove from heat and let stand, covered, for 5 minutes. Serve immediately.

MENU PLANNING

Chapter 16

"WHAT'S FOR DINNER?" is probably the second most frequently asked question in families, but for me, the most frequently asked question is asked by the cook: "What shall I make for dinner?"

When Kuntal and I vacationed on Cape Cod with our families, I marveled at the effortless manner that she pulled together a taco dinner of tortillas, beans, rice, and all of the trimmings. I realized that, despite how often I cook, it rarely occurs to me to make tacos or burritos, because of the fuss I imagine that they involve. Instead, my mind travels along well-established routes. Around 5:00 P.M., I start thinking about making a pasta dish for dinner; then rice and tofu with stir-fried vegetables occurs to me, then the baked-potato-with-salad option. No more than five or six choices go through my mind at that critical moment.

Often we lack the time or energy to create surprising, new dishes and menu items every week; or, perhaps, in a frenzy of turning over a new culinary leaf, we scout up some new recipes, only to discover when it's time to cook that we can't find the information that we so diligently gathered.

This chapter provides a solution to the "what to cook?" dilemma. Everything is here at your fingertips; all you have to do is identify the season, the mood you're in, and the amount of time available, and you're on your way. Two weeklong menus are provided, one for the autumn/winter season and one for spring/summer. There are also collections of quick-cooking choices, ethnic/regional dishes, and special holiday meals.

PRINCIPLES OF MEAL PLANNING

An important principle of meal planning is to include a wide spectrum of food flavors and textures with the understanding that while we eat to be nourished, we also eat for flavor and taste. Using foods with a wide array of tastes also helps us to include most of the nutrients that are needed for a balanced diet.

At Kripalu, we frequently use the guide to planning and flavoring foods featured below. It was developed by Hansaraj, a longtime Kripalu chef, and it contains information about the flavors and qualities of foods to use in combination and about the nutritional components of vegetarian foods.

A Cook's Guide to Planning and Flavoring Foods

A balance of flavors, qualities, and nutritional components comprise every well-planned meal. Use this guide to select ingredients for cooking a particular dish or to balance a dish if certain elements have been used in excess.

Flavors

Sweet: sweeteners, coriander, cardamom, basil, nutmeg, mirin.

Sour: citrus, vinegars, pickles, tamarind, umeboshi.

Salty: pickles, tamari, soy sauce, miso, kelp, dulse, bouillon, umeboshi.

Bitter: dark greens, parsley, grapefruit, sesame seeds, fenugreek seeds.

Pungent: gingerroot, garlic, pepper, scallions, hot spices.

Qualities

Heavy: cheese, seitan, casserole, mashed.

Light: parsley, celery, alfalfa sprouts, salad, tossed.

Smooth: tahini, puree, blended.

Crunchy: nuts, seeds, coconut, cereal, grain, topping, roasted.

Thick: kuzu, arrowroot, gel, agar-agar, sauce, roux.

Thin: liquid, juice, broth, boiled.

Moist: oil, marinade, dressed.

Dry: flour, crust, baked.

Nutritional Components

Protein: tofu, tempeh, seitan, yogurt, cheese, beans, nuts, seeds, eggs.

Complex Carbohydrates: rice, millet, oats, flours, pasta, beans, potatoes, roots, winter squash, bread, toast.

Simple Carbohydrates: fresh fruit, fruit juices, cooked fruit, dried fruit, carrot juice, beet juice, jellies, jams, sweeteners.

Fats/Oils: nuts, seeds, tahini, nut butters, cheese, yogurt, vegetable oils, sour cream, ghee, butter, whole milk, cream, coconut oil, lecithin, palm oil.

Water: broth, soak water, mineral water, tea, coffee, sauces, smoothies, juices.

> ## HOW TO BALANCE FLAVORS IN A DISH
> - ***Too salty:*** *add sour or water (or tofu or potato).*
> - ***Too sweet:*** *add salt and a touch of bitter and/or sour.*
> - ***Too pungent:*** *add oil, salt, and a touch of sweet.*
> - ***Too sour:*** *add sweet and a touch of bitter.*
> - ***Too bitter:*** *increase all of the other flavors — easy on pungent.*

Although the foods listed above can often be placed in more than one category, the guide helps identify the major components in the vegetarian diet. Use the guide in cooking to balance qualities by adding foods or using techniques that emphasize a complementary quality. For instance, if a dish turns out too thick, add liquid (thin). If it's too dry, add oil (moist) by marinating, sautéing, or dressing the dish. If it's too heavy, lighten it with some fresh parsley or lightly cooked celery.

FOOD COMBINING

Volumes have been written about which foods should be eaten together and which combinations should be avoided to maximize nutrition and minimize indigestion. Different schools of thought abound, and there is no single approach that can take into account everyone's needs, which vary with considerations of age and constitution, as well as with preferences and beliefs about nutrition. So I offer very general guidelines, aware that even some of the menus in this chapter may go beyond what might be considered optimal food combining.

> ## GENERAL FOOD-COMBINING GUIDELINES
> ***1. Fruits are best eaten alone or with other fruits.***
>
> ***2. Vegetables and proteins combine well.***
>
> ***3. Grains and vegetables combine very well.***

Basically, food combining is a question of timing — the less complex the food, the less time it takes to break down in the digestive tract. Fruits and simple sugars are digested quickly, vegetables relatively quickly. Grains take more time, and oils and heavy proteins the most time. It's best to avoid combining foods that are digested quickly with those that take a long time to digest, because such combinations set up a scenario for fermentation, gas, and bloating.

There are also nutrient-combining considerations. Grains and vegetables are sources of incomplete protein; they contain many, but not all, of the different amino acids that the body needs to synthesize human protein. Eating different sources of incomplete protein together makes for complete protein.

PREPARING FOOD AHEAD

Many of our recipes can be prepared in advance and can be frozen, defrosted, and served during a busy week. Particularly suitable are stews and similar dishes, such as *Seitan Stew, Tofu Stew, Chickpea Stew, Seitan Stroganoff,* and *Tofu Pot Pie.* A number of pasta dishes can also be prepared ahead, including *Baked Macaroni and Cheese Casserole, Squasharoni, Noodle Pie,* and *Spinach-Cheese Lasagna.* Also, try *Berkshire Pie, Tofu-Spinach Quiche,* and *Bulgur-Walnut Loaf.* In addition, consult the menus for special occasions in this chapter; many of the recipes can be cooked in advance, frozen, then defrosted on the special day.

MENUS

Below are two weeks of menus for breakfast, lunch, and dinner. They are divided into two seasons: spring/summer and autumn/winter. The spring/summer menus include lighter, easier to digest foods, including summer vegetables and fruits, salads, dips, pastas, and grains. The autumn/winter menus include dishes that are more complex. They take longer to digest, help stave off the cold, and include warming grains and beans and winter squashes and vegetables.

SPRING/ SUMMER MENUS

BREAKFAST
Apple-Banana Smoothie, 41
Almond Coffee Cake, 38

LUNCH
White Bean-Escarole Soup, 55
Chickpea of the Sea, 186
Mixed Greens with Carrot-Ginger
Dressing, 210

DINNER
Pad Thai Noodles with Spiced
Peanut Sauce, 104, 75
Collards with Brown Rice Vinegar
and Tamari, 167

BREAKFAST
Basmati Rice Pudding, 30
Chandrakant's Secret Chai Recipe,
324

LUNCH
Potato-Leek Soup, 50
Vegetarian Caesar Salad, 175

DINNER
Noodle Pie, 111
Spinach, Radicchio, and Watercress
Salad with Lemon-Sesame Dressing,
177, 218

BREAKFAST
Cantaloupe-Honeydew Juice, 205
Oatmeal-Nut Scones, or
Banana-Walnut Muffins, 37, 35
Tea

LUNCH
Grilled Tofu Cubes with Sweet
Mustard Sauce, 89, 77
Tabouli, 191
Mama D's Coleslaw, 184
Earth Bread, 237

DINNER
Baked Macaroni and Cheese
Casserole, or Squasharoni,
106, 108
Arame with Spinach, 169
Baked Onions, 156
Swedish Ginger Cookies, 292

BREAKFAST
Amasake French Toast, 34

Raisin Sauce, 31

Tea

LUNCH
Carrot-Ginger Soup with
Chives, 47

Spiced Basmati Rice, 319

Vegetable Masamba, 152

DINNER
Tofu-Basil Lasagna, 102

Mixed Greens with Balsamic
Vinaigrette, 220

Everything Bread, 237

Strawberry Mousse, 295

BREAKFAST
Muesli, 26

Boston Brown Bread, 256

Tea

LUNCH
Creamy Zucchini Soup, 51

Hummus Among Us, 201

Carrot and celery sticks

Tabouli, 191

DINNER
Grilled Tempeh with Broccoli, 96

Red Onions and Dulse, 155

Tossed Salad with Cool Cucumber
Dressing, 209

BREAKFAST
Hot Cinnamon Soymilk
Pudding, 293

Toasted Anadama Bread, 240

Ginger-Sage Tea, 42

LUNCH
Pasta Primavera Salad, 194

Green Beans and Garlic, 374

DINNER
Southern Fried Tofu, 91

Scalloped Potatoes, 160

Confetti Kale, 168

Peach Pie, 270

BREAKFAST
Pineapple-Grapefruit Juice, 205

Pan Corn Bread, or Poppy
Seed Bread, 253, 260

LUNCH
Cauliflower-Cheddar Cheese Soup,
48
Cold Sesame Noodles, 196
Grilled Vegetable Medley, 149

DINNER
Broccoli-Walnut Polenta, 87
Chicory Salad with Sesame Dressing,
178

AUTUMN/ WINTER MENUS

BREAKFAST
Oatmeal
Toasted Raisin Bread, 241
Tea

LUNCH
Black Bean Soup, 54
Tofu Reuben, 118

DINNER
Spinach-Cheese Lasagna, 100
Tossed Salad with Walnut-Miso
Dressing, 214
Pecan Sandies, 291

BREAKFAST
Apple Crisp, or Oatmeal-Nut
Scones with jam, 40, 37
Tea

LUNCH
Vegetable Creole, 150
Khichari, 323

DINNER
Berkshire Pie, 110
Mixed Greens with Pumpkin
Seed Dressing, 215
Eight-Grain Bread with
butter, 244

BREAKFAST
Carrot, Celery, and Apple
Juice, 205
Scrambled Tofu, 32
Soysage, 33

LUNCH
Cream of Tomato Soup, 52
New Orleans Subs, 388

DINNER

White Miso-Ginger Soup, 58

Kung Pao Tempeh, 98

Indonesian Rice Salad, 192

Beet Nishime, 157

BREAKFAST

Millet-Carrot Cereal, 27

Banana Bread, or Bavarian Bread,
257, 239

Tea

LUNCH

Bulgur-Walnut Loaf, 135

Baked Wakame and Vegetables, 153

Roasted Rosemary Red Potatoes, 159

DINNER

Tomato-Cheese, White, or Broccoli-
Pesto Pizza, 121, 122, 122

Mixed Greens with Umeboshi Scallion
Dressing, 216

BREAKFAST

Spiced Yogurt Nog, 41

Cranberry-Mandarin Muffins, 36

LUNCH

Split Pea Soup, 57

Tofu Pot Pie, 112

DINNER

Red Lentil Pâté, 140

Asapao Rice, 130

Cajun Turnips and Greens, 166

BREAKFAST

Yogurt with sliced fruit

Almond Coffee Cake, 38

Tea

LUNCH

Millet Croquettes with
Beet-Horseradish Sauce, 136

Umeboshi Cabbage Wedges, 158

Whole-Wheat Sourdough Bread,
251

DINNER

French Onion Soup, 49

Spaghetti Squash with Tofu and
Autumn Gravy, 338

Mixed Greens with Green Goddess
Dressing, 224

Wheat-free Gingerbread Cake, 281

BREAKFAST
Tomato-Celery Juice, 205
Upma Cereal, 28
Toasted Whole-Wheat Bread with
cream cheese, 236

LUNCH
Shepherd's Pie, 332
Carrot-Currant Salad, 183

DINNER
Tofu Pot Pie, 112
Mixed Greens with Umeboshi
Beet Dressing, 211
Mocha Walnut Cake, 276

QUICK COOKING:
7 DINNERS IN 30 MINUTES

For those times when you need to make something magically appear.

1.
*Fettuccine with Sun-Dried
Tomatoes and Feta Cheese, 109
Green Beans and Garlic, 374*

2.
*Tofu Reuben, 118
Cucumber-Dulse Salad, 179*

3.
*Southern-Fried Tofu, 91
Herbed Brown Basmati Rice, 129*

4.
*Tofu in Orange Pepper Sauce, 92
Soba Noodles with Arame, 170*

5.
*Udons in Miso with Daikon and
Watercress, 358
Tossed Salad with French
Dressing, 221*

6.
*Tempeh Barbecue, 99
Collards with Brown Rice Vinegar
and Tamari, 167*

7.
*Eggplant Provençal, 86
Mixed Greens and Orange
Salad, 176*

ETHNIC/REGIONAL MENUS

Here are menus that feature the flavors of the South, Asia, and the Mediterranean. Each menu is composed of recipes that deliciously complement each other.

CAJUN

Greens Gumbo, 66
Red and Black Bean Chili, 64
Jambalaya Rice, 131
New Orleans Greens Salad, 173
Jalapeño-Cheese Corn Bread, 254
Pecan Pie, 274

MEXICAN

Mexican Corn Chowder, 63
White Bean-Tortilla Casserole, 361
House Salsa, 227
Almond Rice, 132
Guacamole, 200
Garnishes of lettuce, olives, tomatoes, onions
Tofu Sour Cream, 79

JAPANESE

Tofu Yung, 95
Seitan Teriyaki, 346
Norimake Casserole, 384
Plum Sauce, or Sweet Mustard Sauce, 76, 77
Cinnamon Soymilk Pudding, 293

INDIAN

Madrasi Red Lentil Dahl, 306
Gujarati Mixed Vegetables, 308
Punjabi Cucumber Raita, 311
Golden Basmati Rice, 312
Cilantro Chutney, 310
Shiro, 313

ITALIAN

Italian Lentil Soup, 56
Antipasto, 199
Linguine in Red Vegetable Sauce, or in Uncle Pasquale's Marinara Sauce, 354, 70
Mixed Greens with Tofu Cheese and Creamy Italian Dressing, 198, 225
Focàccia Bread, 247
Rain Forest Bars, 287

GREEK

Couscous with Chickpeas and Lemon Tahini Sauce, 138, 77
Greek Salad, 174
Dolmati, 390
Tofu-Spinach Triangles, 342
Almond-Date Rolls, 407

Holiday Feasts

Here are eight full menus for holidays and special occasions. Since these require more elaborate preparation, you will need to gather the recipes and plan your shopping and cooking time, so everything is ready on the big day. Consider dividing the menu among those items that can be cooked and stored well in advance, those that need to be made the day before (e.g. baked goods), and those that must be made on the day of the event (e.g. barbecued items and tossed salads). Be sure that you have adequate cookware and storage containers; it helps to have casserole dishes or baking pans that you can easily transfer from refrigerator to oven to table.

Spring Solstice Party

Light and Lively Stir-Fry with Tofu, 344
Wild Rice Pilaf, 133
Tricolor Terrine, 330
Tossed Salad with Feta-Garlic Dressing, 223
Herb Biscuits, 255
Black Forest Cake, 277

June Graduation

Baked Tofu with Mushrooms and Scallions, 94
Indian Home Fries, 316
Steamed Asparagus with Tofu Hollandaise Sauce, 78
French Baguettes, 249
Strawberry-Rhubarb Pie, 267

Fourth of July Picnic

Cheese-Nut Burgers, 117
Mardi Gras Slaw, 185
Potato Salad, 190
Mixed Greens with Bleu Cheese Dressing, 222
Olive Relish, 229
Swedish Rye Bread, 246
Berry Cobbler with Vanilla Custard Sauce, 276, 298

Labor Day Barbecue

Easy Gazpacho, 366
Seitan Kabobs, 371
Roasted Portabella Mushrooms, Peppers, and Zucchini, 381

Rice and Wheat Berry Salad,
193
Mardi Gras Slaw, 185
Chocolate Chip Supremes, or
Maple Oatmeal-Raisin Cookies
with vanilla ice cream,
289, 290

THANKSGIVING DINNER

Golden Brown Tofu, 90
Sweet Rice and Chestnuts, 134
Grilled Vegetable Medley,
149
Mashed Millet with Cauliflower,
352
Autumn Gravy, 80
Herbed Cheese Bread, 242
Pumpkin-Chocolate Pie, 272

HANUKKAH DINNER

Hot Beet Borscht with Sour Cream,
376
Potato Latkes, 379
Mixed Greens with Parsley-Garlic
Dressing, 219
Stuffed Cabbage in Tomato-Raisin
Sauce, 377

Kasha Varnishkas with
Shiitake Mushroom Gravy,
356
Apricot Kugel, 391

CHRISTMAS DINNER

Seitan Stroganoff, 88
Herb Biscuits, 255
Confetti Kale, 168
Baked Onions, 156
Candied Yams, 164
Peasant French Bread, 248
Mocha Walnut Cake
with Soy Cream,
276, 299

NEW YEAR'S DAY BRUNCH

Pineapple-Grapefruit Juice, 205
Tofu-Spinach Quiche, 114
Toasted bagels
Carrot-Cashew Spread, or Tofu,
Olive, and Scallion Spread,
202, 203
Fig Bread, or Prune Bread,
258, 259
Chandrakant's Secret Chai Recipe,
324

HERE'S TO THE CHEF AND A SATISFYING DINING EXPERIENCE!

Chapter 17

NOW THAT YOU have prepared some of the healthy and delicious recipes in this book, you are ready to eat. But before you sit down to enjoy the fruits of your labor, there's something to be said about eating and about preparing yourself to enjoy the food you have wholeheartedly prepared.

At Kripalu, we practice what we call "conscious eating." Conscious eating means, among other things, chewing carefully and completely, so that food is adequately prepared for digestion and assimilation. Another aspect of conscious eating involves paying attention to the signals of the body about what kind and how much food it needs at any particular time. If you're not paying attention to your body's messages, you're much more likely to eat out of habit or from the temporary stimulation caused by external messages, such as advertising and social convention.

Here's a personal example of an *un*conscious dining experience. I was up early for a workshop that I was leading at Kripalu. Because my assistant was sick, I knew I'd have to hurry to prepare the program room and my teaching materials before the participants arrived. Feeling a bit frantic, I rushed into the Kripalu dining room to get some breakfast. I grabbed a bowl of rice cereal, topped with raisin sauce, tahini, and wheat germ and sat down, attempting to review my lesson plan and gulp down my cereal at the same time.

Suddenly, I nearly gagged. In my haste, I had mistakenly taken a huge serving of miso; instead of raisin sauce. Imagine my shock at tasting something so salty when I was expecting something sweet. Forced to stop what I was doing, I belatedly decided to pay attention to what was on my plate.

How often do we really pay attention to what's on our plate? If you cook a lot, you have probably watched with sad amusement as the meal you so painstakingly prepared in an hour was wolfed down in five minutes. We often have buried the act of eating under distracting routines of radio, TV, phone conversations, newspaper reading, grocery list writing, and refereeing fights among the children.

In truth, eating deserves the same attention and concentration needed to make any activity—be it playing the piano, painting the woodwork, or writing a report—a fully satisfying experience.

FIVE TIPS FOR CONSCIOUS EATING

1. Eat When You're Hungry
We're used to eating for a variety of reasons that have little to do with physical hunger, such as avoiding stress, pacifying emotions, or overcoming boredom. Make it your goal to recognize true hunger and eat only when you experience its signals.

2. Relax Briefly Before Eating
The hunger that you experience when tense or upset is not true hunger. It is mentally induced, designed to provide an outlet for nervousness and tension. Take a few moments before a meal to relax and recognize your body's signals about what and how much to eat.

3. Eat in a Pleasant Atmosphere
Make the place where you eat attractive and just for eating. Create a relaxing environment by setting a clean, uncluttered table, lighting candles, or putting flowers on the table. At the very least, invite yourself to sit down to eat, rather than eat standing or on the run.

4. Concentrate on Chewing
Concentrating on chewing helps you to digest your food and to derive the fullest satisfaction from it.

5. Accept Your Lapses from Conscious Eating
Everyone sometimes eats too much, too little, too quickly, or too absentmindedly. Don't make it a big deal; respond with humor and understanding, using lapses as learning opportunities to help you move toward your goal of appreciating your food.

APPENDIX

GLOSSARY OF SELECTED TERMS

Aduki beans (also called azuki beans): very small, red beans that are the basis of many soups and stews. Macrobiotic and Ayurvedic cooking associate aduki beans with qualities that may help to strengthen the kidneys.

Agar-agar: a sea vegetable derivative used as a thickening agent. It creates a gel- or puddinglike texture. It is high in iodine and trace elements and has the unusual characteristic that it can be reheated and broken back down to a liquid even after it has set up, so that overgelling is easily remedied. It can be purchased in flake, bar, and powder form; the powder is the most congealing.

Ajwan: an Indian spice used in curries and vegetable dishes. A variety of wild celery seed, it is considered helpful to digestion and warming to the body.

Amaranth: a millet-sized seed gathered from a broad-leafed plant. Amaranth has been cultivated for centuries in Central and South America and the Southwestern U.S., and it has recently become very popular as a nutritious, high-protein grain.

Amasake: a drink made from the fermentation of rice. Amasake has a thick, creamy consistency, and it is often used as a sweetener for puddings, pastries, and cereals.

Arame: a thin, dark brown sea vegetable prized for its mild flavor. Arame is a good choice for people just beginning to experiment with sea vegetables. It can be cooked in soups or stews, and it is a good source of protein, vitamins A and B, and trace minerals.

Arrowroot: a starch, derived from a tuberous root, that is used to thicken sauces, stews, and puddings. It has a light, neutral flavor.

Asafetida (also called hing): a strong-smelling spice similar in flavor to garlic. It has been used as a remedy in folk medicine for centuries and is considered especially helpful to digestion.

Balsamic vinegar: an aromatic, resinous vinegar, favored by connoisseurs. It is fermented through a long process that yields an earthy, wine-flavored vinegar.

Barley malt: a grain-based, complex carbohydrate used as a light sweetener. It is easy for the body to digest and assimilate.

Basmati rice: a delicate rice of Indian origin whose name means "fragrant." It can be purchased in both brown and white varieties.

Brown rice: whole-grain rice from which only the inedible hulls have been removed. It is not polished and therefore retains a natural coating of bran that imparts a distinctive, nutty flavor and a chewy texture. Brown rice is a good source of vitamin E, phosphorus, riboflavin, calcium, protein, and fiber.

Brown rice syrup: a malted sweetener made from brown rice and barley. It has a delicate flavor and is easy to digest and assimilate.

Bulgur: a type of wheat that has been lightly cooked, then dried or roasted, then cracked. It makes a nutty hot cereal or side dish.

Canola oil: a vegetable oil that has become very popular, owing to its lack of pronounced flavor and the much-touted presence of omega-3 and monounsaturated fatty acids, which may play a role in reducing cholesterol levels. Also, monounsaturates are more stable than polyunsaturates, which decreases the problems associated with rancidity in oils. With a high smoking point, canola is excellent for baking, sautéing, and deep-fat frying.

Cardamom: a sweet, aromatic spice from India used in curries, stews, and desserts. It can be purchased in pod, seed, or powder form and is most effective when used freshly ground.

Chapati: a round, flat, unleavened Indian bread, usually made of whole-wheat flour and fried.

Chickpeas (also called garbanzo beans): big, oat-colored beans popular in Mexican, Greek, and Indian cooking. They are used in stews, curries, and spreads, of which the most popular spread is hummus.

Cilantro: the leaf of the coriander plant; a lively, pungent green used to season Mexican, Indian, and Mediterranean dishes.

Coriander: an aromatic spice that in Indian cooking is called "the cradle of seasonings," because it balances the hot, pungent herbs used in curries and stews. It is considered a digestive aid and can be purchased in whole seeds or powder form.

Corn oil: a popular vegetable oil with a buttery flavor that works well for baking, sautéing, salads, and popcorn. Because it foams at high temperatures, it is not recommended for deep-fat frying.

Couscous: semolina that has been processed into tiny, pale yellow granules. Since it's been deprived of its bran and germ, couscous is not a whole grain, but it cooks quickly and has a delicately pleasant taste.

Cumin: a spice with a hot flavor and an earthy aroma, used frequently in Mexican, Indian, and Cajun cooking.

Dahl: a soup made from legumes and a variety of hot, pungent, and salty seasonings. It is often the centerpiece of an Indian meal.

Daikon: a large, white radish with a tangy, sometimes hot, bite. It can be served raw in salads, cooked in stews, or simply steamed. Daikon is a staple of Chinese and Japanese cooking, and it is known medicinally for its cleansing and detoxification properties.

Dulse: a rich, red sea vegetable that grows in cool waters. It is a source of protein, iron, chlorophyll, fiber, and vitamins A and B.

Endive: a bitter, leafy herb used in salads and soups.

Filé powder: a bouquet of ground, young sassafras leaves and a variety of other spices and herbs, used to season soups and greens.

Garam masala: a hot, sweet spice used in Indian cooking. It is a combination of cardamom, cinnamon, coriander, peppercorns, cloves, and sometimes cumin.

Ghee: a cooking oil made by clarifying butter.

Ginger: a hot, pungent spice widely used in cooking. It contains calcium, potassium, iron, and phosphorus. Ginger stimulates digestion and circulation and is frequently used as a tonic and a digestive aid.

Gomasio: a condiment made from salt and toasted sesame seeds.

Goma-wakame: a condiment made from salt, toasted sesame seeds, and wakame, a nutritious sea vegetable.

Granulated cane juice: a minimally refined sugar with a taste and texture similar to brown sugar. The most commonly available brand is called Sucanat.

Hiziki (also called hijiki): a dark sea vegetable with thick, spaghettilike strands. It is a source of calcium, protein, iron, vitamins A and B, and trace minerals.

Kelp: a sea vegetable, similar to kombu, that contains iodine, potassium, calcium, magnesium, phosphorus, iron, and vitamins A, B, C, and E.

Khir: a thin pudding made from rice, sweetened milk, and almonds. It is served as a dessert for Indian meals.

Kombu: a wide-leafed sea vegetable that is harvested by hand, folded into strips, then dried. It is a good source of calcium and potassium. Kombu is used in soups and stews and when pickled or marinated, as a condiment.

Kuzu: a vegetable starch used as a thickener for soups, stews, and puddings. Helpful to digestion, it is frequently used as a medicinal agent.

Millet: a tiny, round, yellow grain used in soups, stews, and stuffings. It is considered more alkaline and less acid than other grains in its effect on digestion.

Mirin: a lightly fermented vinegar made from sweetened sake. Its mildly sweet flavor is useful in desserts, grain dishes, and stews.

Miso: a high-protein paste made from the mash of fermented soy beans and (usually) fermented grains. It's used to impart a salty flavor to broths, soups, and stews.

Muesli: a breakfast cereal made from soaked rolled oats, raisins, and almonds.

Mung beans: tiny, round, green beans with a light, pleasant flavor. They are used in stews and soups and when sprouted, in salads and main dishes.

Nori: a sea vegetable, high in vitamin A, protein, and trace minerals, processed into dark green or brown sheets. Nori is toasted and used to wrap sushi, rice balls, and fish.

Norimake (literally, "nori-roll"): a Japanese-style appetizer or entrée of rice and other ingredients (tofu, scallions, celery, carrots, gingerroot, umeboshi paste, etc.) rolled in sheets of nori.

Nutritional yeast: a bright yellow condiment made from processed, malted yeast. It is is known for its ample B vitamins, including vitamin B_{12}, and is sprinkled on salads, vegetable dishes, and tofu dishes.

Oat milk: a nondairy milk substitute made from cooked oats, blended with water.

Olive oil: an oil produced from the pulp of olives and used in salad dressings, sauces, and light sautéing. It comes in two types: "virgin" olive oil is a first extraction; it is mechanically pressed, not heated; "pure" olive oil is a second extraction, which requires heat and pressure. Virgin is considered a higher grade than pure, but pure grades have good stability and can be stored unrefrigerated, while virgin grades are less stable. Like canola oil, olive oil is high in monounsaturates.

Peanut oil: a cooking oil high in saturated fat with the characteristic taste of peanuts that makes it an excellent oil for deep-frying, sautéing, peanut sauces, and peanut butter cookies.

Pesto: a green sauce made from fresh basil, olive oil, Parmesan cheese, pine nuts, oregano, and other seasonings.

Puri: a puffy, fried Indian wheat cake.

Quinoa: a hardy, nutritious grain known as the staple of the Incan civilization in South America. It is high in protein and is a source of vitamin E, phosphorus, calcium, iron, and several B vitamins.

Rice milk: a beverage made from rice and water. It is easy to digest and has less fat than cow's milk or soymilk.

Rice syrup: a light sweetener made from rice. People with allergies to corn, wheat, or barley sweeteners can use rice syrup successfully.

Rice vinegar: a light, mild vinegar made from rice and used extensively in Chinese and Japanese cooking.

Safflower oil: a popular vegetable oil that is versatile, because it does not have a strong, identifiable flavor. It does have a short shelf life, however, and should be refrigerated.

Saffron: the stigma of a crocus (*Crocus sativus*). The orange or red strands, used in small amounts, give a yellow color and an aromatic flavor to many dishes, especially rice dishes. It is the world's most expensive seasoning, because each strand is picked by hand.

Sea vegetables: highly diverse plants harvested from the sea. These vegetables are an excellent source of calcium, iron, phosphorus, magnesium, and vitamin B_{12}, which can be difficult to obtain in a vegetarian diet. Sea vegetables include arame, dulse, hiziki, kombu, kelp, nori, and wakame.

Seitan (also called wheat meat): a wheat product from which the bran and starch have been removed through processing so that only the gluten remains. It is used as a nutritious meat alternative in soups, stews, and other dishes.

Sesame oil: a highly flavored, pungent, and somewhat nutty-tasting oil that can be purchased in light and dark varieties. The dark variety has a distinctive, smoky flavor, because it is extracted from roasted sesame seeds. Both varieties are highly stable and can withstand high cooking temperatures, so they're good for deep-fat frying and stir-frying.

Shiitake mushrooms: large, dark mushrooms with a wide cap and a long stem. Shiitakes are a staple of Asian cooking; in macrobiotic cooking, they are also used medicinally in teas.

Soba noodles: Japanese noodles made from buckwheat or a mixture of buckwheat and whole-wheat flour. They require a slightly longer cooking time than noodles made from refined flours.

Soybean oil: an oil with a very strong flavor. It is most commonly used in baking, where its flavor can be masked by the presence of other ingredients.

Soy cheese: a nondairy processed cheese made from tofu, soymilk, soy oil, and other ingredients. Soy cheese can be purchased in cheddar, Parmesan, and mozzarella varieties. It has the same melting characteristics as dairy cheese.

Soymilk: a vegetable-based beverage derived wholly from soybeans and water. It has less fat, fewer calories, and more iron than an equal portion of cow's milk. It is helpful for people with lactose intolerance. Its two major disadvantages: it has less calcium than cow's milk, and it is much more expensive.

Sprouts: seeds or legumes soaked in water to grow tiny vegetable tendrils. Sprouting changes the seed or legume into a carbohydrate-rich vegetable, full of vitamins A and C and trace minerals. Favored sprouts for use in salads and cooking are from alfalfa, mung bean, buckwheat, lentil, soybean, and chickpea.

Sucanat: see granulated cane juice.

Sunflower oil: a medium-flavored oil very similar in flavor and content to safflower oil. It is one of the few oils indigenous to North America.

Tahini: ground sesame seed paste. Tahini spreads like a more liquid version of peanut butter, and it is very high in fat and protein.

Tamari: aged, concentrated soy sauce used as a flavoring. It can be purchased in wheat-free and low-sodium versions.

Tempeh: a rich, fermented soy product that is high in protein, low in saturated fats, and as easy to prepare as meat or fish. It is also a good source of iron, calcium, and B vitamins.

Tofu: a protein-rich curd made from soymilk. Since it is neutral tasting, it tends to take on the characteristics of whatever foods that it is cooked with. It can be served raw, steamed, broiled, stewed, roasted, or baked or blended into salad dressings, spreads, or whipped toppings. Tofu can be purchased in soft, firm, and extra-firm versions.

Udon noodles: thick, flat, Japanese noodles, usually made from whole-wheat flour.

Umeboshi paste: a salty, red paste made from pickled (umeboshi) plums. Umeboshi paste is a staple in Japanese cooking, and it is considered to have many medicinal qualities, including aiding the digestion.

Umeboshi vinegar: a sour, salty vinegar of reddish purple color made from the fermentation of umeboshi plums.

Vagar: a combination of Indian spices sautéed in ghee or oil. It is blended into casseroles, rice dishes, and stews to add flavor and heat.

Wakame: a sea vegetable high in iron, calcium, sodium, magnesium, protein, and vitamins A, B, and C.

Wasabi: the ground root of a small green plant used as a condiment that imparts a very fiery flavor. It can be purchased in powder form that reconstitutes with water.

Zest: the colored part of a citrus fruit's outer skin. It is shaved or peeled off and used as a flavoring.

BIBLIOGRAPHY

Baker, Cherie. *Naturally Delicious Desserts.* New York: Ballantine Books, 1985.

Brody, Jane. *Jane Brody's Good Food Gourmet: Recipes and Menus for Delicious and Healthful Entertaining.* New York: Bantam Books, 1990.

Colbin, Annemarie. *The Natural Gourmet.* New York: Ballantine Books, 1989.

Editors of East West Journal. *Shopper's Guide to Natural Foods.* Garden City Park, N.Y.: Avery Publishing Group, Inc., 1987.

Hagler, Louise. *Tofu Cookery.* Summertown, Tenn.: The Book Publishing Company, 1991.

Kripalu Center for Yoga and Health. *Kripalu's Self Health Guide: A Personal Program for Holistic Living.* Lenox, Mass.: Kripalu Publications, 1993.

Levitt, Jo Ann, Linda Smith, and Christine Warren. *Kripalu Kitchen: A Natural Foods Cookbook and Nutritional Guide.* Lenox, Mass.: Kripalu Publications, 1992.

Morningstar, Amadea with Urmila Desai. *The Ayurvedic Cookbook.* Wilmot, Wisc.: Lotus Light Press, 1990.

Ornish, Dean. *Dr. Dean Ornish's Program for Reversing Heart Disease.* New York: Ballantine Books, 1990.

Perry, Rick. *The Hurricane Kitchen.* Camden, Maine: Yankee Books, 1988.

Rombauer, Irma and Marion Rombauer Becker. *The Joy of Cooking.* New York: A Plume Book, 1973.

Somerville, Anne. *Fields of Greens: New Vegetarian Recipes from the Celebrated Greens Restaurant.* New York: Bantam Books, 1993.

Stanchich, Lino. *Power Eating Program: You Are How You Eat.* Miami, Fla.: Healthy Products, Inc., 1989.

The Moosewood Collective. *The Moosewood Restaurant Cooks at Home.* New York: Simon and Schuster, 1994.

The Moosewood Collective. *Sundays at Moosewood Restaurant.* New York: Simon and Schuster, 1990.

Wigmore, Ann. *Ann Wigmore's Recipes for a Longer Life.* Wayne, N.J.: Avery Publishing Group, 1991.

Sources

For more information and a free catalogue of these and other sources for yoga and personal growth, write or call Kripalu Distribution, PO Box 2218, Lenox, MA 01240. tel: 800-448-3445, fax: 800-448-3302.

Kripalu's Self Health Guide: A Personal Program for Holistic Living. Create a healthy lifestyle with this comprehensive, holistic guide to health and well-being. Softcover: 250 pp.

Why Do Yoga: What Will It Do for Me?: A Discussion of the Medical Benefits of Yoga with Jeffrey Migdow, M.D. An inspiring and entertaining video, featuring the director of Kripalu Center's Yoga Teachers' Training Department. Includes an entire yoga practice that you can do without ever leaving your chair! Videotape: 30 minutes.

Discovering Kripalu Yoga with Nancy Foust (Megha). These two 30-minute yoga sessions provide a gentle and energizing introduction to the practice of yoga. Videotape: 60 minutes.

Mealtime Meditations. Make your mealtime a relaxing experience with this inspiring guide that will change your relationship with food. Audiotape: 50 minutes.

Kripalu Center offers a variety of programs throughout the year in yoga, health and wellness, personal growth, and spiritual attunement. For program information, call 1-800-967-3577.

To order sourdough breads from Richard Bourdon's mail-order firm, Bread and Stuff Bakery, write or call:
Richard Bourdon
Bread and Stuff Bakery
PO Box 812
Housatonic, MA 01236
tel and fax: 413-274-6346

INDEX

ABOUT THE AUTHOR

Atma Jo Ann Levitt, M.A., R.N. is a writer, counselor, and lecturer who has had a longtime interest in promoting health and well-being—from her expanded role as nurse to her involvement with stress management, personal growth, and holistic health education. As an 18-year resident of the Kripalu Center, she pioneered many of its personal growth programs, directed the popular Health for Life Program, and served in an administrative and editing capacity for the Center.

Atma coauthored *Kripalu Kitchen,* published in 1980, and also wrote *Sounds of the Sacred: Chants of Love and Prayer,* as well as pamphlets and short pieces related to health and personal growth issues. She lives in western Massachusetts.